ASSESSMENT IN CHRISTIAN HIGHER EDUCATION

Rhetoric and Reality

D. John Lee and Gloria Goris Stronks
Editors

UNIVERSITY
PRESS OF
AMERICA

Lanham • New York • London

Calvin Center Series

Library of Congress Cataloging-in-Publication Data

Assessment in Christian higher education : rhetoric and reality /
D. John Lee and Gloria Goris Stronks, editors.
p.   cm. — (Calvin Center series)
Proceedings of a conference held at Calvin College, April 1993.
Includes bibliographical references.
1. Church colleges—United States—Congresses.   2. Church
colleges—United States—Evaluation—Congresses.   I. Lee, D. John.
II. Stronks, Gloria Goris.   III. Series.
LC427.A88   1994   377'.8'0973—dc20   94–9171 CIP

ISBN 0–8191–9408–5 (cloth : alk. paper)
ISBN 0–8191–9409–3 (pbk. : alk. paper)

 The paper used in this publication meets the minimum requirements of
American National Standard for Information Sciences—Permanence
of Paper for Printed Library Materials, ANSI Z39.48–1984.

Contents

Section A: Issues

Section B: Research

Section C: Research Briefs

Epilogue

List of Figures

List of Figures

List of Tables

Foreword

This book is the product of the Calvin Center for Christian Scholarship (CCCS) which was established at Calvin college in 1976. The purpose of the CCCS is to promote creative, articulate and rigorous scholarship that addresses important, theoretical and practical issues. Such scholarship would focus on areas of life in which it may be expected that a Christian position could be worked out and for which previous Christian scholarship has been too parochially expressed, too superficially developed or too little in accord with Christianity itself.

The present volume is a result of the work of D. John Lee and Gloria Goris Stronks, who received a grant from the Calvin Center for Christian Scholarship to host a conference that would produce the book. The conference was held at Calvin College in April, 1993.

The central question posed in this volume is, at once, of great theoretical interest and of great practical consequences because it is being asked by most, if not all, college administrators: how can we know if the education promised in our mission statement is actually taking place? Despite the considerable consequences that turn on answering that question, the field of assessment in higher education is relatively new. The case studies and critical analyses to follow in this volume will, one hopes, help to bring some clarity and coherence to the various studies that have been done and to suggest lines of inquiry for future research.

Since the time of the conference, Professors Lee and Stronks have worked with the authors on a thorough revision of their conference papers. The contributions of some conference participants do not appear in this volume. The CCCS presents this book with the hope that it will be of interest to scholars and of use to college administrators.

Grand Rapids   Ronald A. Wells
February, 1994   Director, CCCS

Acknowledgments

We are grateful to the board of directors of the Calvin Center for Christian Scholarship for making this project possible. Ronald Wells, the Director of the Center, provided administrative and moral support throughout our work. Kate Miller and Donna Romanowski, the Center's staff associates, arranged many details of the conference at which the ideas in the book were refined, prepared the manuscript for publication, and kept us free of organizational hassles so that our work could proceed smoothly and on schedule. It is our hope that in this time of uncertainty about assessment, this book will help others work out a truly Christian vision of assessment as it applies to their own colleges.

D. John Lee and Gloria Goris Stronks

Introduction

Gloria Goris Stronks and D. John Lee

The word "assessment" means different things to different people. To some, an assessment refers to the value that has been placed on their property for the purpose of determining market price or taxes. To others, assessment refers to a set of clinical measurements used to evaluate a person's psychological condition. In higher education, there is no agreed upon definition of assessment, so it may be more appropriate to think about assessment as a "movement." Assessment in higher education is a movement concerned with evaluating outcomes. But, how the evaluation is done or what outcomes are considered varies tremendously. Even the contributors to this book use the word "assessment" differently. However, this variety in meaning and use, although it may be confusing, is not unfortunate. So long as there is diversity among colleges and universities, there will be diversity in approaches to and perspectives on assessment.

Christian colleges and universities are in the process of trying to understand what the term "assessment" means to their campuses. While, admittedly, the focus on assessment at these institutions is partly a result of pressure from accreditation agencies, it also arises from an honest attempt to determine the extent to which the stated or implied goals for student learning and development are being met.

The decade of the eighties introduced the topic of assessment in higher education; the primary motive was to inform the public about the quality of learning at colleges and universities. Assessment was intended to promote accountability, to ensure that institutions at the tertiary level were providing opportunities for learning as effectively and efficiently as possible. Assessment was to help answer the question, "Is the money set aside for higher education being used productively?"

Later came the notion that a byproduct of assessment was the promotion of needed instructional change within institutions of higher education. This way of thinking about assessment linked evaluations of student learning to curriculum revision and to faculty becoming more effective teachers. In some respects, this motive for undertaking assessment of learning was to suggest that the competence of the faculty was under scrutiny. Assessment was now also used to help answer the question, "How can the faculty be teaching more effectively?" and "Does the curriculum really educate students for our world today?"

Christian colleges and universities share the concern for effectiveness and efficiency, both in use of resources and in instruction. In addition, these institutions claim that they help students think about how their Christian faith relates to every area of life -- in the classroom, in extracurricular activities, on the playing fields, in human relationships, and in service opportunities around the world. They have a long-standing commitment to the ideal that their brand of higher education leads to changed lives. They assert that the Christian college or university experience is one which not only enables the student to come to know the subject, but also to come to know his or her own story, and the Christian story, as illuminated by the subject. The Christian college can create a space for learning in which obedience to truth may be practiced. Assessment helps a Christian college or university demonstrate its faithfulness as an organization committed to a biblical view of student learning and development. It does so by finding answers to questions about students. To what extent does the college or university contribute to student learning and development? Do students successfully acquire the knowledge and competencies we intend? Are our graduates prepared for the next step, whether that is graduate school or jobs? Are there ways we could improve our combinations of courses and campus life to achieve greater intellectual maturity and higher performance? When asked what one question they would most like to have answered concerning their students, faculty in one Christian college said, "Above all, we would like to know whether our students truly understand worldviews and how their faith relates to the worldview that we say provides a framework for thinking at this college."

This book approaches the topic of assessment in Christian higher education by considering the issues and research. The first section relates assessment directly to the tasks implied by the mission of the college and suggests ways in which the design and implementation of assessment programs can help in carrying out that mission. David Brandt explains why assessment in Christian colleges can be extremely complicated but is also necessary and satisfying. Nicholas Barker and Harry Pinner describe seven ways in which academicians commonly deceive themselves concerning their institutions and remind us that the ultimate test of institutional effectiveness comes in the quality events which are yet to take place in students' lives. Therefore, any assessment plan must consider the input of the past, the value added in the present, and the events of the future.

A central claim of Christian higher education is that the Christian college or university experience will help students' faith to grow and mature. There is a growing body of research concerning how college affects student religious attitudes, and Rodger Rice effectively summarizes those findings. His analysis of the conclusions about what happens to students' religious conviction when they are exposed to higher education is a necessary background for our present work in assessment. Rice's critical review is particularly important in that it provides a direction for the much needed future research, along with the warning that our institutions must be prepared to take action when performance fails to live up to our high rhetoric.

One part of the curriculum which should most clearly reflect the intention of the college for student learning is the general education component, or the "core," as it is sometimes called. The general education component is that part of the curriculum which all students are required to study and it seems reasonable to assume that colleges intend certain outcomes and developments as a result of that common study. Gloria Goris Stronks provides a model for use in ongoing assessment of the effects of the general education component or core curriculum on student learning and development.

The second section of the book consists of several examples of research concerning the effect of Christian liberal arts colleges on student learning and development. John Van Wicklin, Ron Burwell, and Richard Butman report on a longitudinal study of their students, many of whom come to college deeply committed to their limited experience and resistant to ideas which fall outside a relatively narrow latitude of acceptance. The researchers follow the development of these students as they move through the college years and describe their progress or lack thereof. The longitudinal study of D. John Lee and Paula Smalligan Foster considers the memories and assessments that students had of their college years. This study is interesting because it also includes the voices of alumni who have been out of college for three years. Lee points out the importance of cross-cultural and experienced-based learning and encourages a "process" rather than "product" orientation when it comes to thinking about and measuring Christian maturity. Both of these longitudinal studies raise important questions which will surely keep faculty and administrators from allowing themselves to be complacent about what is happening on their campuses. Steven Timmermans describes the way knowledge of student learner characteristics can improve both instruction and student performance. With the goal of improving educational practice in mind, Harold Faw and Harro Van Brummelen analyzed the content and types of questions found in final examinations. They also investigate how instructors plan their course components as they relate to the attainment of the college mission. Their research demonstrates how a scrutiny of the nature of final exams, together with the resulting reflection and discussion with faculty, may lead to course revisions that more clearly reflect the goals of the college.

Section C contains three research briefs which should prove useful to most Christian college or university assessment programs. The literature on the development of moral reasoning in college students is extensive. Steven McNeel introduces this research and reports some data on a few Christian college samples using James Rest's *Defining Issues Test*. Next, a team at Bethel College (MN), led by anthropologist Harley Shreck, shares their ethnographic method of reading student culture. Research of this nature may prove essential to assessment. It not only provides a baseline of where our students are, but reveals some essential dimensions of student life which are often ignored or denied in curricular and cocurricular planning. Finally, Bayard Baylis and his colleagues report the results of the 1990 *Cooperative Institute Research Program* (CIRP) questionnaire for a combined sample of ten Christian colleges' entering students. Their factor analysis revealed an interesting model which can also be used to provide some baseline measures for assessment programs.

David Guthrie closes our discussion with a theology of assessment. A doxology is a hymn of praise and glory used in worship. Thinking of assessment as doxology, Guthrie convincingly argues that institutional assessment brings praise to God in that it helps a Christian college come to terms with its faithfulness as an organization committed to a biblical view of student development.

Assessment on any campus always begins with the questions faculty and administrators raise concerning student learning and development. The research reported in this volume, however, shows clearly that assessment programs themselves must always be under scrutiny because initial assessment attempts will raise new questions, at times even showing that the original questions were not the ones that deserve our primary attention. Theories of assessment, the frameworks in which assessment occurs, and practices of assessment must always inform each other, if assessment is to be as effective and efficient as we intend.

When we look back on our work in the year 2000, it will be interesting to look again at the relationship between the rhetoric we hear from faculty and administrators in our Christian colleges and universities and the reality of student learning and development. Will instruction, curriculum, and campus life have improved? Will anything have changed as a result of our discussions and activities concerning assessment?

Section A: Issues

1. Assessment: Mandate or Privilege?

David S. Brandt

Higher educators have, for the past several years, considered assessment one of the most important, but most difficult tasks confronting them. The 1993 annual meeting of the North Central Association, held recently in Chicago, was characterized by a somewhat pessimistic mood regarding assessment. A well-attended session, conducted by the panel which reviews all assessment plans, told us that they had reviewed twenty plans. Ten of those received a passing grade from the panel, and only one was graded exemplary.

Faculty members who are often not thrilled about institutional assessment spend many hours regularly assessing students. In fact, most faculty members consider themselves experts on the subject. We academicians are convinced that we know how to grade. We admit that it is difficult and sometimes traumatic, but we know how to draw the lines. It is interesting that something we do routinely in the classroom and consider ourselves to be "good at," presents such a problem when it confronts us on an institutional level. We sometimes grouse about the need to assign grades and we even write articles in opposition to the giving of grades. We suggest that they do not tell the whole story, that they are not fair, but few would argue seriously that we should do away with grades, much less that we should stop evaluating our students in some appropriate way. For example, if I inform an appropriate faculty committee that a colleague has assigned an *A* grade to all members of a class, the response is one of outrage. Such "grading" is considered to be unfair and unjust to the students in that class. Furthermore, where are our standards?

To begin our discussion of assessment, we need to address three questions: Why do we grade our students? Why should we do assessment at Christian liberal arts colleges? Why are we hesitant about assessment?

Why Do We Grade Our Students?

It is not often that a faculty member takes the time to ask the reason for grading. It is something which is so deeply ingrained in our academic culture that we don't even need to ask why we go through this often painful exercise. My experience indicates the following three reasons for providing student grades.

The most immediate pressure to grade students probably comes from the "outside." Graduate schools and employers both seem to demand a transcript with grades. Since we all wish to get our students enrolled in the best graduate schools or to get them placed in the best positions, we want them to "look good" in the eyes of those who read the transcripts. In fact, it may well be that this outside pressure has also been the greatest stimulus to nation-wide grade inflation.

We grade students for purposes of comparison. We are part of a highly competitive society where winning is often everything. Students want to know how they are doing. Faculty members want to know how this student or this class compares with previous students or classes. It is important to all of us to say that students from my school do better than students from your school. The competitive aspect of grading may be, especially in North America, the strongest reason why we assess students.

There is, of course, another reason, and I wonder how often we establish assessment techniques to implement this third reason for grading. Grading is seen as a usually summative task. We seldom take the developmental aspect of grading seriously. In *The Active Life*, Parker Palmer (1990) writes about "the healing power of failure." Palmer writes:

> Our culture puts such a premium on success and such sanctions on failure
> that we find it hard to affirm the rightness of failing at a good cause to
> affirm the creativity that failure can contain. Most of us still treat failure as
> terminal just as we were taught in school where an *F* in a course was a final
> verdict on which there was no appeal. (Palmer 1990, 89)

He goes on to say, "the paradox is that failure may turn to growth while success can turn to self-satisfaction and closure" (89). I am sure that each of us would affirm this principle in our private lives.

We, of course, often learn most from failures. But how do we know we have failed if we do not evaluate? Courses, teachers, and students all need feedback. None of these should be static. Each should be changing and growing. Evaluation should be helpful, to the faculty member as well as the student. Such a statement makes many of us smile. We suspect that students seldom care what we write on a paper once they have seen the grade. Their concern is to maximize grade rather than learning. Many a faculty person has no intention of modifying a course from one semester to the next. Our goal is to teach the course and complete it and then get on with our scholarship activities. In my opinion, however, the real reason for assessing or grading students is to provide formative feedback that leads to growth.

Both student and teacher have much to learn. Too seldom do we deliberately grade students formatively, and we certainly do not set out to seek failure in order to find out where we are weak and how we can grow.

As I view the current assessment movement, I see very similar forces at work. Increasingly, the "outside" demands it. Accreditors and legislative bodies want to know how we rate. There is one issue of *U.S. News and World Report* that we all read. Did we "make it" or not. The competitive element in our society is alive and well in higher education; but once again, as with courses, the very best reason for assessment is to improve who we are and to provide increasingly excellent education for our students. Kay Schallenkamp, a member of the North Central review panel, suggested that the most neglected aspect in the assessment plans the panel has read so far is the formative function. We need to "discover" our "failures."

Why Should We Do Assessment at Christian Liberal Arts Colleges?

The Christian liberal arts college is critical for the furtherance of God's Kingdom. We have on our campuses large segments of the church of tomorrow. Increasingly we will also influence the current adult church through non-traditional educational efforts. If there is anything at the end of the twentieth century that needs to be done right, it is Christian higher education. We need to know what we are doing and regularly evaluate it to make sure that we are effective as God's agents in the world. If anyone in higher education ought to be motivated to change in order to improve, it is us. We are dealing with issues that are of ultimate importance and therefore cannot waste time nor delay positive change.

Much of the assessment emphasis sought by accrediting agencies relates to the academic area. Our catalogs, however, suggest that we seek excellence in affective as well as cognitive areas. We claim to be educating the total person which means that academic measures are not sufficient for our assessment. We do far more to our students than most schools do. As a result, assessment becomes more complicated, but also more satisfying. Our plans for assessment must include ways to measure our influence on students' personal and spiritual lives as well as on their intellectual development. When we think of testing, we usually think about objective instruments that are preferably multiple choice to aid in scoring. In order to measure our influence on students' personal and spiritual lives, we may need to develop narrative instruments which tell stories rather than results in numbers.

I regularly lead what we call at Bethel an "administrative fellowship group." This is a time when I meet with approximately ten students each week where we talk and get to know each other. By the end of a semester or a year with such a group, I know these students quite well. I have wondered what it might be like to keep a weekly journal about those groups, to write about change, process and growth in the lives of that group of students (such a journal would, of course, also show much about myself), to record the look on a student's face when she or he "gets it," to note the different kinds of comments a student makes today compared with six weeks ago. I am convinced that we don't deliberately look for such assessment nor do we clearly record it for future reference.

Higher education is responsible to a variety of constituencies. We have responsibility not only to the various accrediting and governmental agencies, but to our own ecclesiastical constituencies as well. We are required to demonstrate that we are fulfilling our missions to regional accreditors, disciplinary accreditors, and governmental agencies just like any college or university. Much more important in the long run is the fact that we also need to demonstrate the fulfillment of our mission to churches, boards, donors, parents, alumni and other friends who care that we are maintaining the intellectual, personal and spiritual impact on the lives of our students. Parts of our assessment might not be of interest to some constituencies but become vitally important to others. I believe that we owe our constituents accountability. They deserve to know how their gifts are being used and how the students they send us are being educated.

The quality of our assessment might become particularly important to some of our secular constituencies where Christian institutions are suspect. For some time we have moved very close to the center of the cultural stream of this country. That appears to be changing rapidly and will likely continue to change. If we stay true to the faith statements and lifestyle statements that currently exist, these peculiarities will turn many parts of the politically correct educational establishment against us. There are crucial parts of political correctness that are also biblically mandated. There are other areas, however, where current political correctness would diverge from biblical values and practices.

I am somewhat hesitant to suggest the next reason for our kind of school to do assessment. We are probably not equally guilty, but I have encountered enough of it that I am willing to risk the generalization. The Christian college needs to do institutional assessment very well because there exists among us an inferiority complex. I don't think that we ourselves know how good we are. In Christian colleges faculty in some departments are surprised when a colleague decides to accept a position at their school even though they "could go anywhere they would like to." I have talked with students who have said to me "after all, I am only at (blank) college." This is true in spite of the fact that each one of our schools has a list of highly successful alumni, powerful faculty members, both in the classroom and in scholarship, and outstanding students who will be visible and important influences in the future. It is imperative that we document our quality not only for the good of those on the outside but for our own well being. I believe that we are institutions of high educational quality whose stories deserve to be documented and told widely.

Why are We Hesitant About Assessment?

To bring a major initiative to our campuses at a time when resources are very scarce always raises the question of how much the effort will cost. Any attempt to reallocate resources from existing programs to something new like assessment will surely be resisted by many. Assessment costs money. I feel that we are in a situation where we cannot afford to do assessment poorly. We need to use those assessments that already exist on our campuses and add new programs of assessment carefully and efficiently. Assessment needs to be a community effort that includes all faculty and administrators so that no one or no one group bears the burden to the exclusion of others. The problems relating to the expense for assessment should drive us to seeking efficient ways of doing assessment rather than seeking ways to avoid assessment.

There is always the argument that in assessing we are interfering with faculty autonomy in the classroom. We have come to a time of collaboration where it would be to everyone's advantage for all of us to work together. If we use assessment for formative evaluation in addition to summative evaluation, then this process can only encourage and help the classroom rather than hurt it.

On most campuses everyone knows who is effective and who is not. What we don't do well is to document this knowledge. As a result, many of us are hesitant to get into the assessment business for fear that we will be shown to be among those who are not doing the job very well. If, however, it is true, as I contend, that we are fine institutions and that the purpose of assessment will be formative rather than summative it seems to me that all of us would welcome assessment to document our quality and to provide feedback for positive change. For example, two specific faculty members with whom I have worked during my years in academic administration reacted differently when confronted with low student opinions of their classes. Quickly one provided reasons why these perceptions were low, why they were not likely to change, and why the instrument was not good. The other received the information thoughtfully and asked, "Can you help me?" The

latter individual has changed methodology as well as his general attitude
toward his classes. Today students perceive him to be well above average as
a classroom instructor. He is proud of his classroom work and his teaching
has changed from something he "has to do" to something which is a source
of joy for him. To some extent, at least, every teacher can be helped to
improve.

Conclusion

I would like to suggest some simple exercises to help faculty think about
assessment. Begin by thinking about and considering your alumni. Think of
the teachers, doctors, ministers, business people, homemakers, and maybe
even a few college professors who have passed through your department.
How did they get to be so good? I suggest that, in large part, you "did it to
them." Attend one of your end-of-season sports banquets to see what has
happened to the student athlete. I think you would learn much, especially if
that particular team did not have a successful season. Listen to the senior
who played four years but never started. Listen to the students report on
spring break missions trips in chapel. Talk with your advisees about their
spiritual growth while in school. At commencement, think about who these
students were four (or six) years earlier. You will be wonderfully surprised
and will find these students, or former students, ministering to you.

All of these activities are assessment activities. Learn how to document
them. You will feel encouraged and you may find out what you would like
to change. All assessment programs should be distinct, reflecting each
individual institution. The purpose of institutional assessment is to enhance
the education provided to our students. Assessment may lead to some
decisions that not every person will like; but I encourage you to get involved
in the process at your institution. The goal of enhancing our education ought
to excite us, especially those of us at Christian institutions.

Reference List

Palmer, P. J. 1990. *The active life.* San Francisco: HarperCollins.

2. The Gentle Art of Self-Deception: Assessment in Christian Colleges

Nicholas P. Barker and Harry A. Pinner

Declining faculty work load, rising tuition costs, and crowded or closed classes are just a few of the many criticisms being hurled at higher education today. They all are part of the current trend to point the finger of accountability at the system of higher education. While institutions of higher education have long guarded the turf of academia and reminded the business-minded that you cannot run a college like a business, the business principle of consumer satisfaction has crept into our hallowed halls. Faculty and administrative work habits and motives are being examined and questioned by legislators and parents. The demand for accountability is strong and many institutions are having trouble reconciling that demand with their programs. A long look at the printed reason for existence (the mission statement) might give many institutions even more reason to fear this rising call for accountability.

Colleges and universities that take seriously the call for accountability may find in assessment their best means of holding themselves accountable and satisfying others who hold them accountable. In the simplest of terms, assessment can be reduced to a two-fold test. First, we might ask the faculty, "What is this institution trying to accomplish?" and see if there is uniform agreement. If so, we could ask the second question: "Are we accomplishing it and can we show the public our proof?" This test captures the need to have a stated mission, have it understood, have it effectively implemented, and have documentation of that effectiveness. Anything less is not good enough in today's consumer environment.

Assessment of student outcomes has become the standard means of attempting to reconcile the measurement of our results with the reason for our existence. Assessment involves the ongoing development of a plan, the implementation of a process, and the ultimate examination and adjustment of the product -- higher education. However, assessment as a major tool for evaluation and improvement has subtly led to serious self-deceptions on the part of Christian college faculties and administrations.

How do college administrators and faculty members deceive themselves? The sources of self-deception are many and varied, and perhaps academicians are more seriously liable to self-deception than the ordinary run of people because we are so loath to consider ourselves less than objective, analytic, and intellectually omni-competent. We not infrequently entertain the illusion that we are not subject to being "conned," even by ourselves. After all, if we educated types are not smart enough to see life clear and whole, who is? Not only our pride, but other forces operate in the direction of self-deception. We sometimes fall in love with our analysis of a part of the field and miss other parts, we sincerely and zealously pursue what we do well and enjoy doing, politely ignoring other necessary tasks; and we, busy and important people all (like Chaucer's Man of Law, who "was a busy man, but seemed busier than he was"), work quickly to get tasks finished and off our desks onto other people's desks, failing to take time-demanding complexities into account. Few human beings find it easy to resist self-deception, especially where self-flattery and self-interest intrude. And so, though we may satisfy colleagues, accrediting agencies, and even ourselves, we fall short of the value for ourselves, our institutions, and our students of the genuine and lasting benefits of assessment.

We shall examine seven common and frequently overlapping self-deceptions, spending considerably more time on some than on others. The first four of these the Christian shares with other college and university administrators and faculty members; the last three are the peculiar property of Christian higher education. The first is based on confusion about the end to be served by assessment. The second involves inadequate attention to, or distorted understandings of, the institutional mission statement. Closely connected with the second is the third, which involves debates over quantitative assessment and qualitative assessment. Fourth is a self-deception arising out of a trendy determination to focus on outcomes to the exclusion of inputs. To the fifth, sixth, and seventh we shall give the labels Academic Success, Academic Success Plus, and Christian Academic Perspectives. We shall begin our discussion of each of these seven self-deceptions with an illustrative dialogue between a faculty member and an academic administrator.

We shall conclude the paper by positing what we see as the only satisfactory kind of assessment, the only one we regard as free from self-deception.

I. The End to be Served by Assessment

Administrator: We need to institute a student outcomes assessment program so that we can measure how good a college we really have here. And then we can prove it to our students, parents, churches, and donors.

Faculty Member: There you go again -- always worrying about how we look to the constituency. You just confirmed my suspicion that assessment is nothing more than a buzzword for public relations. All you want is to parade before the public our entering students' SAT scores, the percentage of earned doctorates on our faculty, and the number of our students who go on to graduate school.

Administrator: Now wait a minute. I said an assessment program would help us measure how good a college we really are. I don't believe in presenting a picture of the college that's out of accord with reality. Good assessment simply ensures that our public-relations efforts are accurate and have integrity.

Faculty Member: I'm all in favor of that. But level with me for a minute. Don't we *really* need to implement an assessment plan because our regional accrediting association has made that a requirement for continued accreditation?

Administrator: Well, that's true. But I still believe deep down that assessment is a good thing and that it would be good for us to do it.

Faculty Member: I'm not so sure it's a good thing, but I do know that I don't want to teach at an unaccredited college.

What is the chief end of assessment in higher education? Even if our faculty member and administrator were to reach such tenuous agreement as is implied at the end of their conversation above, they would be self-deceived if they thought that they adequately understood the ends to be served by assessment. The chief end of assessment is not to produce accurate public relations publications or to satisfy the requirements of the regional accrediting association. Indeed, assessment serving these other ends will most likely prove an impediment to the chief end of assessment, which is the improvement of the college for the benefit of future students. When a college engages in assessment primarily for public-relations purposes, the focus is

almost certainly going to be on the college's strengths; when a college
engages in assessment for the sake of the improvement of the college, the
focus will frequently be on the college's weaknesses. Similarly, college
personnel undertaking assessment primarily for the sake of accreditation will
work hard to meet an externally determined deadline, heave a sigh of relief
when the task is finished, rejoice if they receive approval, hope that the next
intrusion by the accrediting association will be a long way off, and set aside
all thoughts of improving the college.

How does assessment contribute to the improvement of the college? It
does so by measuring the college's level of success in achieving its goals and
by promoting the development and implementation of strategies for doing
better what it now does not do very well. Assessment for other ends is like
assessment for the sake of measurement alone, which accomplishes nothing.
Ongoing assessment for the sake of continuous feedback into the system,
feedback that leads to the encouragement of successes and the correction of
deficiencies, is what is needed.

II. The Institutional Mission Statement

Faculty Member: I can buy into this assessment business if you agree to go
back to the college's statement of mission. I was really impressed with the
high ideals the founders of this college had when they wrote our mission
statement. In fact, that was one of the main reasons I decided to come here
to teach. And it's clear that everybody here really believes in the mission
statement.

Administrator: I know what you mean. And I really appreciate the mission
statement too. It's very inspirational. But I'm not at all sure that we can
translate our mission statement into an assessment program. You said it
yourself when you spoke of the founders' "high ideals." It's awfully hard to
determine whether we are living up to such lofty goals.

Faculty Member: I thought the mission statement was supposed to be the
basis for everything we do around here. If assessment can't be tied to the
mission statement, I doubt if assessment belongs here.

Administrator: Would you settle for an assessment program that enabled us
to compare ourselves with other colleges that have many of the same goals we
have? For example, wouldn't it be a good thing to know whether our
graduates can write as well as State's graduates?

Even if our friends reached an uneasy truce at this point, they would be
gently deceiving themselves concerning the importance of assessment. In

fact, they would have so trivialized and simplified assessment as to make it only a superficial instrument for college comparisons. Such a plan reminds us of a quotation from Calvin and Hobbes.

Calvin: Here's an interesting article. The top five gum brands are compared in terms of flavor retention, elasticity, bubble capacity and chewing rebound. The computer graph shows the results, compensating for various saliva acidities. If you know your pH, this really helps you choose the proper gum for your chewing style.

Hobbes: What kind of nut would *care* about all this?!

Calvin: *Everyone!* This is hard data! It lets you quantify your enjoyment!

Hobbes: I thought fun was supposed to be *fun.*

Calvin: Well, *I* prefer to trust the experts.

Perhaps Calvin has finally missed the mark. Neither bubble gum nor academic assessment results should be perceived as dogma. However, Hobbes might have been more accepting of Calvin's data had he understood the reason for chewing bubble gum. Mission and purpose must be central for assessment results to have any value.

The Southern Association of Colleges and Schools mandates that an effective assessment process include the following: 1) the establishment of a clearly defined purpose appropriate to collegiate education, 2) the formulation of educational goals consistent with the institution's purpose, 3) the development of procedures for evaluating the extent to which these educational goals are being achieved, and 4) the use of the results of these evaluations to improve institutional programs, services, and operations (Southern Association of Colleges and Schools [SACS] 1992, 16).

The whole process of assessment and its outcomes rest entirely upon the college's purpose, which not only would include goals common to all colleges and universities, but would stress goals characteristic of Christian higher education, and, more particularly, goals peculiar to one particular college. An institution's statement of mission should have major impact on the planning, process, and product of an assessment plan.

The Purpose Statement of Covenant College claims a commitment to help our students "see creation as the handiwork of God...," to seek "to bring every thought and act into obedience to Him; to reclaim the creation for God and redirect it to the service of God and humanity..." and "to see learning as a continuous process and vocation..." (Covenant College 1992a, 11).

Either our work on these goals is worthy of planned effort, careful assessment, and intelligent improvement, or the goals themselves are merely expressive of vague and directionless emotion. If an institution's mission statement does not at least imply criteria by which faculty members' activities and the students' development can be assessed, the mission statement almost certainly needs serious revision. If, on the other hand, a worthy mission statement is ignored in the assessment program, there is a high likelihood that someone has sacrificed importance for ease of measurement, significance for superficial clarity. Which brings us to...

III. The Quantity/Quality Debate

Faculty Member: You know what bothers me most about assessment? It's the assumption that the most important things in life and in education -- things like holistic learning and spiritual growth -- can be measured.

Administrator: Why can't they be measured? Won't you admit that if we had adequate pre-testing and post-testing, we could determine whether a student at the time of graduation knows the names of more of Shakespeare's plays and characters -- or more chemical elements, or the anatomical makeup of more invertebrates, or more systems of psychotherapy, or the main presuppositions of more of the world's great philosophers -- than she did at the time of matriculation? If so, value has demonstrably been added, the college has done its job well, and we can probably find out how we accomplished that feat and attempt to improve upon it next year.

Faculty Member: Sure, one can always measure quantities. But you're fooling yourself if you think you can measure the most important elements of higher education. How can you determine whether that same student has grown in her ability to apprehend and apply these easily measured quantities? Can she really think about them? Can she relate them, take them apart, put them together, evaluate them, appreciate their nuances, put them to use? Isn't it quite simply impossible to do any meaningful assessment of these, the truly significant values of higher education?

Administrator: I care as much as you do about these deeper values. But what's wrong with measuring, and taking accountability for, quantifiable items? Besides, I disagree with your contention that quality cannot be measured. Look at this quotation from an article in the *Chronicle of Higher Education:*

> ...I refuse to believe that people who can detect and measure minute ripples
> in the fabric of the universe as it existed billions of years ago cannot also

determine the quality and quantity of their own product -- learning by students, faculty members, and others. Such a project may be a major research challenge in itself, but surely not an impossible one. Controversial, political, and unpalatable, perhaps, but *not* impossible. (Langenberg 1992, A44)

Faculty Member: OK. I give up. I realize that assessment is here to stay, and I'm willing to give it a try. Let's see if we can compromise and put together a really sound system of assessment that has academic integrity....

To give up on the attempt to assess quality and settle for a merely quantifiable program is to lapse again into self-deception. But here we enter one of the major topics of debate among both those who welcome assessment and those who are still fighting it. Some ask, "Can you measure quality?" while others ask, "How do we measure quality?" In either case, quality must be defined if we can expect to measure effectiveness.

E. Grady Bogue and Robert L. Saunders chronicle the history and purpose of assessment in *The Evidence for Quality* (1992). They ask how one is able to improve the quality of education if quality cannot be defined. But where is one to find a definition of quality?

In *Zen and the Art of Motorcycle Maintenance* Robert Pirsig likens the measurement of quality to a train pulling boxcars of fruits and vegetables. For him, quality is to be found not in the trip itself but rather in the delivery of the fresh fruit and vegetables: "Quality couldn't be independently related with either the subject or the object but could be found only in the relationship of the two with each other. It is the point at which the subject and object meet. Quality is not the thing. It is an event" (Pirsig 1979, 239).

While Pirsig provides little help in the definition of quality for higher education, he may have pointed us in the right direction. The true relationships between the subject and object come together not in the four-year trip of education, but after graduation. The quality events can be found in the life of the graduate. It is the daily event of bumping into the world with a new set of perspectives and experiences which will affect the results of that world-contact.

There is a strange tension between the desire to measure quantifiable events on the trip leading to the conclusion that quality has been defined, and the value of measuring the outcomes at the end of the trip, yet feeling that since those outcomes were not quantified, the results were inconclusive. Some assessment plans are so caught up in the need to quantify such easily measured outcomes as are reflected in Graduate Record Exams and Major Field Achievement Tests that the true test of quality is ignored. Other institutions get so bogged down in trying to determine how quality can be measured that they fail to measure anything.

Bogue and Saunders offer a more helpful resolution to this tension between quality and quantity:

> We do not subscribe to the notion that every worthy and desirable outcome of American higher education will yield to measurement. But we do hold the conviction that quality can be defined, that quality can be measured, and that quality can be used to improve our impact on students and their growth as well as to enhance programs and services (Bogue and Saunders 1992, 2).

Not surprisingly, the key to that definition lies, once more, in an institution's statement of purpose or mission. Bogue and Saunders suggest that the source of quality can be found in "conformance to mission specifications and goal achievement within publicly accepted standards of accountability and integrity" (Bogue and Saunders, 20). If quality is the success of mission, it can be measured.

The process of assessment, while helping us determine our effectiveness in the academic disciplines offered and providing us with the information to modify and improve our programs where needed, will not address quality and therefore real effectiveness unless it is based upon our mission.

Arthur Holmes, in *The Idea of a Christian College*, suggests that the distinctive characteristic of a Christian college "should be an education that cultivates the creative and active integration of faith and learning, of faith and culture" (1975, 16). Not only does he define our distinctiveness, he has identified that upon which we must measure quality.

Bogue and Saunders make a parallel observation: "Quality undergraduate education consists of preparing learners through the use of words, numbers, and abstract concepts to understand, cope with, and positively influence the environment in which they find themselves" (Bogue and Saunders, 13). They have no idea where their worldview fits in this process, but it is present as they call on graduates to affect culture and society.

Like most Christian colleges, Covenant College got caught in the debate between quantity and quality. We became victims of our own debate and became paralyzed so that neither quantity nor quality was measured. Some reluctantly acknowledged the need to participate in this useless endeavor as our accreditation was on the line, and attributed little other practical value to the exercise. Others knew that such a process might prove helpful in the further development of curriculum and instruction, but were not sure how much weight to give the findings.

The true debate about assessment should not be whether it is needed and for whom we perform this function. That debate is over! The debate ought rather to be over such questions as: How can we effectively enter into this process? What can be measured? How should it be measured? How should those measurements be interpreted? How should that information be applied to the curriculum and instruction?

We must not approach the quantity-quality issue as an either/or proposition. How can we do any less than to seek in some way to measure our effectiveness in meeting the lofty goals in our mission statement and to improve in areas that call for improvement, whether they are quantities or qualities?

IV. The Input/Output Debate

Administrator: On the most elementary level, we can see how much better we are than we were three years ago: our entering freshmen this year have an average SAT of 1052, as compared with 1020 in 1991, 1015 in 1990, and 995 in 1989. Also, the earned doctorates on our faculty have gone up from 65% to 70% in the same period.

Faculty Member: Inputs like those have no necessary connection with the outputs of education. Or didn't you mean what you said earlier about value-added assessment -- about the outcomes of students' experiences here?

Administrator: I'll admit that some of our best teachers -- the ones that deeply influence our students -- don't have Ph.D.s.

Faculty Member: And I'll admit that students with higher SAT scores are generally better motivated to learn than students with lower SATs.

Administrator: Still, you have a point. Our assessment program should focus not on inputs but only on outputs.

In this spirit of bonhomie they gently fall once more into self-deception. To be sure, it took higher education too long to realize how empty could be the bragging of elite schools about their impressive inputs. See, for example, Alexander W. Astin's *Achieving Educational Excellence*, Chapter Two: "Why Traditional Views of Excellence Are Counterproductive," (Astin 1985, 24-59). Astin encourages us to ask whether the highly selective elite schools deserve much credit for putting out highly motivated and intelligent graduates who were, after all, highly motivated and intelligent when they matriculated.

There is value, however, in looking not only at outputs but at inputs and processes as well. Using Pirsig's illustration of the fruit and vegetable train, our knowing the quality of the fruit and vegetables that were loaded onto the train and the travel conditions to the delivery point should enable us to make some predictions concerning the event that will take place at delivery. It would be hard to expect a customer to be satisfied with the delivery if the quality of the fruit and vegetables was bad from the very beginning or if it was bruised or frozen in transit.

Assessment plans should continue to examine the ingredients that become part of the process and will surely have an effect on the level of effectiveness. We fear that too many schools will become so engaged in outcomes measurements that they will fail to measure the importance of hiring, developing and retaining qualified faculty members. Every assessment plan should include a section on inputs demonstrating the value of beginning with quality and developing quality.

Even the truism that we should measure students' learning rather than professors' teaching needs to be examined more critically than is often done. If it can be demonstrated, for example, that classroom discussion actively involving the student produces more, better, and longer-lasting learning than formal lectures (see, for example, Astin, Chapter Six: "Student Involvement: The Key to Effective Education," 133-57), we may safely assume that a faculty employing considerable amounts of interactive discussion in their classes are producing more learning in their students than a faculty relying far more heavily on monologic lectures.

Assessment at its best takes into account both inputs and outputs. Starting with the mission statement, it presents a vision of how the students should turn out. Then it reasons backwards to the ingredients that would most likely produce such outcomes.

For example, the authors of this paper are both in agreement with Covenant College's commitment to "help students better understand and appreciate ethnic and cultural diversity..." (Covenant College 1992b), but we hold to completely different tactical positions for implementing that goal. One would attempt to provide that understanding through classroom instruction and cross-cultural involvement out of the academic environment, while the other would place more weight on the recruitment of minority and international students.

Though the ultimate criterion for quality is, of course, a matter of outputs, we should consider inputs as penultimate criteria if we can be certain they help produce the outcomes. If, for example, a Christian college has established as a goal the production of a certain percentage of graduates going on to become Christian missionaries, it would not be irrelevant to identify as a problem the college's failing to require Christian belief of at least a similar percentage of entering students. Likewise, if a Christian college has committed itself to the development of Christian thinking on the part of its students, the college would do well to hire faculty members capable of modeling Christian thinking.

Let us assume that our friends on the faculty and administration successfully work out their concerns and establish a system of assessment that puts together the measurement of inputs and outcomes and the measurement of quantity and quality, a system that focuses appropriately on the college's mission statement and on the improvement of the college for the sake of the students. Even then they are deceiving themselves if they think that their resolution of these issues will result in a good measure of their institution's effectiveness as a **Christian** college. Correcting the self-deceptions already discussed might well give us a false sense of security and cause us to miss the most important aspect of assessment for a Christian college.

The crucial question is, how can we prove our effectiveness in meeting our purpose -- to help a student not only know more, but to think about those facts and concepts as Christ would have us think about them? The student must be able to do more than relate them, evaluate them, and appreciate their nuances. He must be equipped to put them to uses compatible with God's mercy and justice. Have we measured a student's ability to see the world as God's world and to respond to his knowledge accordingly?

This is the greatest self-deception in Christian college assessment -- to act and assess as others do and to fail to measure that which sets a Christian education apart from any other type of educational experience. Assessment must be integrative if it is to measure effectiveness in a Christian college. Our penchant for self-deception will be all the more pronounced if we congratulate ourselves on having achieved two kinds of integration -- the integration of our concerns for quantity and quality and the integration of our concerns for inputs and outputs. To rest satisfied with resolution of the quantity-quality tension and the input-output tension is woefully inadequate.

How can we as Christian college faculty members or administrators practice assessment that is both satisfactorily integrative and free from the usual pitfalls of self-deception? Let us look at three ways of assessing the effectiveness of a Christian college. The great likelihood is that, by default or design, Christian educators have already chosen or will choose one of these three.

V. Academic Success

Administrator: What we have to do is take a genuinely accurate look at how our students measure up *as students*. I'm so tired of having people think that because we're a Christian college, we're not academically sound.

Faculty Member: I couldn't agree with you more. This is, after all, a college -- not a camp, a mental hospital, or an orphanage. So we must measure our *collegiate*, our *academic*, success.

Administrator: Now we're getting somewhere. But you're the expert here. How should we go about it?

Faculty Member: We need to measure the academic outcomes of our students. We'll compare them with the national norms or do pre- and post-testing to determine the value added. We'll find out if our students know their disciplines and have mastered the tools of oral and written communications, critical thinking, and reading comprehension.

Administrator: All right! Let's roll up our sleeves and get to work.

If you take this approach, you might be able to hold your academic head high and prove that your college is not an inferior institution. It is just not different. Clearly, though this may integrate measures of quantity and quality, and measures of input and outcome, it is not integrative as Christian colleges intend to be integrative.

If we settle for this type of assessment, we are most likely guilty of succumbing to the pressure of an accrediting agency and building an assessment exercise. Such a plan would not measure real quality as defined by Bogue and Saunders, for the distinct mission of the institution would be ignored. While most accrediting agencies will have little regard for or understanding of the peculiar aspects of the mission of a Christian college, we should. To measure the academic success of our students and not measure that part of our mission is to fail the test of effectiveness.

However, while this type of assessment plan would not be complete as it does not measure effectiveness in meeting mission, it will become the style and foundation for the successful plan which we shall describe later. We must be careful not to ignore this important aspect of our mission, the academic development of our students, but we must also realize that this is but one ingredient in an effective assessment plan.

VI. Academic Success Plus

Faculty Member: Though I insist that this institution is, first and foremost, a college, I'll admit that it is not *just* a college.

Administrator: I'd rather put it this way: a *Christian* college operates, and must operate, on the basis of a broader and richer definition of "college."

Faculty Member: What you're saying is that to be worthy of the name "Christian college," we must be not only academic but spiritual.

Administrator: Exactly! And, as far as assessment is concerned, we have every reason to measure not only our students'*academic* success, but their *spiritual* success as well.

This approach goes one step further than the last. A college might measure not only the academic aspects of the program, but also the spiritual maturation of the students. This might provide information to determine if attendance at the institution has had a positive effect on a student's spiritual condition.

This approach fosters several self-deceptions. The ability to separate academic, social, and physical maturation from spiritual maturation will present a major hurdle in this approach. If a student's calling while in college is to be a Christian student, would it not be the case that her spiritual success would at least in some respects be inseparable from her academic success?

Pascarella and Terenzini present some compelling study results in *How College Affects Students*. They cite a 1987 study by Funk and Willits and a 1977 study by Astin which confirm earlier studies indicating that college students tend to show less interest in religious affairs during their college years. Astin "concluded that shifts toward greater secularization are probably a function of both normal maturation and college influence" (Pascarella and Terenzini 1991, 293).

If these changes described by Pascarella and Terenzini also hold true for students in Christian colleges, and we would assume that at least the direction is probably accurate, it would become increasingly difficult to measure the students' spiritual growth. Even if the normal trend of decreased interest in religious issues was curtailed, it would be impossible to measure the true value added. This becomes all the more complicated if the student sees her spiritual calling as the need to develop her academic abilities to their best potential.

Another possible danger in attempting to measure the spiritual growth of the student is found in the setting of expected results. Every outcome assessment measurement must start with mission as reflected in the expected results and quantified by the assessment instrument. Assuming that spiritual maturation is part of the mission of a college that would employ this approach, what would be the expected outcome? Would one measure the length and frequency of devotions? Could we perform some quantifiable pre- and post-test of spirituality and spiritual activities?

At Covenant College we have developed a perception survey given to seniors to ascertain their feelings about the college's impact on their understanding of who God is and of what God wants of them, and their felt need to participate actively in the biblical change of culture and society. They are also asked to weigh the impact of nineteen items on their spiritual life. This information can help us measure the influence of the institution on their spiritual lives, but it is not an attempt to measure their spiritual lives or maturation.

Sanctification is a process that depends upon the grace of God, not time and grade. Referring to Pirsig's idea that quality is the point at which the subject and object meet, quality would then be the time when a child of God meets with his God. It is not the reflection of activities, church attendance frequency, or number of spiritual activities.

The desire to know if students are being positively influenced in the Christian life is a valid one. However valuable that may be in the evaluation of programs, it does not provide much use in a direct measure of effectiveness. Even if the results are positive on both counts, academic and spiritual influence, an institution can assume it has functioned well as a college and perhaps even as a church but will have none the less failed to measure the fulfillment of its integrative mission.

VII. Christian Academic Perspectives

Administrator: The more I look at this whole subject, the more unsettling I find it. For example, I have for years bragged about how we integrate faith and learning at our college. But do we?

Faculty Member: I think we really do.

Administrator: Can we prove it?

Faculty Member: Whether we can or can't, aren't we at the hub of what assessment really ought to be?

Administrator: I think you're right. We need to measure the extent to which our students integrate their Christian faith with their academic disciplines.

Faculty Member: Yes. We need to see if their academic perspectives are truly Christian. Have they really come to understand what it means to be a *Christian* poet, a *Christian* historian, a *Christian* biologist, and so forth?

Administrator: And, more generally, have they, to use Blamires' and Niebuhr's phrases, come to possess a Christian mind that perceives the relationship between Christ and culture?

Faculty Member: Or, to use Wolters' way of putting it, do they see the effects of creation, fall, and redemption on every area of study?

What self-deception lies in this approach? Isn't a Christian worldview, an integration of our Christian faith with all areas of learning and life, what our colleges are primarily committed to? Surely we are close to what many of us regard as the heart of Christian higher education. And it is certainly a better approach to assessment than the previous two: it far more adequately relates the mission and the effectiveness of an institution; it measures both academic outcomes and the perspectives that the students and graduates bring to their disciplines, their lives, and their place in society.

Let us continue to develop some of the virtues of this approach. For example, building on the theory that inputs still provide a major impact on outputs and should therefore be attended to, we would suggest an input measurement. If a Christian college's mission statement defines an integrative approach to faith and learning as an element of the learning process, the faculty might be asked to chronicle the manner by which they accomplish this in their teaching. It would be time well spent to engage the faculty in discussions concerning the types and levels of integrative approaches appropriate to the various disciplines.

Gloria Goris Stronks makes an interesting observation in "Assessing Outcomes in Christian Higher Education." She writes that "up to this time assessment has been in the direction of finding out what an institution stands for and what those who work at the institution are doing. The new direction in assessment is an attempt to determine how much students learn in a given college and how their thinking has changed as a result of that college experience" (Stronks 1991, 94). We would suggest an extension of that observation.

If quality is the measurement of the effectiveness of college mission, and integrative thought is a part of that mission, quantity of learning and change of thinking are just the beginning of quality measurement. Such institutions also need to know the results of those things learned and of the new approach to thinking. How has a change in thinking been demonstrated by the student?

During a recent Global History lecture at Covenant College the students' understanding of presuppositions was challenged. The professor was lecturing on the impact of the Industrial Revolution and the emergence of a global society. He read the following quotation from *Capitalism and Progress* by Robert Goudzwaard:

> In such a social structure an orientation toward a set vertical direction of life does not make any sense. Instead, a horizontal orientation dominates; the purpose of development and expansion is directed to earthly possibilities. For instance, in an unadulterated capitalist society regulations regarding just prices are naturally considered as unlawful interventions in the market mechanism. For that reason, the first barrier which necessarily must be removed was the one of the church and heaven. The vertical orientation of life had to be transformed into a predominantly horizontal one. (Goudzwaard 1979, 11)

The professor challenged the students to think about vertical concerns. If God is sovereign over all of life, should not the horizontal orientation be open for review from a vertical direction? A discussion followed which included the right or wrong of overcharging for rent in a hurricane area. Since the demand was high, the market seemed to allow for major rent increases. Horizontal thinking without vertical interruption would support this kind of action. One might question such practices in light of scripture.

Teaching of this sort can provide students with the necessary tools to examine their discipline, current events, and all of life from a biblical perspective. A college must determine that the professors hold such a biblical perspective, are teaching students to recognize and properly handle such a perspective, and are challenging students to practice and use this new outlook on life -- a world and life view built on the Scriptures. But this is only the input.

Louis Voskuil's use of G. Linwood Barney's analysis of how culture functions may prove helpful in our attempt to measure our graduates' role in transforming culture. He writes:

> Each culture is a series of layers the deepest of which consists of ideology, cosmology and worldview. A second layer which is closely related and probably derived from it is that of values. Stemming from both of these layers is a third layer of institutions such as marriage, law, education. These institutions are a bridge to the fourth and surface layer of material artifacts and observable behavior and customs. This layer is more easily described and more easily changed. (Voskuil 1988, 9)

It may be possible to examine our graduates as they work through these various levels of culture. Each of them will contribute to the totality of culture, and the effectiveness or ineffectiveness of our institutions will be present in that contribution. To be able to measure that contribution becomes the challenge for a college that takes seriously the call to become effective and demonstrate quality as defined by mission.

At Covenant College, we have set a graduation requirement of an undergraduate thesis in the student's discipline. This project has changed names and format over the years but remains the capstone of the undergraduate experience. The Senior Integration Project (SIP) is a "written thesis or project which will provide an opportunity to explore and analyze a problem in the student's major field in the light of Christian philosophy" (Covenant College 1992a, 31). The student will be graded on her treatment of the academic topic, her communication skills in both the written thesis and the oral defense, and her ability to demonstrate that a biblical perspective is the foundation upon which observation and critique are made.

This form of assessment brings with it serious consequences. Not only must the faculty understand and be able to communicate a Christian philosophical position by which the discipline can be taught and understood; they must also be able to recognize the emergence of the student's approach and ascertain the quality of her understanding of biblical foundations. Two people may approach the discipline from different directions and both may be biblically based. This becomes a learning experience for both teacher and student and an opportunity to challenge the student to continue developing this pattern of thought in all aspects of learning and living.

It may sound as if we are commending, indeed praising, what we have labeled the seventh form of self-deception. If so, it is understandable. We do derive considerable satisfaction from the discovery that some, perhaps many, of our students have managed to apprehend the Christian academic perspectives we believe to be so important. But we have also, more often than we would care to admit, found ourselves terribly discouraged by the discovery that some of these very same students have gone on to do very little with what they have learned, to misuse it in snobbery, mean-spiritedness, and arrogance, or to cast it aside and pursue such painful and destructive paths as alcoholism, materialism, marital infidelity, and even atheism. Perhaps you have had the same experience. What has gone wrong here? Is there no escape from assessment involving self-deception?

We have outlined seven self-deceptions in Christian college assessment. We discussed the end to be served in assessment or the why of assessment. The second self-deception was the disregard of the mission statement in the development of the assessment plan. Thirdly we examined the quantity/quality debate which often leads to assessment paralysis. The fourth self-deception was the tendency to overlook the value of inputs in the assessment process. The fifth and all too common Christian college deception is to assess academic quality in an attempt to dispel the fear of mediocrity. In a desire to demonstrate the spiritual element of mission, some Christian colleges fall into the sixth self-deception of striving to measure spiritual growth as an academic add-on. The final self-deception involves the right process, an integrative approach to assessing an integrative mission, but remains too narrow in focus because of timing.

Even those graduates who can demonstrate some familiarity with the tools of integrative thinking are just beginning to explore the world. Let us return once more to Pirsig's train full of fruits and vegetables. The quality events that Pirsig describes and we as Christian college faculty and administrators seek are yet to take place. When our graduates marry, or remain single, develop friendships, rear children, make their way in the marketplace, and participate in a host of other events that weave the fabric of society in which they live, then they will give us opportunity to assess our programs. The ultimate test of institutional effectiveness comes in those quality events.

John H. Westerhoff makes a somewhat similar point in his distinctions among instruction, education, and formation. We maintain that a Christian college must undergo assessment with regard to all three, and cannot be content with success only in instruction (which "aids persons to acquire that knowledge and those abilities useful for responsible personal and communal Christian life in church and society") or even with success in both instruction and education (which "aids persons to reflect critically on their behavior and experiences in the light of the gospel so that they might discern if they are being faithful and when they might need to change their behavior"). The Christian college has the high calling of going beyond instruction and education to formation, which "aids persons to acquire Christian faith (understood as a particular perception of life and our lives), Christian character (understood as identity and appropriate behavioral dispositions), and Christian consciousness (understood as that interior subjective awareness or temperament that predisposes persons to particular experiences)" (Westerhoff 1992, 266-67). Indeed, we would go so far as to say, with Westerhoff, that a Christian college should see itself as dedicated to nothing less than "the formation of Christians" (278), and should assess itself as such.

The outcomes from even the most adequately integrative approach must be measured in these areas of life and living if an institution wants to measure real effectiveness and therefore quality. We grant that after considerable time has elapsed, feedback may sometimes be difficult to apply in easily determined improvements, but we believe that anything less than this is seriously inadequate. We must develop an assessment plan that considers the inputs of the past, the value added of the present, and the quality events of the future. Such a plan offers freedom from these many assessment self-deceptions and permits the continued development of quality. Student academic outcomes cannot be separated from life-long perspectival issues if a college's adherence to an integrative mission statement is to be judged effective. A mission statement that stresses the integration of biblical revelation with thinking, learning and living demands an integrative and long-term assessment process. Let us clear our minds of self-deceptions. Let us not profess one way and assess another.

Allow us to offer a footnote to this subject. This book is dealing with both the theory and the practice of assessment in Christian higher education. We Christians in higher education are still discussing the why's and starting on the how's of assessment. The American public will not wait much longer. The call for accountability may well lead us down the path of a national assessment program which will give less than lip service to the mission of a Christian college, and we may be expected to embrace the same mission as every other college, as defined by the public pressures of the day.

The opening paragraph of the *Report of the NAICU Task Force on Education*, released in December, 1992, reads as follows:

Higher education is a strategic investment in the future of our nation and public officials are demanding greater accountability from colleges and universities. It seems virtually inevitable that this will result in a national program of assessment at the collegiate level, and that NAICU members will not be exempt from it (NAICU 1992, 1).

The report goes on to call for action to seek public policy "respecting and protecting the freedom of institutions to define their own missions, clientele, curricula and educational policies" (NAICU 1992, 1). The mission statement of most NAICU schools will not be in jeopardy as long as they seem aimed at producing graduates who can contribute to the economy and demonstrate a minimum of basic skills associated with a baccalaureate degree. Christian colleges may, for the first time, have to defend the value of teaching from a biblical perspective.

Covenant College has been accredited and reaffirmed and has gone through substantive change examinations, but had never faced the need to defend our mission until recently. When the visiting team reviewed our assessment plans for our Master in Education program, they interpreted our expected outcomes as less than acceptable for master's level work because of the inclusion of perspectival issues. It took much convincing to move their attention to those areas of academics which facilitated our approval.

The need to measure our effectiveness as Christian colleges who want to graduate students with biblical perspectives on education and all areas of life and with fully productive Christian lives is greater now than ever. Yet we are now facing our most serious challenge to prove the educational value of such a pursuit. In this context quality and effectiveness must be measured in relation to our mission and we must remain true to our mission.

Let us get on with the process of assessment with academic and biblical integrity. We need to redefine the word "excellence" for a public that is crying for less but needs more.

Reference List

Astin, A. W.   1985.   *Achieving educational excellence.* San
   Francisco: Jossey-Bass.

Blamires, H.   1978.   *The Christian mind.* Ann Arbor: Servant.

Bogue, E. G. and R. L. Saunders.   1992.   *The evidence for quality.*   San
   Francisco: Jossey-Bass.

Covenant College.   1992a.   *Academic bulletin.*

Covenant College.   1992b.   *Institutional effectiveness, annual report, 1991-
   92.*

Goudzwaard, R.   1979.   *Capitalism and progress.*   Grand Rapids: Eerdmans.

Holmes, A. F.   1975.   *The idea of a Christian college.*   Grand Rapids:
   Eerdmans.

Langenberg, D. N.   1992.   Point of view.   *The Chronicle of Higher
   Education 39,* (22 September): A44.

National Association of Independant Colleges and Universities. 1992. *Report
   of the NAICU task force on education.*

Niebuhr, H. R.   1956.   *Christ and culture.*   New York: Harper
   Collins.

Pascarella, E. T. and P. T. Terenzini.   1991.   *How college affects
   students.*   San Francisco: Jossey-Bass.

Pirsig, R. M.   1979.   *Zen and the art of motorcycle maintenance.*   New
   York: Quill.

Southern Association of Colleges and Schools.   1992.   *Criteria for
   accreditation.*

Stronks, G. G.   1991.   Assessing outcomes in Christian higher
   education. *Faculty Dialogue* 14:91-105.

Voskuil, L. 1988. History: Sound and fury signifying nothing? *Pro Rege* 16(3): 2-12.

Westerhoff, J. H. 1992. *Schooling Christians: "Holy experiments" in American education.* Grand Rapids: Eerdmans.

Wolters, A. R. 1985. *Creation regained: Biblical basics for a reformational worldview.* Grand Rapids: Eerdmans.

3. How Protestant Evangelical Colleges Affect Student Faith and Worldview: An Assessment Review

Rodger R. Rice

Assessment in higher education can no longer be ignored. People from inside and outside the academy are asking hard questions about the value and effectiveness of higher education. There are over 3,000 colleges and universities in the United States. Of the 600 or so which retain some tie to a Christian denomination or constituency, about 125 make a claim to be "Christ-centered" liberal arts colleges. This distinctive is often described as a commitment to helping students think about relating Christianity to every area of learning and life (*Consider a Christian College* 1990, 4). In this chapter, I review what assessment has been attempted on these "Christ-centered," or what I will refer to as Protestant evangelical colleges. These colleges, which were once described as untouched by the academic revolution (Riesman 1981), cannot dodge the assessment movement.

Protestant evangelical colleges make bold claims about their positive effect on student faith and worldview. And although assessment within these colleges is in its infancy, some serious efforts to generate evidence of their effect on students has been ventured. This chapter proceeds in four parts. First, it reviews Pascarella and Terenzini's (1991) recent summary of the research on how the college experience, particularly at church-related colleges, affects students' religious attitudes. Second, it examines two reports based on James Davison Hunter's Evangelical Academy Project (Hunter and

Hammond 1984; Hunter 1987), a pioneer assessment effort that focused on thirteen evangelical colleges. Third, it reviews two assessment dissertations conducted subsequent to Hunter's provocative study that challenged his interpretations concerning the Protestant evangelical college's effect on student development.

This review only covers research which considered several institutions simultaneously. Although useful to their respective institutions, conclusions based solely on single case studies do not provide the type of plausible evidence assessment demands. While the differences between Protestant evangelical colleges are significant, their similar claims concerning the integration of the Christian faith and learning allow some generalization. Comparative and multiple-institution studies are legitimate, necessary, and needed.   The fourth part of this chapter suggests guidelines for future assessment research of Protestant evangelical colleges.

Student Religious Attitudes: A Summary of Research

Ernest Pascarella and Patrick Terenzini's (1991) summary of the last 20 years of assessment research is indispensable. They reviewed the results of over 2,600 studies to answer the question of how college affects students. In summarizing the changes during college in student attitudes and values in general, they wrote:

> If one theme underlying changes in values and attitudes during college is that they tend to be supportive of or at least consistent with observed changes in cognitive growth, a second theme is that the changes also coalesce around a general trend toward liberalization. Considering consistent changes in the areas of sociopolitical, religious, and gender role attitudes and values, it would appear that there are unmistakable and sometimes substantial freshman-to-senior shifts toward openness and a tolerance for diversity, a stronger 'other-person orientation,' and concern for individual rights and human welfare.   These shifts are combined with an increase in liberal political and social values and a decline in both doctrinaire religious beliefs and traditional attitudes about gender roles. The clear movement in this liberalization of attitudes and values is away from a personal perspective characterized by constraint, narrowness, exclusiveness, simplicity, and intolerance and toward a perspective with an emphasis on greater individual freedom, breadth, inclusiveness, complexity, and tolerance. (Pascarella and Terenzini 1991, 559-60)

The liberalizing effect of college applies to higher education in general. The differences in student outcomes attributable to distinctive institutional characteristics (e.g. mission, size, selectivity, etc.) or "between-college effects," are minimal. Pascarella and Terenzini continue,

...the body of evidence reviewed casts considerable doubt on the premise that the conventional, if substantial, structural, resource, and qualitative differences among schools are translated into correspondingly large differences in average educational effects. In short, similarities in between-college effects would appear to vastly outweigh the differences. (Pascarella and Terenzini 1991, 589-90)

There is little consistent evidence to indicate that college *selectivity*, *prestige*, or *educational resources* have any important net impact on students. Nearly all the variance in learning and cognitive outcomes is attributable to individual aptitude differences among students attending different colleges. Only a small part is uniquely due to the college attended (Pascarella and Terenzini 1991, 592). Whether or not the college is *church-related* (not just Protestant evangelical) is one of these modest predictors. There is some evidence to suggest that when student body selectivity is held constant, church-related colleges tend to retard development of secular values and attitudes (597). But again, the church-related nature of a college accounts for only a small portion of the total variance.

Pascarella and Terenzini specifically wrote about the effect of college type on student religious attitudes and values:

Few studies shed any light on the effects of various kinds of colleges on changes in students' religious attitudes and values. In probably the strongest studies on this point, Astin found (net of other personal and background factors) significantly greater than expected decreases in conventional religious affiliation and in religiousness (that is, praying and reading the Bible) among students attending selective or prestigious schools. These declines were most evident in prestigious, nonsectarian, four-year colleges. Declines also appeared to be greater than expected at large universities and public two-year colleges. The likelihood of changing toward no religious preference was also highest at so-called elite institutions. Astin replicated these findings in two separate follow-ups. Attending a Protestant, Catholic, or all-men's college, however, tended to suppress changes in religious affiliation. In addition, while Catholic school attendance also tended to retard declines in religiousness, somewhat greater slippage was associated with Protestant college attendance.

Other studies provide similar evidence....Rich and Jolicoeur (1978), ...did, however, find reason to believe that attendance at a secular institution produced greater declines, while enrollment at a church-related college tended to produce increases in religious orthodoxy.

Nonetheless, and although the evidentiary base is small, it seems reasonable to conclude that institutional characteristics probably do play a role in the degree to which religious preferences, attitudes, values, and behavior change during college. It seems equally clear that the nature and extent of those differences vary substantially across kinds of institutions, with selective institutions apparently exerting the strongest and most consistent effects in the direction of reduced formal religious affiliations and religiousness. (Pascarella and Terenzini 1991, 303-304)

In sum, declines in religiousness are not as great in Protestant and Catholic colleges compared to public and nonsectarian private college, although the declines are greater in Protestant than Catholic colleges. Only one study (Rich and Jolicoeur 1978) uncovered an increase in religious orthodoxy at church-related colleges.

Interestingly, Pascarella and Terenzini suggested that there may be some institutional variables, not yet conceptualized or measured, which would yield greater between-college effects or better distinguish institutions on student outcomes. They stated:

There is evidence in several areas that institutional context -- a college or university's educational and interpersonal climate (and subclimates) -- may more powerfully differentiate among institutions in the extent of their influence on student change than do the typical descriptors. Different conceptualizations of institutional "environments" and analyses of subenvironments may reveal greater between-institution differences than are now apparent in the research literature. (Pascarella and Terenzini 1991, 589-90)

It is possible to summarize the findings of Pascarella and Terenzini on how college affects students religious attitudes and values into four points:

1) During college, students in general experience intellectual growth and liberalizing of attitudes and values, including "doctrinaire religious beliefs." Religious decline or secularism is greater with men than women and greater with high-ability students. These effects persist after college, channeling graduates into postcollege lives that reinforce their values and thus increase the likelihood of being passed on to their children.

2) Despite wide differences among colleges and universities, they do not translate into large differences in how students are affected, in fact, the similarities outweigh the differences.

3) There are modest "between-college effects" relative to selectivity and secularism. That is, while selective, prestigious institutions are not more effective in achieving learning and cognitive outcomes (differences are due to student ability), there is consistent evidence (weak to moderate) that they do have an edge in effecting secularism. In contrast, students at church-related colleges do not become as secularized to the same extent as those students who attended selective prestigious universities or college. Higher education secularizes, with secular institutions having a greater impact than church-related ones.

4) The institutional context, environment, climate, or culture can differentiate colleges on student outcomes and, with different

conceptualization, has the potential of revealing stronger between-college differences in future studies.

Student religious attitudes and values are weakened as a result of attending college. But, Protestant evangelical colleges claim to strengthen the Christian faith of their graduates. Is this an inconsistency? Is the rhetoric not supported by reality?

Hunter's Evangelical Academy Project

During 1982-83, James Davison Hunter surveyed samples of students attending nine evangelical colleges as well as three large-enrollment religious studies classes at the University of California at Santa Barbara. The focus of this Evangelical Academy Project (EAP) was to explore the values and attitudes of a college-age cohort of evangelicals and, by doing so, to explore the cultural and political temperament of the coming generation of evangelicals.

The results of the college surveys first appeared in 1984 as a co-authored journal article (Hunter & Hammond). But, it was not until 1987 when Hunter's book, *Evangelicalism: The Coming Generation* was published that leaders of evangelical higher education took notice of his research. The conclusions Hunter drew from his empirical results were not exactly complimentary of the effects evangelical colleges were having on their students. Indeed Hunter's data suggests that there is more rhetoric than reality when it comes to Protestant evangelical colleges fulfilling their mission as distinctively "Christian" liberal arts colleges.

What was Hunter's conclusion? Protestant evangelical colleges are not strengthening the Christian faith of their graduates, but in fact are doing exactly the opposite. As already reviewed, previous social research had supplied convincing evidence that higher education secularizes. Exposure of students to higher education weakens the grip of religious convictions on a student's life. Hunter identified three factors which contribute to this secularizing process: (1) the "nature of the activity itself," for example, the fostering of independent and critical reflection, (2) exposure to faculty or the professorate, "one of the most secularized group of workers," and (3) the social environment of higher education which is "often the very first social world many students inhabit that is entirely detached from the cognitive and moral coordinates of their childhood, and it invariably plays a part in weakening the credibility of adolescent religiosity" (Hunter 1987, 171). That is, the goals, the people, and the social context of higher education all work together to directly challenge adolescent religious conviction. Hunter's data suggested that the Protestant evangelical college or university is no exception. "[...I]nferring from freshmen through senior comparisons, there is a consistent decline in adherence to various aspects of the Evangelical world view" (172).

While on the surface one would thus imagine the Protestant evangelical college curriculum, faculty, and culture to be different, it is really not different at all. In fact, Protestant evangelical higher education undermines and weakens, instead of buttresses, the traditional religious and cultural orthodoxy of conservative Protestantism. Hunter argued that the Christian liberal arts curriculum is more liberal than Christian. He also found that the faculty are "less committed to the theological and cultural traditions of the Evangelical heritage than their students." Furthermore, faculty see their task as one of "liberation" and "sense that true and vital Christianity depends upon a debunking of many of the traditions of conservative Protestantism" (Hunter 1987, 175-176). And, because the social environment of many evangelical colleges is highly insulated, there is no threat to the student's worldview and it begins to erode under the secularizing forces of the curriculum and faculty. Hunter's argument about the erosive nature of evangelical colleges' social environment needs further explanation.

Hunter argued that college environments differ "in the degree to which the college community is protected or insulated from anything which would threaten the symbolic integrity of that community" (Hunter 1987, 176). Hunter proposed an "insularity index" based on two indices: the requirements of faculty and the criteria for student admissions. All nine evangelical colleges surveyed in the EAP required signed statements of faith from their faculty members, and six required comparable assurance from entering students. These six colleges were referred to as "highly insulated." The other three colleges not only permitted non-evangelicals to enroll but also actively recruited "seekers" and had admission policies that permitted a designated proportion of "seekers." Thus, non-evangelicals at these three schools were there by design and these three schools were labeled "moderately insulated." Public universities, which cannot discriminate on the basis of religion in hiring or admitting students, were assumed to have "low insularity."

What Hunter found with respect to campus insularity was startling. Using correlations between his "insularity index" and measures of evangelical orthodoxy and worldview, Hunter argued the following:

> One might suppose that the more highly insulated campus would be far better able to accomplish its mission of protecting orthodoxy than the moderately insulated or, especially, the noninsulated settings, and that the secular campus would present a nearly impossible situation for the evangelical intent on being true to his or her faith.... [But], the more intent Evangelical higher education is on preserving the integrity of its traditions, the less successful it is. (Hunter 1987, 176-77)

Meanwhile, evangelical students on noninsulated or secular campuses actually have their Christian worldview strengthened! Hunter's explanation is that, in highly insulated evangelical colleges, there is no external threat to the student's worldview. The social environment of such colleges is perceived to be safe, so that one's defensive posture can be relaxed. The setting of the evangelical college allows for the relaxation of cognitive defenses, but "it is in the safety of this setting that the erosive effects of education can take place. In this case, the threat is not external and visible but internal and, by and large, unperceived" (Hunter 1987, 177). Thus, according to Hunter, highly insulated environments do not resist secularization but actually facilitate it!

In contrast, evangelical students in the low insulated public university setting are continually reminded of the vulnerability of their beliefs. No doubt the secular campus is a threat to the evangelical worldview, but it is also a "a trial by fire" (Hunter and Hammond 1984, 229). The recognition of the minority status of their convictions relative to competing perspectives fosters a "fortress mentality" among the strongly committed. In such a situation the believer's identity as a believer is accentuated and reinforced. In this context, the evangelical becomes even "more" evangelical.

Hunter concluded his comparison of campus environments by insularity by pointing out the following irony of Christian higher education:

> Contemporary Christian higher education...produces the unintended consequences of being counterproductive to its own objectives, that is, produces individual Christians who are either less certain of their attachments to the traditions of their faith or altogether disaffected from them. Education, to the degree that it is not indoctrination, weakens the tenacity with which Evangelicals hold on to their world view. In sum, Evangelical education creates its own contaminating effects. And the more Christian higher education professionalizes and bureaucratizes (that is, the more it models itself institutionally after secular higher education), the more likely this process will intensify. (Hunter 1987, 178)

If Hunter is correct, the future of evangelicalism in the United States is dismal. If the mission of evangelical higher education is to train leaders of the evangelical movement, and such training actually erodes students' commitment to their faith, then the inner vitality of the tradition is threatened. An implication of Hunter's conclusion is that perhaps evangelical higher education with all its colleges, universities, seminaries, and support organizations (e.g. mission/service agencies, publishing houses, etc.) should be dismantled. The secular public and private colleges and universities, according to Hunter, are more effective in maintaining the evangelical worldview.

Hunter argued that "the loss of binding address" is at the heart of the dissolution of evangelical faith and worldview. To him, a healthy evangelical community would possess cultural strength:

> ...defined by how deeply [the culture] is ingrained in the consciousness of those who live within its boundaries. When strongly institutionalized it is buried so deeply into the self that its meanings are understood implicitly--as a taken-for-granted certainty. *There is no need or compulsion to reflect upon its significance or to ponder its mysteries* [emphasis mine]. Indeed, any effort to articulate its total meaning would fail, for what is known explicitly is superficial, like an outcropping which reveals only a tip of a rock of enormous mass. (Hunter 1987, 210)

Hunter appears to be saying that a strong culture is an unreflective one and that reflection is the beginning of the culture's dissolution and eventually the loss of binding address. This happens in part "because the implicit meanings of culture succumb to the modern imperative of analysis, reflection, and introspection -- what Philip Rieff has called the 'therapeutic attitude'" (Hunter 1987, 210). The modern predilection toward reflection results in the separation of the self from the institutions that give it form and substance. From the condition of subjective detachment, what was once taken for granted is now re-evaluated, and there is a loss of "the feeling of serene certainty." The traditional culture and worldview of evangelicalism has lost its binding address, then, when "truth is no longer something unconsciously assumed but is something to which one must consciously and intellectually assent" (211).

The Evangelical Academy Project was a bold effort and Hunter deserves commendation from the evangelical community. No previous research of its magnitude had been conducted on students of Protestant evangelical colleges for the purpose of examining the effect of higher education on students' faith and worldview. Hunter's inclusion of a sample of evangelical students at a public university for comparison was wise and critical for interpreting his results. We are indebted to him for not only raising the questions he did, but also for conducting the research to answer those questions. Leaders of the Christian community, and especially those of evangelical higher education, have been reluctant to support and conduct this kind of research. Hunter's project showed that this research is possible, needed, and more ought to be done.

Hunter's results do not contradict the general findings of Pascarella and Terenzini (1991). Students at Protestant evangelical colleges experience some erosion of their evangelical worldview, or some liberalization of their religious attitudes and values. This finding is quite consistent with the studies reviewed earlier. However, his finding that the orthodoxy of the evangelical students attending a public university increased was a surprise. By contrasting this finding with the declines in religious commitment of students attending evangelical colleges, Hunter made an ordinary effect of church-related higher education appear quite extraordinary. The public university sample of evangelical students was, in my judgment, flawed and was unwisely used as a comparison to the evangelical college samples. I shall say more about this flaw in the next section.

Critique of Hunter's Project

Hunter's Evangelical Academy Project has several methodological and conceptual weaknesses which challenge the interpretations and conclusions he drew from his data. Identifying these weak points should help prevent the same pitfalls in future investigations. My critique involves six comments which, although interrelated, will be presented separately.

1) *Hunter's cross-sectional methodology is suspect.* Although not unacceptable in social science research, Hunter's use of freshmen-to-senior comparisons based on one-time only surveys to reflect change in religious beliefs during college is a weak methodological design to support his argumentation. In order to draw longitudinal conclusions from cross-sectional data, a researcher must assume that the freshmen and seniors are equivalent to one another, which is a very tenuous assumption. A number of factors, such as student selectivity, could greatly influence cross-sectional results. Terenzini describes the limitations of the commonly used cross-section design:

> Such designs have a number of limitations, however, including the need to assume that current seniors, at the time they matriculated, were similar in important respects to current freshmen -- a questionable proposition. Such designs also leave selective dropout during the college years uncontrolled. Not all students who begin college will finish it, and students who complete a college program, compared with those who do not, are likely to have higher aptitude and achievement records and greater commitment to college. Given such self-selection during the college years, freshman and senior groups score means would probably be different even if the two classes had been identical at the time they entered college. Any changes over the period in admissions standards or recruiting strategies might also have produced initially nonequivalent groups in the two classes (Terenzini 1988, 655).

Thus if a researcher is interested in how college students change during and as a result of their college experience, the stronger research design is a panel (sometimes referred to as a cohort) of the same students with repeated measurement over college years. Longitudinal research is very expensive, the reason why cross-sectional surveys are often used in lieu of the panel study. But even with the use of a cross-sectional research design to approximate the results of a panel of college students, there are techniques available to help reach the correct conclusions, or at best to avoid erroneous findings. Terenzini (1988, 655) suggested the following ways to reduce the nonequivalent-groups problem inherent in the cross-section design: controlling for age and entering academic aptitude through statistics, matching, or both. Another option is to use samples of freshman and senior students of the same age. These are preferable, if imperfect, alternatives to the typical, unadjusted, cross-sectional design, according to Terenzini. Hunter employed no such techniques in his study.

2) *Hunter's study did not distinguish between change or growth in students and college effect.* For adequate research on college effects, Astin (1977) advised that observed changes in students over time must be seen as having two major components: "the first is change resulting from the impact of college; the second is change resulting from other influences, such as maturation and the environment outside of college" (Astin 1977, 5). Relative to the study of religious attitudes and values and the distinction of maturation versus college impact, Astin wrote:

> Once students enter college, the trend is clearly toward greater secularization of religious beliefs. Are these changes merely developmental for persons in this age range, or does the college experience contribute to the changes? Results with age of the entering students suggest that secularization is in part maturational. (Astin 1977, 58-59)

A longitudinal study of the effect of church-related higher education on students' religious beliefs should use techniques for sorting out the effects of maturation versus the college experience. Hunter's study, since it was not longitudinal, could not do so.

3) *Implicit in Hunter's approach is the assumption that evangelical students' religious beliefs and worldview change according to some linear and regular fashion.* But, does student faith really develop this way? In her book, *The Critical Years*, Sharon Parks, focusing on the young adult years, introduced a rather complex model of how faith develops. About her own model, she offered this caveat: "One of the most serious limitations of this model is the possible implication (and not infrequent charge) that the activity of faith is being represented as linear and fixed, rather than as the dynamic, multidimensional, creative process that it is in reality" (Parks 1986, 95). Concentric circles, spirals, and moving pictures, she wrote, would be better metaphors for capturing faith development. A longitudinal study employing personal interviews would enrich the quality of information on how students change during college. Discussing the permanence of college effects, Astin offered the following counsel:

Long-term longitudinal studies show that differences in students' political attitudes, beliefs, interests, and career aspirations persist over relatively long periods of time. What is not clear from these studies is whether *changes that may be specifically attributed to the college experience* persist over time. This ambiguity can only be resolved with well-controlled longitudinal studies covering long periods. (Astin 1977, 209-10)

The same advice applies to students' religious attitudes and beliefs. Longitudinal studies of evangelical college students will tell much more about the future generation of evangelicals, but the question of what impact graduates of evangelical and non-evangelical colleges have on the church needs to be researched in a variety of ways as well.

4) *Hunter's sample of students from the University of California at Santa Barbara to represent "low insularity" was not representative in at least two ways.* First, it was not a random sample of the students attending the university, but a purposive sample -- students in a religious studies course. It is risky to compare random with purposive samples, particularly if a criterion variable coincide with the sample boundaries. That is, evangelical students at a public university enrolled in a religious studies course are most likely going to be assertive and defensive about their Christian beliefs and values. Second, the university sample was reported by Hunter to have a gender ratio of two females to every male: i.e. the sample was 67% female. Hunter admitted to the poor representativeness of this sample, but he used it nevertheless to contrast with the evangelical college samples and to draw crucial conclusions in his argument. Other research has shown consistently that religious declines during college are less among women than men (cf. Pascarella and Terenzini 1991). The sample's abundance of women drawn from religious studies classes made for a very biased set of university evangelical students for comparison with the stratified random evangelical college samples. Therefore, upon closer inspection, it is *not* surprising that the religious orthodoxy of the evangelical students sampled at his university was high. By comparing this sample with students attending Protestant evangelical colleges, Hunter accentuated the difference in a direction to support his own agenda.

Assessment research on Protestant evangelical colleges will need comparative data from public institutions. Every effort should be made to ensure representative sampling. One possible strategy is to develop partnerships with faculty at public universities and nonsectarian private colleges to participate in joint assessment projects.

5) *Insularity is a key concept in Hunter's argument, but his operational definition was pretentious and confounded.* In order to index how open a campus was to a plurality of worldviews, Hunter used the hiring and admission policies of each college or university. His public university was

assumed to be "low insulated" because it could not select or screen out faculty or students on the basis of religion. Six of the Protestant evangelical colleges he sampled were dubbed "high insularity" since they required a faith statement of their students and faculty; the other three colleges which had a "seeker" quota policy were described as having "moderate insularity." However, evangelical colleges are not as secluded as they are often portrayed by the media. Many of these colleges regularly invite speakers and visitors to campus who represent a wide variety of worldviews. Also, the mass media in North America precludes any campus, evangelical or other, from high insularity. Likewise, public universities are not as open to all worldviews as much as they think themselves to be: intolerance and smugness can be found at public universities as well (cf. D'Souza 1991; Marsden 1992). Public universities campuses are also strewn with pockets of insularity, homogenous support groups that enable many to survive in a pluralistic environment.

Hunter's definition of insularity was confounded by academic selectivity. Many of the evangelical colleges Hunter sampled were not only religiously selective, they were *academically selective* as well. Academically selective colleges or universities admit only those students with high grade point averages and test scores. Interestingly, these students also score high on measures of religious apostasy. As Astin stated, "Religious apostasy is reduced in the nonselective Protestant colleges and increased at the selective colleges" (Astin 1977, 235). The more academically selective, the more prevalent the liberalization and secularization are on a campus. Hunter, however, attributed the secularization which occurs to evangelical college students to be primarily due to the high insularity of the campus social environment. A re-analysis would be necessary, but perhaps the secularization Hunter found at the evangelical colleges could be accounted for more by academic rather than religious selectivity.

Perhaps a more representative way to classify evangelical colleges would have been *church-relatedness*. This is a complex variable but several taxonomies have been proposed (e.g. Pattillo and Mackenzie 1966; Ringenberg 1984). Also, measures of *evangelicalism* have been developed (e.g. Smidt 1988; Wilcox 1986) which could be used to classify the faculty and students and offer a percentage of evangelicals in each institution. Whether or not these indices can predict reliable between-college effects needs to be investigated.

6) *Hunter's static view of culture and orthodoxy misrepresents the Protestant evangelical faith and worldview.* A key premise to Hunter's argument is that a strong and vital culture is unreflective, implicit, and taken-for-granted, and that a weak and dying culture is reflective, explicit, and requires assent. Such a posture leads to a rather static view of cultures, including those of faith communities. The following sweeping statement about Western history reflects his premise: "From the Reformation to the late

19th century, conservative Protestantism maintained that binding address on most who professed the faith" (Hunter 1987, 211). Hunter simply ignores the dynamic role played by the intellectual leaders of conservative Protestantism during that period. In the present era, Hunter sees that the intellectual leaders of the conservative Protestant community, the faculty of Protestant evangelical colleges, as the purveyors of modern consciousness, of analysis and reflection, which only contributes to the dissolution of evangelical culture and worldview. The historical and contemporary evidence of the role intellectuals play in the maintenance of conservative Protestantism raises serious questions about Hunter's view of what contributes to evangelical culture's "binding address."

However, Hunter does challenge us to review the role of education in Protestant evangelicalism. Robert Wuthnow (1988) has emphasized that education was a critical factor in the polarization and decline of mainstream Protestantism. John Mulder commented on Wuthnow, with special attention to Presbyterianism, in the following:

> Robert Wuthnow has advanced the thesis that a critical variable in explaining this disaffiliation [from the established church] is the increase in educational achievement among this generation [the post-war baby boomers]. In short, the more likely a person is to have a college education, the more likely that person will be to drop out of the church or never affiliate with one. The correlation is stronger for children of mainstream Protestant backgrounds, less strong for children with conservative backgrounds.
>
> What is unclear about Wuthnow's finding is the meaning of education as an explanation. For example, is it the ideas encountered in higher education that prove to be corrosive of church affiliation and religious identity? Or, is it the experience of socialization in higher education that works contrary to church participation? Is there any difference in church affiliation between those who attend public institutions of higher education and those who attend church-related colleges? Further research is needed.
>
> But what is troubling about Wuthnow's analysis is that it questions mainstream Protestantism's supreme confidence in education itself. The finding is particularly alarming for Presbyterians who have prided themselves on being the pioneers of education and supporting public education and the ideals of the university in higher education. (Mulder 1990, 7)

Hunter argues that it is the *ideas* of higher education that are corrosive. It is the intellectual elite's predilection toward reflection and sense of subjective detachment that weakens the binding address of a faith. The commitment and moral zeal of early Protestantism have been displaced by "sensibility and civility," qualities that characterize pluralistic Protestantism today. To Hunter, not even the fundamentalists, "for whom sectarian incivility in the pursuit of a cause is not troublesome," can escape the loss of binding address effect of the modern world. The sectarian defensiveness of the fundamentalists reflects "an underlying uncertainty about the fate and resilience of the beliefs they espouse. If they were fundamentally convinced that Protestant orthodoxy had a future in the modern world order, there would seem to be less urgency to launch a defensive assault on it" (Hunter 1987, 212-13).

Hunter's evaluation of modern Protestantism and evangelical higher education is dismal: "Unwitting accommodation and sectarian defensiveness, then, are both signs that the traditions and creeds they live for are being transformed. Perhaps more fundamentally, they are also prominent symptoms of the loss of binding address" (Hunter 1987, 213). This statement epitomizes the dilemma of Protestantism's response to the modern, secular world: accommodation or isolation. Evangelical higher education finds itself with two parallel responses: professionalization and indoctrination. To the extent that evangelicals pursue the former, it will accommodate to secular higher education.   To the extent that it chooses indoctrination, sectarian defensiveness and isolation result. Hunter implies that there is no viable middle ground or posture.   Many others have identified this dilemma for Christian higher education, although in perhaps slightly different language. For example, consider the following statement by Mark Noll:

> ...evangelical colleges face many of the problems which confront all private colleges in the late twentieth century.   Financial pressure, the changing nature of governmental support, and uncertainties concerning the number of available students are difficulties as urgent on the campuses of the Christian colleges as elsewhere in private higher education. Yet these may be the least serious issues facing the Christian colleges.
> Far more germane to the purposes for which these institutions exist are questions related to overall academic purpose and to relationships which the colleges sustain with their wider constituencies. The history of Christianity in America, not to speak of its worldwide history, testifies to the precariousness of penetrating Christian thinking. The tendency has ever been present for Christian academics to drift into the secularism of the wider culture or to relapse into the obscurantism of cultic sectarianism. (Noll 1984, 35-36)

Noll implies that there is a middle ground achievable through the process of "penetrating Christian thinking." Hunter seems convinced that reflection and commitment are necessarily enemies and cannot exist together.   The corrective is to see reflection and commitment as complementary contributors to the renewal of traditional orthodoxy.   Assessment research should help us explore the possibility of a middle position for evangelical higher education, a position located between accommodation and isolation, professionalization and indoctrination, secularism and obscurantism, reflection and commitment.

Evangelical College Student Outcomes: Parkyn and Railsback

Since Hunter's project there have been few studies to determine the effects of Protestant evangelical Christian colleges on students. Despite its limitations and weaknesses, Hunter's study cannot be ignored and demands an empirical response. Do evangelical colleges undermine the faith of evangelical students? What is the cultural and political temperament of the coming generation of evangelicals? Fortunately, there have been three research projects, none of which were included in Pascarella and Terenzini's book, which have attempted to tackle the questions Hunter has raised. It is interesting to note that these studies, which employed more reliable methodologies, produced results which challenge Hunter's conclusions, suggesting that evaluating student outcomes is much more complex than implied by Hunter's research. The first study by David Parkyn surveyed alumni from thirteen Protestant evangelical colleges, nine of which made up Hunter's sample. The second is Gary Railback's doctoral dissertation on evangelicals in college, and the third is a longitudinal study by John Van Wicklin, Ronald Burwell, and Richard Butman which is presented in later in the volume. I will limit my review to the research of Parkyn and Railback.

Parkyn's Alumni Surveys

In 1984, five years after graduation, the 1979 graduating classes from thirteen member colleges of the Christian College Consortium participated in a survey conducted by David L. Parkyn (1985a, 1985b). The purpose of this research was to determine the extent to which alumni of these colleges thought that their undergraduate education had influenced their affective development. Parkyn's survey was designed to measure the perceived college-related influence on a set of affective outcomes: e.g. values, attitudes, beliefs, etc. These are in contrast to cognitive outcomes which would include basic skills and knowledge of disciplinary content. The survey consisted of twenty-eight statements developed directly from the mission statements from the member college catalogs. For each statement, the respondents were asked to indicate on a 4-point anchored Likert scale (none, very little, somewhat, very much) the level of influence they thought their undergraduate experience had on a particular aspect of their affective development. Ordered randomly on the survey, the twenty-eight statements represented five developmental areas: aesthetic, moral, personal, social, and spiritual. One additional item was a question which asked the graduates how they perceived the influence of their undergraduate education relative to the influence of other people and activities in their life during their college years. This list of people and activities included parents, early childhood, elementary school, secondary education, college, employment, church, volunteer service, and spouse.

Just over half (54%) of the class of 1979 of the thirteen Consortium colleges completed the survey for a total of 1,631 responses. Overall, the alumni perceived their institutions to have had the greatest positive influence in the areas of moral and spiritual development. The area of aesthetic development received the least positive influence during their undergraduate experience. Not surprisingly, the majority of the respondents ranked their parents and spouse as being the greatest influences in their lives. Undergraduate experience and church were ranked as equally influential ahead of all the other sources of influence listed in the questionnaire. These findings contradict Hunter's findings and support the distinctive claim of Protestant evangelical higher education. But, one has to be cautious in interpreting survey results since they are probably contaminated to some degree by social desirability. That is, it is likely that most alumni are going to respond favorably when evaluating the college to which they gave four years of their lives (and tuition).

While spiritual development was the area of their lives which alumni perceived as being influenced the most by college, there was an item which received a particularly low average rating across the colleges. In essence, the respondents were saying that the college did not encourage them to participate in a church. Parkyn offered this observation in connection to this finding:

> College-church relationships for the Christian liberal arts college are often like the town-gown relationships between many towns and the colleges which are located in them.   There is not always the appropriate level of communication, support, and endorsement from one group to the other. These Christian colleges need to have a higher view of the church, and encourage their students to participate in it. The church, likewise, must have an increased view of the church-related college, and encourage its parishioners to participate in it. (Parkyn 1985b, 73)

In 1987, Parkyn replicated his study with the 1982 class of the Consortium. His response rate for this second survey and the results were almost identical to the first and do not need to be detailed here.

Unfortunately, neither one of Parkyn's studies contained a control or comparison group to consider the question of differential impact. A sample of evangelicals from the same cohort who attended secular institutions and/or did not attend college is necessary before one can assert that evangelical colleges contribute to their students' spiritual maturation. Nevertheless, Parkyn's results are encouraging and should be taken as a modest indication that "Christ-centered" colleges are having some success in achieving their objectives. His research also suggests the direction for future research on the impact of evangelical colleges on student development. In the conclusion of his dissertation, he concedes what his study did not make clear: i.e. that studying alumni perceptions does not illumine *how* colleges influence their student's faith development. It is one thing to demonstrate that significant changes can take place during a Christian higher education. It is quite another thing to show what kind of experiences and relationships are responsible or act as catalysts for growth to occur.

Railsback's Dissertation

Gary L. Railsback's doctoral dissertation was designed to examine the impact of college environment on the moral and religious values of students who identify themselves as "born-again Christians." It consisted of secondary analysis of two surveys administered by Alexander W. Astin and the American Council on Education (ACE) and the Higher Education Research Institute (HERI) at the University of California, Los Angeles. The first was the Cooperative Institutional Research Program (CIRP) Freshman Survey completed in the fall of 1985 yielding a sample of almost 300,000 first-time, full-time freshmen enrolled at 350 U.S. four-year colleges and universities. Then, in the summer of 1989, a Follow-Up Survey (FUS) was mailed to a random sample of the original 1985 freshmen, most of whom had now graduated. Twenty-one percent of the sample, or 4,266 graduates returned their FUS questionnaire to HERI (Railsback 1993, 49). This longitudinal design, which looks at the same students when they first entered college and then when they graduated, enables the researcher to observe changes in the same cohort over a four-year period.

One of the regular questions on the Freshman Survey is "Are you a born-again Christian?" (response options were yes or no). Although this question had been asked in previous CIRP surveys, the summer of 1989 was the first time it was included in a Follow-up Survey. By cross-tabulating the responses to these questions, Railsback was able to create a measure of change and stability of religious commitment. "Maintainers" were those students who indicated "yes" to the born-again Christian question both as freshmen and four years later as graduates. This group, reflecting stable religious commitment, consisted of 16% of the follow-up sample. "Converts," or those who responded "no" to the question as freshmen but "yes" four years later, made up 4% of the sample. "Dropouts," or those who said "yes" to the question as freshmen but later as seniors said "no," made up 6% of the sample. And finally, the "never born-again," group, who consistently said "no" to the question about being a born-again Christian, comprised 74% of the sample.

The key hypothesis that Railsback wanted to evaluate was whether or not the evangelical college is a better environment than the public or secular college for maintaining the religious commitment and values of the evangelical movement. Using the CIRP and FUS, Railsback had access to a host of predictor variables to use in regression equations, which he categorized into five groups: (1) demographic; (2) religious; (3) attitudes; goals; and values; (4) self-ratings; and (5) college environment. The last category included the variable of institutional type, permitting comparisons of students attending public and private universities, public and non-sectarian private four-year colleges, Black colleges, Catholic colleges, and Protestant colleges. In addition, Railsback was able to identify those students who had attended member colleges of the Christian College Coalition, a coalition of over 75 Christian liberal arts colleges. All of the Consortium colleges whose graduates Parkyn surveyed are also members of the Coalition. With this information, he could compare the results of Coalition college students with those attending other ("non-Coalition") schools. In other words, he was able to categorize students into equivalent comparison groups, something Hunter had failed to do using a poorly selected sample of evangelical students attending one public university.

The results of the secondary analysis were not surprising but very important in response to Hunter's research. Christian College Coalition colleges and universities, which make up only 2% of the all institutions of higher learning in the U.S., enrolled approximately 12% of all the born-again college freshmen in 1985. Thus, Coalition colleges have higher concentrations of born-again students than non-Coalition schools. Of the freshmen enrolled at Coalition colleges in 1985, 81% said they were born-again, but at non-Coalition schools only 20% of the freshmen said "yes" to the born-again question.

In contrast to Hunter, Coalition colleges appeared to be more effective than non-Coalition schools at maintaining religious commitment and strengthening the evangelical faith and worldview. Coalition schools showed the highest percentage of students who maintained born-again status (76%), whereas public universities had the lowest percentage of "maintainers" (14%), and for all non-Coalition institutions the percentage was 16%. Railsback found that on Coalition campuses the "dropout" rate of born-again freshmen after four years was 6% compared to 28% at non-Coalition schools. Converts were more frequent at Coalition schools who showed an overall gain of 1% of born-again students from freshman to graduation. But, non-Coalition schools experienced an overall decline of 8% in born-again respondents. Railsback also conducted several other analyses looking at the relative impact of Coalition colleges on self-reported religious beliefs, attendance of religious services, academic growth, and several social and political attitudes. In all cases, he concluded a positive impact of the Coalition college environment on conservative Protestant evangelical beliefs and values.

However, Railsback's results were not so clear when he employed Astin's (1991) Input-Environment-Output analysis, which uses multiple regression to predict criterion variables for various subgroups of the sample. In Astin's methodology, the difference between the predicted value and actual value of the dependent variable is the estimated effect of college experience. Railsback reported that he used this methodology to predict born-again status, evangelical beliefs, and academic growth for Coalition and non-Coalition colleges, but the results were inconclusive. A major limitation was the small sample of Coalition college students.

Railsback's data is important but also has its limitations. Using how students respond to the question "Are you a born-again Christian?" when they are freshmen and then four years later as graduates is one way to measure what effect higher education has on religious commitment. But, how valid is such a measure for assessing *change* in a person's religious beliefs and values? Other research has shown that the question itself is effective in distinguishing evangelicals from non-evangelicals, but is this question effective in identifying *change* in religious commitment? To what extent did the change categories of "converts" and "dropouts" merely collect students who had forgotten how they thought of themselves four years before? Also, Railsback's categories imply that people who answered "no" to the born-again Christian question were not Christians. Research by Smidt (1988) and Wilcox (1986) on the correlates of the born-again question in a variety of national surveys has shown nuanced results. Obviously, more research needs to be done measuring faith commitment and change.

Guidelines for Future Assessment of Protestant Evangelical Colleges

The assessment research reviewed in this chapter show that Protestant evangelical colleges' effect on student faith and worldview is mixed. Unfortunately, Hunter's one-sided conclusions are being accepted uncritically. For example, Peter Berger, in his book *A Far Glory* (1992), refers to Hunter's research twice to support his own prediction that the evangelical right, like most mainstream Protestants, "will inevitably come to accept the beliefs and values of the new middle-class culture" (Berger 1992, 60). Relying on Hunter, Berger points to evangelical seminaries and colleges as a contributor to the "cognitive contamination" of evangelicalism, its loss of a spirit of conviction and self-confidence, and its succumbing to the forces of secularization. But, if in fact, the effect of these schools is more complex, we need to invite, endorse, promote, and fund assessment studies of Protestant evangelical colleges and make sure the results are published where they can be widely read.

We also need to use a variety of research designs. Longitudinal studies are essential. We must be able to study what happens to individual students during their college years. Further we must use control and comparison groups (e.g. institutional type, gender, and academic ability). In fact, I strongly urge studies that begin with cohorts of subjects in high school and follow them through college and into post-college life. This would require studies like the U.S. Department of Education's National Educational Longitudinal Study (NELS:88) that began with a panel of eighth graders in 1988, testing them every two years. In 1992 they were tested as high school seniors and in 1996 some will be tested as seniors in college and some outside college. Of course, this kind of assessment research is extremely expensive, but I believe the benefits would far outweigh the costs.

We must be careful not to study the college years in isolation. The complete answer to how evangelical colleges affect students must include the study of what happens to them after college. Where do they go, what do they do, and how well do they do it? Of particular interest is the church-college connection.   Does the secularization of the church begin in college, particularly in evangelical colleges, where its leaders are produced? Or do evangelical college graduates help the church resist the secularizing forces of modern culture? In sum, we need to study college effects in a larger context.

Reference List

Astin, A. W. 1977. *Four critical years: Effects of college on beliefs, attitudes, and knowledge.* San Francisco: Jossey-Bass.

_____. 1991. *Assessment for excellence: The philosophy and practice of assessment and evaluation in higher education.* New York: American council on Education and Macmillan.

Berger, P. L. 1992. *A far glory: The quest for faith in an age of credulity.* New York: The Free Press.

Consider a Christian college: A guide to 78 private liberal arts colleges and universities combining academic excellence and enduring spiritual values. 1990. Second edition. Princeton, NJ: Christian College Coalition, Peterson's Guides.

D'Souza, D. 1991. *Illiberal education: The politics of race and sex on campus.* New York: The Free Press.

Hunter, J. D. 1987. *Evangelicalism: The coming generation.* Chicago: University of Chicago Press.

Hunter, J. D., and P. Hammond. 1984. On maintaining plausibility: The worldview of evangelical college students. *Journal for the Scientific Study of Religion* 23(3):221-38.

Marsden, G. M. 1992. The soul of the American university: A historical overview. In *The secularization of the academy*, eds. G. M. Marsden and B. J. Longield, 9-45. New York, Oxford: Oxford University Press.

Mulder, J. M. 1990. *Presbyterians and higher education: The demise of a tradition?* Unpublished address to the Presidents of the Association of Presbyterian Colleges and Universities, Louisville, KY, March.

Noll, M. A. 1984. Christian colleges, Christian worldviews, and an invitation to research. Introduction to *The Christian college: A history of Protestant higher education in America*, ed. W. C. Ringenberg, 1-36. Grand Rapids: Eerdmans, Christian University Press.

Parks, S. 1986. *The critical years: The young adult search for a faith to live by.* San Francisco: Harper & Row.

Parkyn, D. L. 1985a. *Perceived affective outcomes of Christian liberal arts colleges: An alumni survey of the Christian College Consortium.* PhD. diss., Boston College, Chestnut Hill, MA, March.

_____. 1985b. *Research summary: Perceived affective outcomes of Christian liberal arts colleges: An alumni survey of the Christian College Consortium.* Unpublished manuscript available from author, Messiah College, Grantham, PA, June.

_____. 1987. *Longitudinal assessment of affective outcomes: An alumni survey of the Christian College Consortium.* Unpublished manuscript available from author, Messiah College, Grantham, PA, September.

Pascarella, E. T., and P. T. Terenzini. 1991. *How college affects students: Findings and insights from twenty years of research.* San Francisco: Jossey-Bass.

Pattillo, M. M., and D. M. Mackenzie. 1966. *Church-sponsored higher education in the United States.* Washington, DC: American Council on Education.

Railsback, G. L. 1993. *Evangelicals in college: An exploratory study of the change and stability of religious commitment and academic growth among born-again college students at Christian College Coalition and non-Coalition campuses.* Ph.D. diss. UCLA, Los Angeles, CA.

Rich, H., and P. Jolicoeur. 1978. *Student attitudes and academic environment: A study of California higher education.* New York: Praeger.

Riesman, D. 1981. The evangelical colleges: Untouched by the academic revolution. *Change,* (January/February), 13-20.

Ringenberg, W. C. 1984. *The Christian college: A history of Protestant higher education in America.* Grand Rapids: Eerdmans, Christian University Press.

Smidt, C. 1988. Evangelicals within contemporary American politics: Differentiating between fundamentalist and non-fundamentalist evangelicals. *Western Political Quarterly* 41(3):601-620.

Terenzini, P. 1988. Assessment with open eyes: Pitfalls in studying student outcomes. *Journal of Higher Education* 60:644-664.

Wilcox, C. 1986. Fundamentalists and politics: An analysis of the effects of differing operational definitions. *The Journal of Politics* 48:1041-1051.

Wuthnow, R. 1988 *The restructuring of American religion: Society and faith since World War II.* Princeton, NJ: Princeton University Press.

4. Assessing the General Education Component of the Curriculum in Christian Higher Education

Gloria Goris Stronks

I was teaching a class of senior-level students last semester and recognized in the group a young woman who had come to me for advising during her freshman year. One day as we were leaving the classroom, I commented on the difference four years had made in her life. We talked for awhile and then she said, "When this class began, each day I would sit there and wonder if you remembered our meetings back then. One of the things you told me then was that I must always prepare for meetings with my instructor. You said I must make notes about what I wanted to ask and show that I had done a good deal of thinking about what we were to talk about. You talked about the need for providing supporting evidence for my opinions so that I wouldn't appear to be talking off the top of my head. During this semester I have wondered more than anything whether you remembered me from that time as being the same person you know now. And I wondered what you would think about the change."

William Perry (1981), in an essay on today's students, suggests that while it may be a great joy for students to discover more complex ways of thinking and seeing, the simpler way they used to think was where their hopes and aspirations rested. In leaving the simpler ways of thinking behind, which is part of the process of growth, there may be moments of grief and nostalgia and a need for reassurance that what is happening is a result of legitimate growth. It takes a little time for one's courage to catch up with one's mind. Perry suggests that in moments of major growth, the instructor can serve as a bridge linking the old self with the new: "My instructor knew me then and knows me now."

Most faculty in Christian colleges believe that part of their task in educating students is to help them become aware of the changes and development in their thinking. The original meaning of the verb "to assess" was to "sit down beside while evaluating," and the best instructor-student relationship includes that element.

Christian colleges are presently in the process of trying to understand what the term "assessment" means to their campuses. There are faculty who greet this talk of assessment with defensiveness, suspicion, and even fear. It was so much easier to teach in college twenty years ago before we had available landmark books such as *Forms of Intellectual and Ethical Development During the College Years* (Perry 1980) and *Involvement in Learning* (Study book on the Conditions in Excellence in American Higher Education, 1984). Faculty members knew exactly what their jobs were and what was expected of students. And all of it could take place behind closed doors with very little fuss. Assessment is perceived as coming from outside the closed doors and invading the instructor's territory...reason enough for fear and distrust.

Suspicion is heightened because there is a feeling that "we've been led down a path like this before." The perception is that assessment is the hot topic of the 90s but, in the long run, it will turn out to be meaningless paperwork. We must recognize the very real possibility that if our assessment projects are poorly planned or managed without adequate supervision and funding, that is exactly what will happen.

Why Effects of General Education are so Difficult to Assess

Most colleges have engaged in some kind of assessment of their majors and programs, but there is an important aspect of college life that has gone unattended in terms of assessment. That aspect is assessment of learnings in the general education component of the curriculum. At most of our colleges we spend a considerable amount of time discussing and planning the required courses of the general education component. At some colleges it is called the "core" of the curriculum, with the assumption that moving through that core will ensure that students have common understandings upon which future instruction and learnings will build. We, quite properly, usually begin our discussions concerning general education with a statement of goals concerning what will happen to students as a result of having participated in that component of the curriculum. General education committees, however, tend to write goals in ways that will win the approval of the faculty and, as a result, the goals are written with such lofty outcomes in mind that any attempt to assess whether we have accomplished them is defeated because of their unrealistic nature.

The difficulty is, as Astin (1978) points out, that a student is not "produced" in a college in the same way that a bicycle is produced in a factory. One simply cannot say that if we do these things in college classrooms, they will produce the specific outcomes we have in mind. Students come to us as people who already have a great deal of experience and it is our task to help them develop from that point. Astin suggests that an industrial model of higher education does not serve well as a pattern for us. While it is possible to assess the impact of a manufacturing plant by the number and quality of its products, the actual impact of a general education component is not reflected in the grades the student received in courses. Neither is the total impact of the college on a student necessarily reflected in the student's scores on graduate school tests nor even in their scores on college standardized achievement tests.

According to Astin, we might look to a medical model rather than an industrial model to understand higher education. The main function of medicine, as of education, is to improve the condition of the patient. However, some patients do not recover as a result of the treatment, just as some students do not learn as a result of what is considered to be effective instruction. Some patients recover in spite of the treatment, just as some students learn in spite of ineffective instruction. Medicine and education both strive to bring about change in people. The task of assessment is to measure changes that occur due to the college experience in ways that will help students reflect on those changes and will provide information allowing us to increase the possibility of making changes happen more effectively.

In fact, the factory model of assessment has already created problems on certain campuses. Colleges that began using assessment measures in the mid-1980s tended primarily to use standardized tests or other kinds of evaluation providing only summative information, information that is collected and used to make decisions concerning the overall competence of a program or offering. These colleges experienced a certain frustration because, while they sometimes made changes in courses or programs as a result of the assessment efforts, the ways they chose to assess provided no indication that the overall effect had made a difference in student learning.

A medical model would provide formative information, which is information used to describe for the purpose of improving or forming education. The line between summative and formative assessment is not clearly drawn, but if the purpose of assessment is summative and the future of a program or major rises and falls on the results, the quality of the assessment information must be precise enough to withstand challenges concerning its precision. Therefore, we often use objective tests and numbers to indicate the results of summative assessment. If the purpose is descriptive or formative, such stringent conditions of accuracy may not be necessary since the purpose is to gain impressions which will result in discovering means for improvement.

Summative assessment provides information which appears to be more objective and precise but actually is less helpful in leading to an understanding of the effects of the total program. Formative assessment provides information which appears to be somewhat subjective in that it uses questionaires, essays, and student reports but it is helpful in providing information about learning as a result of the program which cannot be obtained through other measures. If assessment of the general education component is going to make a difference in what we do and how we teach, it needs to be both summative and formative in character right from the start (Schilling and Schilling 1993b). It must be embedded in an understanding of the goals of the curriculum and lead to a clear description of what happens to people as they move through the requirements of general education.

Although all faculty members on a campus may be engaged in student advising and therefore clearly know the course requirements for general education, there is little knowledge concerning what really is happening to students as they move through that component of the curriculum. For example, when I advise students concerning courses, I know that any course they complete will be recorded on transcripts. But what I do not know are the goals, topics, and assignments that are part of those courses I am recommending. I don't even know which books are required. In spite of the fact that I have studied the catalog carefully and know which courses are required of all students for graduation, I am recommending a curriculum I don't really know. Nor do the students seem able to tell me. In a certain sense, students cannot really understand the information gained in a single course or the importance of the assignments to their learning until they see all of it in relation to other courses and other learning experiences. By that time, some of the information cannot be retrieved from memory because it has become invisible to the student.

Schilling and Schilling (1993b) say that if we are going to change or improve an invisible system, we must first make it visible. Descriptive assessment, one kind of formative assessment, has the power to make the curriculum visible, an important first step in seeking improvement. Faculty tend to respect summative or quantifiable assessment of student learning but recognize their inability to use the results in ways that improve the curriculum. At the same time there is a mistrust of formative or qualitative assessment because of the indefinite nature of the results, in spite of the fact that it can give a clearer picture of what really is happening. A combination of the two kinds of assessment is needed and this paper will describe how that combination can lead to a successful plan for assessment in general education.

Descriptive Assessment of General Education

Descriptive assessment is part of formative assessment that occurs in such forms as comprehensive portfolios and intensive student interviews. It plays an important part in making the curriculum visible by showing how the curriculum intersects with the life of the student (Schilling and Schilling, 1993a). Faculty who have conducted extensive interviews with students or who have examined comprehensive portfolios have reported that they are provided with a much clearer view of the total effect their particular college is having on students. They come to know such aspects as: the extent to which campus guest lectures lead to coffee table discussions; classroom instructional methods that help or hinder learning; kinds of assignments that are being given and whether these assignments promote effective learning; aspects of campus life that encourage or hinder students from perceiving themselves as students; the extent to which the total college experience is changing the way students think as well as helping them to have more information to think about.

Students who have participated in portfolio and interview assessments report that the procedure itself has opened the way for additional intellectual growth and self-reflection. The problem with using portfolios and interviews in assessment is that they appear to be inexact. It is difficult to report on the results of this kind of assessment in a meaningful, helpful way. It can be done, but faculty will need instruction in procedures.

An interesting model for using comprehensive portfolios to describe student learning is provided by Western College, a residential, interdisciplinary liberal arts college within Miami University in Oxford, Ohio (Schilling and Schilling 1993a). The plan has been used for providing faculty with information concerning questions such as: What kind of learning experiences are students having as freshmen at our college? What kinds of papers are they expected to write? Do the assignments they are given really promote critical thinking?

Information from the portfolios has also been used at a parent orientation day for providing parents with answers to questions such as: What kind of work will your student do for classes? How will the experience at this college influence his or her values, ambitions, goals, concerns and attitudes? The plan is interesting in that it can be adapted for use at other colleges to provide a wealth of information for any faculty...information that presently is not available to them.

In the Western College Program, sixty students were recruited from a randomly selected sample of incoming freshmen. The students were asked to participate in the project for one year with the agreement that they would be paid $50.00 at the end of the year.

Each student was provided with a strong, three-ring notebook, and was asked to keep a portfolio of all materials produced for class, including homework assignments, tests, projects, papers, and computer exercises. Students were also told to include programs from concerts and plays attended and handouts from guest lectures which they had heard. They were not to be concerned about collecting too much material but rather were to include anything that was part of their lives on campus. The students were told that at the end of the semester they would be required to complete a writing exercise asking them to reflect on their experiences during the past semester. The written exercise would be followed by a structured interview with a faculty member.

For the first round, faculty volunteered to be part of the study. The faculty doing the study had no idea what kinds of things would be collected in the portfolio nor how much would be collected. They were simply told that they would, with the help of the portfolio, gain an impressionistic picture of the students' learning and of the curriculum. Faculty predictions concerning the portfolios were: there will be nothing there because the students won't follow through; it will be all computer print-outs with multiple choice test scores; it will be mounds of papers and homework assignments too thick to fit in one binder (Schilling and Schilling 1993a). The faculty who were involved in the project met in retreat to read the portfolios and identify assignments relating to the goals of the mission statement. The results turned out to be richer in information than anyone had dared predict.

The contents of comprehensive portfolios can be categorized or described in various ways in order that they may yield the information they contain. For example, they may be described by counting the pages and, in this case, the average portfolio turned out to be 121 pages. They can be described by tasks, such as counting the number of assignments requiring or providing instruction in critical thinking.

Portfolios can be described in terms of the number of writing tasks students have completed for which they have received instructional comments for further improvement rather than the traditional remarks with a grade. This is important information for a faculty that is concerned about writing across the curriculum. As the faculty read the portfolios, it became evident that, although students were doing a great deal of writing, there was no evidence of systematic instruction concerning the writing of the research paper. This helped them understand why students were having so much difficulty with the development of the senior research project (Schilling and Schilling 1993b).

The faculty at Miami described their students' portfolios by making a story out of each to show what first-year experiences were like and to describe the curriculum which the students actually encountered. Each story included such details as: the number and types of tests the student had taken; the topic and number of pages of each paper that had been written for specific courses with a sample of the kinds of comments peers or instructors had made; and a description of lab reports and journal entries. The stories would have provided an even clearer description of the first-year experience if they had included campus plays, movies, concerts, and sports activities performed or attended during the year.

The comprehensive portfolio project described by the Schillings is one that could be extremely worthwhile in the assessment of the effect of the general education component. Think how helpful it would be for a new faculty member to be able to read summaries of students' first year experiences. Or how much those of us who have been around for a while could learn about what actually is happening to our students rather than what we think is supposed to happen. If the same portfolio assessment were continued through the four college years, what a rich array of information would be available for faculty to use in decisions for shaping and improving the learning environment.

Another kind of descriptive assessment is the faculty-student intensive interview. The purpose of this interview is to help students learn to reflect on where they are in the process of becoming mature, self-reflective Christians with a keen awareness of the responsibilities that involves. Part of assessment is self-assessment, in that students learn to reflect on their own behaviors and interactions with others, and how all of this aids or hinders their movement toward a life of leadership and service.

Determining What Should be Assessed in General Education

If assessment is to occur as a result of measurement of the effect of the general education component, it is essential that the component has clearly stated goals which link the intended learning and development outcomes to the mission of the college. The broad goals of that component will likely have to be examined and restated to show very clear objectives. The objectives, then, will provide an intention with which the outcomes can be compared. One example of the broadly stated goals might be the following:

The goal of the college is to graduate students who view themselves and others as image-bearers of God and are able to take appropriate, effective action in their social and cultural environment. Students will: a) understand and be able to evaluate their own and others behaviors and emotional responses during social interactions; b) be able to discern when their own interactions and behaviors as well as the interactions and behaviors of others do not correspond with identities as image-bearers of God; c) be able to employ and facilitate effective interpersonal and group interactions within their own culture and in intercultural settings and contexts; d) learn to take responsibility for the development of their own gifts, recognize the gifts and tasks of others, and offer mutual support and encouragement so that all may develop individual and communal gifts for leadership and service.

The goal of the college is to graduate students who can locate themselves within the several traditions that shape their cultural identity. Students will: a) be able to articulate the biblical principles underlying the Christian tradition and also the central features of the tradition in which the college stands; b) be able to discuss the major worldviews and systems of theoretical thought that have historically informed Western culture; c) be prepared to explain the origins and development of the major institutions and practices (political, economic, scientific, social, religious, and aesthetic) of Western civilization in comparison to other cultures.

The goal of the college is to graduate students who have developed competencies which enable them to lead productive lives in the church and in society, both as effective participants and leaders. Students will: a) understand the values, attitudes, and behaviors that reflect an authentic Christian commitment and will be encouraged to adopt these as their own; b) be able to recognize injustice and human suffering and be committed to responding as a function of Christian compassion; c) have participated in out-of-classroom experiences which provide a testing ground for the ideas and values that are part of classroom instruction; d) be able to articulate basic principles of emotional, physical, social and spiritual well-being; e) and will be encouraged to personally adopt practices conducive to healthy Christian living.

The goal of the college is to graduate students who have developed facility in the basic college-level skills such as: systematic and critical reasoning; verbal (writing and speaking standard English), numeric, graphic, and multilingual communication. Students will be able to: a) make reasoned inferences from observations and logical premises and be able to articulate them both orally and in written form; b) recognize problems in a variety of situations, gather information, recognize implicit assumptions, analyze the problems, and apply solutions in various settings; c) speak and read in a language other than English, with an understanding of the culture of that language community.

The goal of the college is to graduate students who have an aesthetic appreciation of nature and culture. Students will be able to: a) discern independently the internal structure, pattern, and organization of works of poetry and prose literature; b) express personal response to the literary, performance, and visual arts in terms of their formal elements and in terms of the student's own personal background; c) relate works to their philosophical, historical, and cultural contexts; d) make and defend judgments of the artistic quality of specific works.

The broadly stated goals should be examined in order to select salient features for the focus on objectives. The five objectives which follow provide an intention with which the outcomes can be compared in an assessment plan. There are likely additional objectives which can be distilled from the goals but that aspect of assessment is part of the ongoing work of the college. Graduates will be able to: 1) articulate the biblical principles underlying the Christian tradition and also the central features of the tradition in which this college stands; 2) have the competencies that are required to do college work and are basic to the life of an educated person; 3) express their beliefs clearly and succinctly in oral and written forms; 4) discern when their own and others interactions and behaviors do not correspond with identities as image-bearers of God; 5) value interactions and behaviors in keeping with a life of Christian citizenship in the world.

Principles for Assessing

After the objectives for general education have been stated in a way that is in keeping with the mission statement of the college, it will be necessary to devise a plan for measuring the effectiveness of instruction in that component of the curriculum. It is particularly important that this plan be carefully thought through because a well-designed plan for assessing the effectiveness of general education can serve as a format and guide for departments in assessing majors and programs. One way of beginning work on the plan is to state basic principles which will guide the planning of assessment in the different areas of the college. Following is an example of such principles.

1. Planning of assessment will involve the faculty, administration, student development staff, and students.

The heaviest involvement in planning of assessment of the general education component will be on the part of the assessment committee and the faculty, although administrators and students will also be involved. Assessment of programs and majors will fall naturally to the departments responsible for those areas. Assessment of outcomes of non-curricular objectives will involve staff and students from the various divisions most heavily, but faculty and administration will also be included.

2.   Planning of assessment will begin with the writing of assessable educational objectives in each area which is to be assessed.

These objectives will reflect the mission statement of the college as well as the competencies and values expected of graduates in general and also in a particular major or program. The objectives will be stated as simply, clearly, and specifically as possible before any measurement instruments are selected for a particular area.

3.   Assessment in each area will be accomplished with a combination of formats because of the need for measuring different objectives.

Selected response tests, such as multiple-choice, forced-choice questionnaires, and matching test items, may be used in assessment and are often preferred by faculty because of ease of scoring. However, constructed-response tests, in the form of sentence-completion, essays, performances, portfolios, and diaries, often more realistically reflect learning. Those responsible for planning assessment should examine instruments already being used to determine how they fit within the comprehensive assessment plan.

4.   All assessment will be done with a view toward using the results of the assessment for program improvement.

5.   Each aspect of the assessment plan will be reviewed at specified points in order to determine whether the information provided contributes sufficiently to assessment.

6.   It will be the responsibility of individuals working in each area that is being assessed to write an assessment report for presentation to the administrator responsible for that area and to the assessment coordinator.

A typical assessment report will include the following sections: a) Objectives. What is being assessed? b) Methods. How are objectives being assessed? c) Results and conclusions. What do the data say? What are the recommendations? d) Future. What questions remain? What new issues need to be addressed in the future? e) Evaluation of assessment. What changes should be made in the assessment procedure for this area? How do the students who were involved in assessment evaluate the assessment procedure?

A Plan for Assessing the Effects of General Education

It would be ideal if the effects of general education could be assessed across the student body. However, because of logistical problems and expense of assessing the entire student body, an assessment plan such as the following could be used with a sample of students until the faculty is able to evaluate its effectiveness.

Initially, a randomly selected sample of 50 freshman students might be selected each year to participate in the four-year assessment project. In order to encourage student participation, the institution might consider paying each student $50.00 for each year of participation. Faculty members would be asked to volunteer or be recruited to participate in the project.

A. Assessment with the use of comprehensive portfolios to provide a picture of the first-year experience.

At the beginning of the freshman year, each of the 50 students will be provided with a strong three-ring notebook, and will be asked to keep a portfolio of all materials, including homework assignments, tests, projects, papers, and computer exercises, to provide a picture of what is actually happening in the first-year courses of the college experience. The portfolio will also include bulletins or programs from lectures, concerts, and plays which the student had attended or participated in during that year. The students will be required to submit portfolio inclusions at five points throughout the year. Upon each submission, they will receive $10.00.

Twenty-five faculty members recruited to participate in the study will receive training for doing so. The faculty will meet individually with their two students at the end of the freshman year for the purpose of reviewing the portfolio and describing the events encountered during the year. After the interview, the faculty member will categorize or describe the contents of the portfolio. The faculty will then summarize each portfolio to provide a picture of a first-year experience at the college. Each summary will include such details as the types of tests the student had taken; the topic and number of pages of each paper that had been written for specific courses, with a sample of the kinds of comments peers or instructors had made; a description of lab reports and journal entries; and a list of campus plays, movies, concerts, and sports activities participated in or attended during the year.

B. Assessment of objectives with the use of interviews and questionnaires

As the students move through the four years, the assessment plan will help them reflect on and demonstrate to the faculty the extent to which the goals of the general education requirements are being met. The objectives which express the intention of those goals in a way that can be assessed, are the ones which were stated earlier.

Objectives three and five. The intentions implied by objective three (expression of beliefs) and five (value) cannot be assessed by means of a paper-and-pencil test. Instead, at the beginning of the sophomore year, each of the fifty students will be interviewed by the faculty member assigned to that student.

Prior to the sophomore interview, the students will be brought together to discuss their reaction to the portfolio project. They will also be asked to write in response to the following (Bussema, Eigenbrood, and Lesage, 1993): 1) Name the three most pressing social issues facing society today. 2) Why are these issues important? 3) How will these issues affect your future? 4) How should a Christian respond to these issues? (A rating scale is available for scoring responses, but use of it would be reserved for future research.)

Upon the submission of essays on each of these matters, the student would make an appointment for a one-hour interview with the faculty member. The discussion between student and faculty member would center on the papers. At the end of the interview, the instructor will write a summary of the content of the interview and place it, along with the student's papers, in the student's file. The interview will be videotaped if the student gives permission.

Objectives one, three, four, and five. Objectives one (biblical principles), three (expression of beliefs), four (discernment), and five (values) will be assessed by having students reflect on their learning experiences. This is the purpose of the junior-level interview, which will occur at the end of the junior year.

Prior to the junior-level interview, the student will be asked to respond to the following: 1) how do biblical principles underlying the Christian tradition and central features of the tradition in which this college stands illuminate your thinking concerning a social issue, such as racism; 2) list the major world views and systems of theoretical thought that have historically informed Western culture; 3) describe the patterns and changes that have occurred in your thinking during your college years. What aspects of your college life have most influenced your thinking? 4) what service activities have you participated in during your college years? Describe your response to those activities.

As before, upon submission of these essays the student will make an appointment for an interview with the faculty member, and the interview will focus on the student's essays. Prior to the interview, the interviewer will read the earlier essays and the summary of the past interview. The student will be encouraged to view the videotape of the sophomore interview.

In no case will the papers or interviews be used for the purpose of keeping the student from moving forward in the curriculum or from graduating. The purpose of these papers and interviews is to help students learn to reflect on their own learning. As with the comprehensive portfolio, the faculty member should gain a clearer idea of the results of the college experience.

C. *Assessment of objectives by senior-level questionnaires.*

Objectives one, three, four, and five.   To provide the faculty with an indication of how exiting students view their education, at the close of the senior year the sample of students will be asked to respond to a questionnaire with items such as the following:

To what degree are you able to: 1) understand and evaluate your own behavior and emotional responses during a social interaction; 2) discern when your own interactions and behaviors do not correspond with an identity as an image-bearer of God; 3) employ effective group interactions; 4) take responsibility for the learning and support of others so that they may develop their gifts; 5) understand the underlying Christian or non-Christian assumptions of enduring ideas and contemporary culture; 6) articulate the biblical principles underlying the Christian tradition and also the central features of the tradition in which this college stands; 7) explain the origins and development of the major institutions and practices (political, economic, scientific, social, religious, and aesthetic) of Western civilization in comparison to other cultures?

Students will respond to each of these questions with a forced-choice, Likert scale.   Assurance that responses to this questionnaire will be anonymous and used only to help the faculty assess and improve the curriculum will likely bring about fairly honest responses.   Having reflected with a faculty mentor, during the junior-level interview, on the results of their years in college, students would be far more capable of responding to such a questionnaire than if they simply did it on their own.

D. *Assessment of objectives with the use of standardized test.*

Objective two.   In order to determine the extent to which the intentions of objective two (competencies) are being met, learning should be measured as it relates to the transferable skills implied by questions such as the following: 1) to what extent are students able to think critically; 2) to what extent are students able to think creatively; 3) to what extent are students able to recognize problems and solve them; 4) to what extent are students able to write effectively; 5) to what extent are students able to communicate orally in an effective manner?

The most effective way of assessing these abilities is likely through the use of a paper-and-pencil test, either standardized or locally-prepared.   While it is true that the locally-prepared test will more clearly reflect the goals of the curriculum, a college that is in the early stages of assessment might do well to experiment with existing standardized tests.   Creating a test is time-consuming and frustrating for novices.

Some tests that might be found adequate are the ACT Comp (short form), ETS Academic Profile, College-BASE, and CAAP. Colleges concerned primarily with the assessment of the effectiveness of the program rather than an assessment of individual students might decide to use the test with only a sample of students. They might begin by piloting one of these tests, perhaps at the entry and exit points. After some experience with standardized tests, the college may decide that the only way to assess their own objectives appropriately is through a locally made test but at that point they will have a clear idea concerning what is involved.

Such a plan for assessing the general education component of the curriculum sounds complicated but, in reality, is fairly simple to organize, as the following table will demonstrate:

Table 4.1
Assessing General Education Component

When	What	Purpose
Beginning of freshman year	standardized test	portrait of first year
End of freshman year	comprehensive portfolio	objective 2
Beginning of sophomore year	paper and interview	objectives 3 and 5
End of junior year	paper and interview	objectives 1, 3, 4, 5
End of senior year	questionnaire	objectives 1, 3, 4, 5
End of senior year	standardized test	objective 2

An assessment such as this would provide a college faculty with a rich array of information leading to a portrait of the learning experiences provided during the student years. It would provide evidence that might be used to improve those experiences. At the very least, those who are responsible for directing learning at the college would know the extent to which what they said would happen to students actually was happening on their campus.

Note: During the course of the 1992-1993 academic year, an ad hoc committee was formed for the purpose of writing an assessment plan for Calvin College. Colleagues who served on that committee with me were the following: David Guthrie (Dean for Student Development), David W. Laverell (Math and Computer Science), Rodger R. Rice (Director of the Social Research Center), Allen L. Shoemaker (Psychology), and Dean A. Ward (English). Many of the ideas in this paper were first presented and refined in conversations with the committee members. I am deeply indebted to them.

Astin, A. W.   1978.   *Four critical years: Effects of college on beliefs, attitudes, and knowledge.* San Francisco: Jossey-Bass.

Bussema, K., Eigenbrood, J. and LeSage, J.   1993.   *Student essay rating scale.* Dordt College, Sioux Center.   (Available from K. Bussema, Psychology Department, Dordt College, Sioux Center, IA 51250).

Perry, W. G.   1980.   *Forms of intellectual and ethical development during the college years.* New York: Holt, Rinehart, and Winston.

_____.   1981.   Today's students and their needs.   In *The modern American college*, eds. A. Chickering, et al., 76-114.   San Francisco: Jossey-Bass.

Schilling, K. L. and K. M. Schilling.   1992.   Summer orientation talk to parents at Miami University,   Oxford, Ohio,   17 June - 9 July. Unpublished.

_____.   1993a.   Point of view.   *The Chronicle of Higher Education.*   24 March: A-40.

_____.   1993b.   Descriptive approaches to assessment: Moving beyond meeting requirements to making a difference.   Western College Program, Miami University, Oxford, Ohio.   Unpublished.

Study Group on the Conditions of Excellence in American Higher Education. 1984.   *Involvement in learning: Realizing the potential of American higher education.*   Washington, D.C.:   National Institute of Education.

Stronks, G. G., D. Guthrie, D. W. Laverell, R. R. Rice, A. L. Shoemaker, and D. A. Ward.   1993.   Assessment at Calvin college.   (Available from Gloria Goris Stronks, Education Department, Calvin College).

Section B: Research

5. Squandered Years: Identity Foreclosed Students and the Liberal Education They Avoid

John Van Wicklin, Ronald J. Burwell, Richard E. Butman

My deeply held belief is that if a god anything like the traditional sort exists, our curiosity and intelligence are provided by such a god. We would be unappreciative of those gifts...if we suppressed our passion to explore the universe and ourselves. (Sagan 1979, 291)

Case #1: Danielle[1]

Danielle did not deliberate too much over her college choice. She had received an application from one other college but never filled it out. She was going to go where her brother went to school. She didn't have a clue about her major, but within a week chose music. She was listening to the song "Sing unto Him" on a local, Christian radio station and decided God was telling her to be a music major. She had no specific denominational preference -- just Christian. Her parents were Evangelical Congregational which she thought was "kinda liberal." She was unsure of her own religious beliefs and didn't appear eager to give them more definition. When asked about her sociopolitical beliefs, she didn't claim to have any views and she didn't appear to be searching for any.

By Danielle's senior year things were quite different. After initially declaring music as her major, she would change her mind three times. She switched to elementary education at the beginning of her sophomore year because she liked working with children and she didn't like being cooped up in a small practice room. After one semester she figured out that children were too young for her, so she then switched to outdoor recreation with a youth emphasis. By the beginning of her junior year she made her final switch to Christian education, with a career goal of full-time Christian ministry. This she stayed with until she graduated on "the five-year plan."

Danielle came to college from Kenya where she had grown up as a missionary kid. She soon learned that she lacked the cultural commonalities of her classmates. She also acquired a new role as representative of "the African" and "the missionary" perspective in class discussions and informal chats with her peers. She simply had to become better informed if for no other reason than to avoid the embarassment of not knowing what she was expected to know. Her freshmen and sophomore years had been a time for casting off her religious beliefs. She did not attend church and was not involved in any religious activities. Near the end of her sophomore year she decided to tag along with some of her friends to an abortion rally in a nearby city. Her friends were going to participate in a demonstration that day. Danielle had not given much thought to the abortion controversy, but a guest speaker at a campus-wide event had awakened her interest. So, she decided to accompany her friends in a supportive role. She got caught up in the spirit of the demonstrations and decided rather impulsively to risk arrest -- she was subsequently arrested. The time between her arrest and hearing opened a new frontier for personal reflection. Having eight months to fret over her pending trial induced much thought about law, morality, and conscience. Moreover, this critical incident became a catalyst for engaging inquiries into religious, political, and vocational topics. Having turned over one stone, how could she leave others unturned?

Danielle went back to Kenya and had some long talks with her mom. Her mom did not agree with her risking arrest, but affirmed the positive changes she saw taking place in her daughter. She changed her major to Christian education upon her return to college and started volunteering in a local church. She began to take her academic work more seriously and she started discussing religious and political topics in earnest with a few close friends. By her senior year, she could articulate well what she believed and where she was headed. Although by no means the epitomy of self-actualization she could at least converse more knowingly about abortion, about contrasts between one-party and two-party political systems, and there were even some new wrinkles in her religious ideology. She could also point up some significant differences between her beliefs and those of her parents while at the same time rediscovering her respect for their love and wisdom.

Case #2: Brian

Brian, like Danielle, did not deliberate over his college choice. He came from a Christian family, went all his life to a Baptist church, attended a small, private, Christian academy, and went to the same Christian camp for over ten summers. In his words, a Christian college "is something I always knew I would do. It was the next step." He wanted to go far enough away to be independent yet remain close enough to go home whenever he liked. The two Christian colleges he considered were both within an hour's drive from home.

Brian was set on business as a major from day one because "my dad is in business, I always did well in business classes, and it comes easy for me." When asked if he would be willing to consider anything else he said, "Not really. I have always known what I wanted to do. It is really the only thing I want to do. I can't really think of anything else I would want to do."

He claims to be Baptist, "and my parents are the same as me." When asked if his beliefs are any different from his parents, his reply is "Not really that I can think of. We really mostly would take the same views on things." He did admit to having some doubts about his faith a few months before college. Some of his "non-Christian...well...Catholic" friends started to challenge him with questions about the necessity of baptism, whether Christ is really coming again, and whether he could ever lose his salvation. They seemed to have some pretty good support for their views which upset and confused him. So he took his concerns to his youth pastor who calmed him down by telling him that he was never going to *know* what is right or wrong. He would just have to believe -- establish his faith -- and go on. Therefor, as a freshmen he was looking for college to establish his faith so he wouldn't be as confused and upset when others would challenge his beliefs.

By his senior year, Brian had stayed the course with his business major. He did drop his initial interest in accounting for personnel management having realized that working with people would suit him more than an isolated desk job. His parents continued to be supportive of his career interests in business but with a little more pressure for him to complete an MBA. In his words "My dad prefers that I get my MBA. He has one. If I could get a decent job, I could stray away from the MBA. I am not really motivated to continue with my education. It is just something they feel I should be doing."

As a senior he was still a Baptist and still could not identify even a small way in which his beliefs differed from those of his parents. There had been much consistency and uniformity between his parents and home church in the way he had been brought up. Until college he had been exposed to only one way of believing. When asked if he got into many religious discussions during college he replied, "I don't get into deep discussions because many of my friends have different beliefs and I am more afraid of getting into a heated argument and then someone will get offended." When asked if he had doubted or questioned his faith in college, he thought that doubt was too strong a word. In high school he was surrounded by strong Christians and had a youth pastor checking up on him every week. In college he was surrounded with many variations of religious belief, and this has made him a little more "open-minded" to other views, although his own views didn't change. As he put it, "I try not to keep thinking they [his friends] are wrong and I am right. I just have to realize there are no hard facts that enable me to know I am right. I just have to have faith to believe in my way. Sometimes I just wish things were more clear cut, but they are not, so I just have to realize it is never gonna be that way. Until the Lord comes and explains it I am never gonna know for sure. I just have to have faith that this is what I believe -- not that they are wrong."

When asked questions about his political preferences or his position on various social issues, there was little change in his responses over four years. In both instances he confessed to know exceedingly little about political matters or even what was going on in the world. He did finally register as a Republican in his senior year "probably because all of the people in my town are Republican. I have been brought up that way and that is the only way to be." As a senior he watched the news mainly to gain a sense of what had happened in his suburban locality. He had little interest or understanding of what was going on in the world at large.   He could not say if his sociopolitical beliefs were any different from his parents because he knew too little about what they believed and he had not acquired many views of his own.

These stories have been excerpted from two of over 100 college students that the authors of this article interviewed over a four-year period. In the fall of 1987, we initiated a longitudinal study of first-year students at our three colleges.   Our primary objective was to probe entry- and exit-level characteristics of college students with respect to psychosocial development, values, and moral reasoning. In the spring of 1991, we conducted a followup assessment with all 75 students from the original cohort who were still enrolled.[2]

Our 100 subjects, drawn from either a computer-generated random list or from volunteers in a large, first-year general education class, represent a combined incoming class of approximately 1400. All subjects were tested within the first three months of the academic year, and there were an equal number of students from each college. The followup assessment, completed during the spring, 1991 semester, includes all 75 members of the original cohort who were still enrolled. The percentages of women in the freshman and followup assessments are 63 % and 61 % respectively, which resembles the gender distribution of our three student bodies.

We used both quantitative and qualitative measures with these students. Our quantative measures included the following: a) Demographics, b) Survey of Major Social Issues, c) the Defining Issues Test and d) the Rokeach Values Survey.

Demographics is a survey used to collect information on relevant background variables including gender, home town size, parental marital status and educational background. With each subject's permission we also gathered information from existing college records such as SAT or ACT scores, rank in class, academic major, career goals, and GPA.

The *Survey of Major Social Issues* is a 36-item opinion survey to which each subject indicates extent of agreement. Items provide information on such variables as freedom of expression, women's roles, minority issues, and ecology (Pace 1975).

The *Defining Issues Test* is a structured response test of moral reasoning on which a student prioritizes a number of responses to moral dilemmas. The test yields a "p score" which indicates the extent to which one gives priority to principled moral reasoning (Rest 1979).

The *Rokeach Values Survey* is a test which consists of two sets of 18 values, one set designated as instrumental values and the other as terminal. Instrumental values are beliefs concerning desirable modes of conduct (e.g. honest, forgiving, logical, helpful), and terminal values represent desirable end-states of existence (e.g. salvation, a world at peace, inner harmony). The subject rank orders each set of values in order from most to least important (Rokeach 1975).

In both the freshman and followup assessments, we also conducted videotaped interviews to gather information of a more qualitative nature concerning identity development, moral reasoning, and cognitive style. The identity status and moral judgment categories were assigned by at least three independent raters at each college with intrainstitutional and interinstitutional reliabilities exceeding .75. In the followup assessment we had each student watch his or her videotaped, freshman interview and comment on perceived changes over the college years. We also administered two additional paper-pencil tests in the 1991 assessment only: a measure of Religious Problem Solving (Pargament 1988) and a measure of learning style called the Learning Context Questionnaire or LCQ (Griffith and Chapman, 1982).

Identity Development

In this paper we focus attention on a central aspect of our longitudinal study, identity development in general and the concept of identity foreclosure in particular. We do so because we are convinced that identity development is one important indicator of the extent to which a student fulfills the objectives of a liberal arts education. Our conviction is congruous with the following observation of Pascarella and Terenzini (1991) in their comprehensive review of college outcome studies.

> Historically, America's colleges and universities have had an educational and social mission to "educate" in a sense that extends beyond the cognitive and intellectual development of students. That broader mission has defined education to include increased self-understanding; expansion of

personal...interests; liberation from dogma, prejudice, and narrow-
mindedness; [and] development of personal...standards.... (Pascarella and
Terenzini 1991, 162)

About ten percent of this volume, one entire chapter, is devoted to studies
which examine self-esteem and identity development as related to the college
experience. We also find support for the value of identity development in a
paper commissioned for the American Association for Higher Education's
Eighth Annual Assessment Conference. In this paper, Fuhrmann and Armour
(1993) claim that by anyone's standards, the essence of liberal learning
includes the development of critical thinking, effective communication,
problem solving, and ethical behavior. Research reviews on the identity
construct (e.g. Muuss 1988; and Bourne 1978a, 1978b) demonstrate that
identity development is positively associated with improvements in the
learning outcomes cited by Fuhrmann and Armour.

The identity construct helps us to understand an important difference
between students like Danielle and Brian. Although both received bachelor's
degrees from their respective institutions, Danielle shows more evidence of
the personal growth and maturity that a liberal arts education is expected to
foster.

According to Erikson (1968), young adulthood is marked by a time of
identity formation during which one seeks to answer the question, "Who am
I?" Although one's identity is formed through trying on various roles and
ideologies, it is more than a simple summation of one's past. As Erikson
observes, identity formation "begins where the usefulness of identification
ends. It arises from the absorption [of identifications into] a new
configuration" (159). The social environment facilitates identity formation by
allowing one time and opportunity for critical reflection, the application of
new ideas, and experimentation with varied roles in an atmosphere free from
excessive anxiety.

Sharon Parks (1986) states that young adults are actively engaged in
composing their images of "self, world, and 'God' adequate to ground the
responsibilities and commitments of full adulthood." This process requires
interactions with peers and adult role models, and increasingly, young adults
are turning to higher education to serve as their "primary community of
imagination" (133-34). She contends that the college years are probably the
best window of opportunity for reshaping one's images because the right
combination of factors exist to enable such a transformation to occur.

The theoretical frameworks of Erikson and Parks are rich and far-
reaching but difficult to translate into researchable entities. For that reason
we chose the identity status model of James Marcia (1980) which continues
to be the most faithful and successful research translation of Erikson with
over 150 published studies (Kroger 1989).

Marcia (1980) has identified four identity statuses, each of which represents a particular coping style with the task of identity resolution. Marcia uses Erikson's concepts of crisis and commitment to define these four statuses. The *identity diffused* individual has not experienced a crisis or made any commitments. The *identity foreclosed* person has made commitments, but has not experienced a crisis. In essence, this person has bypassed identity by holding steadfastly and uncritically to childhood identifications, usually the roles and beliefs of one's parents. The *moratorium* status represents one who is actively seeking commitments by exploring alternatives. The *identity achieved* individual has commitments which are based on personal exploration. In the words of Erikson, the identity achieved person has "subordinated [identifications] to a new, unique Gestalt which is more than the sum of its parts" (Erikson 1968, 158). (See Table 5.1).

Table 5.1
Marcia's Identity Statuses as Related to Crisis and Commitment

	No commitment	Commitment
No crisis	Identity diffusion	Identity foreclosure
Crisis	Identity moratorium	Identity achievement

The term "crisis" is an unfortunate word choice because it connotes something like a "shipwreck experience," an emotional upheaval, or a psychological emergency. While some identity crises may be of that nature, it is more accurate to translate "crisis" as an active engagement with and exploration of alternative and competing roles and ideologies. The areas of meaningful exploration for college students include major and career choices, religious (more broadly, metaphysical) ideology, sociopolitical beliefs and sometimes sexual standards, gender roles and relationships.

The term "commitment" refers to the process of selecting from among meaningful but competing alternatives, and these choices are perceived as highly significant because once selected they are not easily reversed. (It may be helpful to think of what is meant by the word "commitment" in such phrases as marital commitment, institutional commitment, Christian commitment, and commiting suicide.)

Jordan (1971) offers a developmental model of the Marcia statuses that we find useful. She states that most students enter college either foreclosed or diffused. The social independence of college together with the challenges of curricular and co-curricular activity may stimulate personal exploration of alternatives (moratorium) leading to identity achievement by the junior or senior year. Although our work is obviously supportive of identity status constructs, it is important to recognize limitations. With any typology there exists a potential for reification in that one may begin to confuse a simplistic structure for the more complex reality it is supposed to represent. Many individuals fit identity statuses or developmental sequences surprisingly well. Others must be "hammered and squeezed" into one category or another. With respect to developmental sequencing, diffusion or foreclosure may *generally* represent a less desirable level of maturity than moratorium or achievement. Nevertheless, diffusion or foreclosure could be a preferred place for an individual in a particular context. For example, identity diffusion in the ranks of Hitler's Youth Corps might represent more maturity than identity achievement. Conceivably, Einstein's disengagement from a rigidly imposed high school curriculum may have been more compatible with his eventual development of relativity theory than commitment to what his teachers expected of him.

Most of the relevant literature supports the Jordan model of identity status change during college with shifts in the direction of identity resolution, and this is found to be true whether cross-sectional or longitudinal designs are employed (Pascarella and Terenzini 1991, 164). For example, Meilman (1979) and Waterman (1982) observe the largest increases in identity

Table 5.2
Overall Identity Status Assignments

Overall Identity Status	Freshmen Fall 1987 N=74*	%	Followup Spring 1991 N=75	%
Diffusion	27	36.5	5	6.7
Foreclosure	32	43.2	32	42.7
Moratorium	13	17.6	24	32.0
Achievement	2	2.7	14	18.7

* Data on identity was unavailable for one freshman subject.

between the ages of 18 and 23, allegedly because college environments offer students a diversified setting, mentors and role models, and freedom to explore ideas and test their assumptions. Parks (1986) also lends credence to the Jordan model by noting that students typically come to college with rather limited, homogeneous experience which needs to be enlarged. We would add that many of our students come to college *deeply committed* to their limited experience and rather resistent to ideas which fall outside a relatively narrow latitude of acceptance, especially in the area of religious ideology.

In our opening case study, Danielle is clearly an example of a student who entered college identity diffused and was identity achieved four years later. As Table 5.2 illustrates, 80% of freshmen in our study are foreclosed or diffused, and four years later only 49% are assigned to these statuses. Table 5.3, which provides a crosstabulation of freshmen and senior identity statuses for our subjects, reveals that 55% have advanced by at least one identity status in four years. (Advancement assumes that it is meaningful *for most subjects* to arrange statuses in a developmental hierarchy of diffusion or foreclosure, followed by moratorium, followed by achievement.)

Adams and Fitch (1982) note that about one-half of college students remain in the same identity status over a two-year period, 15 to 20% progress by at

---

Table 5.3
Crosstabulation of Freshmen Identity Statuses with those in the Followup Study

Identity Status Freshmen (Fall '87)	Overall Identity Status Senior Followup				Row Total
	Diff	For	Mor	Ach	
Diffusion	*5	10	10	2	27
Foreclosure	0	*17	9	6	32
Moratorium	0	**4	*5	4	13
Achievement	0	0	0	*2	2
Column total	5	31	24	14	74

* Subjects who remained in same identity status in longitudinal followup (29 of 74 = 39.2%).
** The only four subjects who regressed in identity status (from moratorium to foreclosure). The remaining 41 of 74 or 55.4% advanced by at least one identity status by the four-year followup study.

least one status, and 10% experience some form of regression (e.g. giving up on active exploration and returning to the security of identity foreclosure). In our study 39% are in the same status on both assessments (5 of 27 diffusions, 17 of 32 foreclosures, 5 of 13 moratoriums, and 2 of 2 achievers). Over half (55%) advanced by at least one status, and 5% regressed.

It is heartening to observe that over one-half of our subjects advanced their level of identity development. However, if an identity diffused or foreclosed status is truly indicative of one who has not acquired ideological commitments through a process of critical exploration, then almost half of our subjects have not made any significant progress toward identity resolution during college. Brian is an example of a student who was identity foreclosed in both the freshman and followup assessments. One can see from Table 5.2 and from Figure 5.1 that the number of identity foreclosures did not diminish from the freshman to the senior year. These rates of identity resolution are apparently normative (and not, for example, unique to Christian higher education) in that Pascarella and Terenzini (1991) find modest evidence to suggest that "from two-fifths to two-thirds of freshmen may enter college and leave four years later with their identity statuses relatively unexamined" (Pascarella and Terenzini 1991, 202).

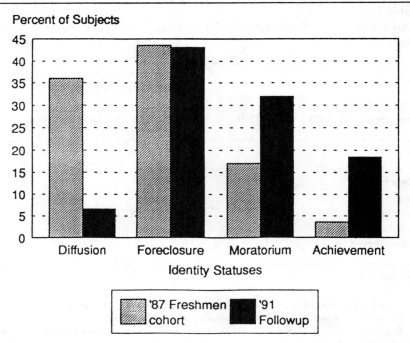

Figure 5.1 Identity Status Distributions: 1987 Freshman and 1991 Followup

What Does it Matter?

To this point we have distinguished the identity statuses *definitionally*. However, one could still ask the question, So what? What difference does it make for one to be diffused, foreclosed, moratorium, or achieved? The most basic way to answer this question is to note that most of the research following Marcia's model has been devoted to finding empirically-derived associations for each of the four statuses. Excellent reviews of this literature can be found in Bourne (1978a, 1978b), Marcia (1980), and Muuss (1988). Although exceptions can be found, this literature clearly supports identity moratorium and achievement as developmentally advanced in comparison to identity diffusion or foreclosure, especially when one steps back from isolated variables and views the profile created by the larger aggregate of research. Since this paper focuses on identity foreclosure, we will state the case from this perspective.

The identity foreclosed student is said to confuse *identification* with *identity*, conforming almost totally with the beliefs of one or both parents. Quite often parents are a "united front" in which one parent's view is indistinguishable from the other's. If a foreclosed student offers supporting rationale for a belief, quite typically this is borrowed as well. There is self-satisfaction here carried to a level of smugness, and the foreclosure's view of even the most complex issue (e.g. a moral dilemma) is cast in black and white terms and quickly dismissed.

The identity foreclosed person is typically a hard-working, "people-pleaser" whose self-esteem can remain high so long as one stays close to one's sources of approval. In that over forty percent of our seniors are classified identity foreclosed, are we sure that there is anything *wrong* with this orientation? Do we really need to do anything about a happy, hardworking student with high self-esteem who stays out of trouble and identifies wholeheartedly with warm, loving, Christian parents? After all, loving, evangelical, Christian parents have it fairly well together, don't they? Haven't these students come to our colleges prepared to work hard, get good grades, and become established by their college experience in the ways their families and churches have mapped out for them?

Identity foreclosed seniors have held fast to uncritical patterns of identification stemming from childhood and early adolescence. Their college experience may have provided them with knowledge and vocational skills, and it may have provided affirmation for the uncritically borrowed ideology with which they entered college. What they have *not* acquired is a transformed image of self and world sufficient to serve as a foundation for adult life. What is wrong with identity foreclosure as an outcome of four years of college is that it represents the loss of *unique* talents and contributions of an *individual* who is not simply a clone of another person.

Orlofsky, Marcia, and Lesser (1973) find identity foreclosed students to be low in personal autonomy and self-directedness and high in their need for social approval. Furthermore, Kroger and Haslett (1988) claim that college students who are foreclosed tend to have object relations structures which limit their psychosocial commitments to areas compatible with earlier identifications. These students may retain their sense of security and self-esteem so long as they remain in friendly and familiar environments. However, they will be vulnerable to shifting circumstances which may place them in diversified surroundings and require them to think and act differently. Although strong in one's beliefs and commitments, to use Marcia's analogy, this person is "rigid and brittle...like glass; if you push at it in one way, it is very strong; if you push at it in a different way, it shatters" (Marcia 1979, 9). It is this rigid as opposed to flexible strength that distinguishes a foreclosed identity from an achieved identity.

An identity *achieved* person may also have a pattern of goals and beliefs that are very similar to one's parents, but the difference is that one's self-image is rooted in personal and critical exploration of alternative goals and beliefs. We believe that Oliver Wendell Holmes captured this distinction when he reportedly said, "I do not give a fig for simplicity on this side of complexity, but I would give my life for simplicity on the other side of complexity" (Parks 1986, 50). Identity foreclosure represents a simplicity on the wrong side of complexity.

Our research with the Defining Issues Test points up a significant deficiency in identity foreclosed students. The DIT yields a "p-score" which is a measure of the relative importance one gives to principled moral reasoning. Rest, Davison, and Robbins (1978) report from a thorough review of DIT studies that the average college student's p-score increases about 10 points during the college years. Similarly, Shaver (1985) found 11 point increases from the freshman to senior year at a conservative, Christian liberal arts college. Studies have also found significantly higher correlations between p-scores and amount of education than between p-scores and age suggesting that the increases are more linked to formal education than to simple chronological maturation (Pascarella and Terenzini 1991).[3]

In other words, DIT increases may be taken as an index of how much progress one is making in moral reasoning as a result of one's formal education. In our longitudinal study we made a specific comparison between two groups of subjects -- 17 "persistent foreclosures" (foreclosed in both the freshman and followup assessments) and 15 "advancers" (foreclosed as freshmen but moratorium or achieved four years later). The "advancers" increased in DIT p-scores an average of 11.5 points (41.2 to 52.7). The "persistent foreclosures" (of which Brian is an example) increased by *seven-tenths of one point* (38.4 to 39.1). This is interesting because it suggests there may be something about an identity foreclosed orientation which limits the personal growth that can result from one's formal education and co-curricular experience. (See Figure 5.2 below.)

We also examined all 32 foreclosed seniors in contrast to the 24 senior moratoriums on several of the measures used in our study. This represents a "pre-crisis" and "mid-crisis" comparison, and it also compares those with borrowed commitments and those presently searching for commitments. The foreclosed seniors were found to have significantly lower DIT "p-scores" than senior moratoriums (For -- 41.2; Mor -- 51.7); p < .007). With respect to Kohlberg's moral judgment stages, 30 of 32 foreclosed seniors were in stages 3, 4 or 3-4 transition (a conformity orientation), and the other two were in stages 1 and 2 (personal expediency). In contrast, one-third of senior moratoriums (8 of 24) were in stage 5 or 4-5 transition (moving toward principled moral reasoning.

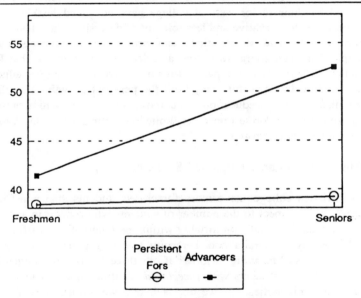

Figure 5.2 Persistent Foreclosures and Advancers: DIT "p scores" in 1987 and 1991.

On the Pace Scale of Major Social Issues, the senior foreclosures were more conservative on many issues, and tended to be less tolerant of diversity. For example, in contrast to senior moratoriums, they were less apt to agree that married women with small children should be allowed to follow their own interests (p < .01), or that we need more women in government (p < .05).

They were also more apt to believe that anyone regardless of color who works hard can get ahead in life ($p < .01$), and that minorities receive equal treatment from the police and in the courts ($p < .005$).

On the Rokeach Value Survey, senior foreclosures placed significantly lower priority than senior moratoriums on the values of broadmindedness (For -- 11.5; Mor -- 6.8; $p < .001$), and imagination (For -- 12.7; Mor -- 9.6; $p > .01$). These differences are interesting because a student in a moratorium phase is actively exploring alternatives and trying to form or "imagine" better conceptions of reality. A significant difference in LCQ scores was also found. On this scale, lower LCQ scores are in the direction of a cognitive style referred to by Parks (1986) as authority-bound dualism, and higher scores are in the direction of relativism or commitment in the context of relativism. Senior foreclosures had significantly lower LCQ scores than senior moratoriums (For -- 3.88; Mor -- 4.30; $p < .04$).[4]

In summary, this research suggests that students who remained identity foreclosed by their senior year of college have advanced less in cognitive style, are more conservative and less tolerant of diversity, place less value on broadmindedness and imagination, and are more conforming and less "principled" in their moral reasoning and decision-making. In that DIT p-scores tend to increase as one participates in the process of higher education, an identity foreclosed posture may limit the personal growth value that can occur with a liberal arts education. In that over 40% of our senior sample are foreclosed, the cumulative impact of limited and narrowly focused learning becomes a significant matter.

Christian Colleges and Foreclosed Students

Do Christian colleges have more foreclosed students than non-Christian colleges? With respect to the number of students who remain in a *pre-crisis identity,* we appear to fall comfortably within the range of "two-fifths to two-thirds" cited by Pascarella and Terenzini (1991) for colleges in general. However, it is still meaningful to ask if our three Christian colleges have a greater number of students with *foreclosed* identities than do most secular colleges and universities. If we do, is it that we attract more foreclosed students because of our homogeneity and greater institutional commitment to "in loco parentis" responsibilities? Furthermore, do we do less well in promoting the identity development of the foreclosed students that we have? Would they be "better off" if forced to face the greater diversity of lifestyle and belief to be found within a secular college setting?

Comparisons with other institutions are tenuous at best. First of all, most of the identity status research is insensitive to age and year in college as variables for control, and there are exceedingly few, well-constructed longitudinal studies. Secondly, most of the longitudinal and cross-sectional work available is 15 to 20 years old which suggests the possibility of confounding by changes in the sociocultural milieu. Furthermore, most of these studies use few subjects and do not take the necessary precautions to ensure representativeness of their respective college populations. Finally, identity status assignment depends on a subjective interview procedure. Without training tapes and computations of interinstitutional reliabilities (such as were done for our combined sample), there is a great possibility that we would be comparing apples with oranges.

Given these formidable qualifications, we will speak to the questions we raise concerning Christian colleges and identity foreclosed students. Our percentage of freshmen with foreclosed identities is 43.2% with the percentage of foreclosed occupational, religious, and political identities being 29.7, 66.2, and 37.8 respectively. The percentage of freshmen occupational, religious, and political foreclosures reported by Waterman and Goldman (1976) on a representative sampling of Hartwick College students is 29.6, 36.5, and 16.3 respectively. (Hartwick is a independent, nonprofit college of approximately 1400 students.) Our percentage of seniors with foreclosed identities is 42.7% with the percentage of foreclosed occupational, religious, and political identities being 37.3, 40.0 and 33.3 respectively. The percentage of senior occupational, religious, and political foreclosures reported by Waterman and Goldman (1976) for Hartwick students is 35.2, 17.3, and 16.3 respectively. Cushing (1971) reports a rate of foreclosure among juniors and seniors at SUNY (Buffalo) as 21.2%, and Meilman (1979) cites a rate of foreclosure for 18-year-olds as 24% and for 21-year-olds as 16%. It would appear that our senior foreclosure rate is high by the comparisons that we are able to make. (See Table 5.4).

The comparison to the Hartwick College sample (Waterman and Goldman 1976) is very interesting. Our freshman and senior foreclosure rate for occupational identity is almost identical. For religious and political identity we have a similar rate of decline in identity foreclosure from the freshman to the senior year, except that we have twice as many foreclosed subjects in both categories at the outset. If anything can be derived from the comparison it would be that a conservative religious college may attract greater numbers of students with foreclosed identities. Beyond that there is insufficient evidence to demonstrate that we are any better or worse in assisting foreclosed students to advance their level of identity development.

Discussion

Theories which cover the adolescent and young adulthood years stress a developmental shift from an uncritical reliance upon *Authority* to a emerging *inner* voice and *self-selected* authorities.[5] The 49% of our senior sample (Table 5.2) who are pre-crisis with respect to identity development have not

Table 5.4 Comparison of Percentages of Occupational, Religious, and Political Foreclosures *Hartwick College and Our Three Colleges

Type of Foreclosure	Hartwick College		Three Colleges	
	Freshmen	Senior	Freshmen	Senior
Occupational	29.6%	35.2%	29.7%	37.3%
Religious	36.5%	17.3%	66.2%	40.0%
Political	16.3%	16.3%	37.8%	33.3%
Foreclosed identity	**--	--	43.2%	42.7%

*   134 freshmen at Hartwick College from either the class of 1970 or 1971 completed the identity interview. 59 of 134 completed a senior followup assessment.

** Percentages not available for overall identity foreclosure in the Hartwick sample.

made this developmental shift. The other 51% have either made this shift (identity achievement) or are in the process of doing so (moratorium). What should we think about this? Should a 51% success rate be viewed as failing, much as if one had received a 51% on an exam? How could our general education curricula, let alone major and minor courses, not reach half of our students at a personal level? How could half of the student body remain identity diffused or foreclosed in the face of co-curricular programs supervised by student *development* personnel?

Perhaps this is a case of the glass being half empty or half full. Should we chide ourselves for being pessimistic when we have as much right to be optimistic? There is at least some consolation, as we noted earlier, that identity development among students in Christian higher education appears comparable to that of secular colleges and universities. Pending contrary evidence, we should feel as secure in what we are doing as anyone and pleased with our successes but not perhaps to a point of complacency. There will always be room for improvement.

In that most of our seniors in *precrisis* identities are foreclosed, some may wonder if this status is truly a problem for Christian believers. For our students, *religious* identity foreclosure most often represents commitment to conservative, evangelical beliefs in the *absence* of crisis, questioning, or doubt, and many Christians shy away from doubt when applied to the arena of faith. Questioning religious belief equates with attacking God, and doubt is seen as a disavowal of the claim that one can *know* God and be *assured* of salvation. In some circles, real questions are discouraged but phony questions, with readily apparent answers, may be allowed. Taylor (1992) provides an example of phony doubt in the "Christian" movie which

> allows twenty minutes or so of rebellion and "questioning God" on the part of its young protagonist, to be followed, as surely as day follows night, by twenty minutes of finding the way back to God and a happy ending. (Taylor 1992, 31)

We support the claim that *genuine* doubt or questioning should not be suppressed but made to serve faith. As Taylor observes,

> normally doubt is seen as sapping faith's strength. Why not the reverse? Where there is doubt, faith has its reason for being. Clearly faith is not needed where certainty supposedly exists, but only in situations where doubt is possible, even present. (Taylor 1992, 81)

We believe that identity foreclosure, characterized by borrowed commitments and the absence of critical inquiry, is a legitimate cause for concern -- even in the area of religious ideology.

If one is interested in initiating a quest for factors that promote identity formation in the context of higher education, then a classic study by Chickering (1969) is a good place to begin. His observations are based on a five-year, longitudinal study of institutional and student characteristics related to identity development at a number of small colleges. Chickering claims that the small college may have an advantage over the large university in the development of *community*. Erikson's (1968) psycho-*social* theory emphasizes the importance of community in the process of identity formation. Identity requires a mutuality of personal exploration and social affirmation by peers and mentors in order for identity achievement to occur. Chickering claims that identity development is best fostered when students are residential as opposed to commuter and can live in close interaction with persons of diverse backgrounds where spontaneous, meaningful discussions occur and close friendships can form. In the classroom he claims that identity development is best fostered when the educational experience reduces pressure for highly competitive, academic achievement, substantive feedback is given to each student regarding personal strengths and weaknesses, and the classroom reward system is based more on cooperative completion of assigned tasks. Faculty foster identity development when they are accessible to students, authentic in their relationships with students and are reasonably knowledgeable about the students that they teach.

The Chickering material is almost twenty-five years old. Does current research support these findings? Astin (1993) has recently updated his findings on college students through a review of over 20 years of data collection in his nationwide, Cooperative Institutional Research Project (CIRP). He claims that the most important factor influencing student growth and development during the college years is the peer group, and that beliefs tend to move in the direction of the dominant values of the student's peer group. Beyond that, he claims that the faculty represent the second greatest overall influence on student development. He distinguishes two important variables that characterize faculty in American colleges and universities, research orientation and student orientation. Faculty with a student orientation tend to be from smaller, private, four-year colleges which foster a sense of community, they have positive attitudes toward general education, and they allocate more time to teaching and advising than to research and writing, and supervising undergraduate research. He also highlights several student variables which appear to have a positive impact on student learning. These include time devoted to study, cooperative learning, independent research projects, giving class presentations, taking essay exams, having class papers critiqued by teachers, frequent student-faculty interaction, and frequent student-student interaction. Factors negatively related to student learning include commuting, working off-campus, multiple-choice exams, and watching TV. In summary, Astin claims that the personal development of undergraduates is aided by active engagement with the undergraduate experience and frequent and meaningful interaction of students with faculty and other students -- factors which are congruent with the psychosocial balance in Erikson's theory.

One theme that runs through the research-based work of both Chickering and Astin is the need for a community of faculty and peers that offer *a balance of challenge and support* integral to the objectives of liberal education. Too much challenge without support may make it difficult to sustain learning in the face of powerful dissonance, while at the same time make it tempting to discount, defend, or retreat. Too much support or homogeneity with little challenge may not nudge one out of apathy or complacency.

Parks' (1986) observations about the role of the professor in promoting meaningful learning lend support to this argument. She claims that faculty members should have both the capacity and responsibility to serve as centers of conflict, bringing out from their respective disciplines "with real power and seriousness those subjects which are...major aspects of reality" (Parks 1986, 141) no matter how threatening may be the contradiction of new ideas with those long and comfortably held. However, she claims that professors must do more than simply raise dissonance or inquisitiveness. She says,

> It is part of the educator's task to initiate the learner into a discipline of definition and critique so that the nature of the dissonant, the unresolved, and the mysterious is clarified. (Parks 1986, 142)

This process of elucidation should not be limited to the classroom. The professor on a mission to "push the little boats away from the dock" should be available outside of the classroom to assist the student in the painful process of rebuilding her worldview. Parks is in harmony with this process when she states that

> if the moment of conflict is to be sustained so as to make possible a new composing of truth and faith, the conflict must be held in a "context of rapport" which is to say, held in community, in communion, in trust. Teachers must have staying power. The conflict is creative only if one is not left alone with it, or otherwise has to defend against it. We can face the largest challenges before us only together. (Parks 1986, 145)

Dissonant ideas seem to be most effective in engaging student attention when they lie within a latitude or boundary of acceptance or at least tolerance. This implies however that a professor needs to know some things about students in order to stimulate the right kind and amount of conflict. It also suggests that the most radical environments are not necessarily the most growth-producing ones. For example, a Christian student in the secular university classroom of a radical professor may simply discount much of what is said, hinging such dismissal on the professor's widely divergent value system. By contrast, on a Christian college campus, the professor is at least initially assumed to be of like mind and faith making any process of discounting more difficult to defend.

Some might argue that teaching faculty are to provide the challenge, and that the reason we hire so many student development folk (most notably the counseling department) is to provide whatever support is needed in terms of damage control. However, these functions are not to be dichotomized. Challenge and support must come from everywhere in the college environment. Faculty members need to be mentors as well as dissonance-raisers, and a mentor is more than a distant but attractive role model. True mentors inspire learning not only by their challenging classroom rhetoric. They acknowledge, affirm, and give greater definition to the student's vaguely sensed images and dreams. They inspire, as Levinson (1979) observes, through an blending of parent and peer roles, enough the parent to represent the advanced level toward which the student strives, and enough the peer to overcome any generational hindrances to the establishment of rapport.

Faculty are not the only mentors, there are also coaches, counselors, chaplains, deans, and upperclass students who are tutors, peer counselors, orientation leaders, and resident assistants. Furthermore, student development professionals challenge as well as support by pushing students beyond comfortable limits toward the acquisition of such qualities as endurance, responsibility, differentiation, intimacy, active listening, and caring confrontation.

The learning style that seems most compatible with identity development is *active learning*. Active learning is a quality to be found *in the learner*. It is important to recognize that the mind of a seasoned, active learner can operate successfully with a professor who lectures relentlessly. Even with a knowledgeable but dreadfully boring professor, an active learner is busy taking notes, forming new images, raising questions for clarification, and integrating the lecture material with assigned readings and past personal experience.

The instrinsically motivated undergraduate student may be able to learn *in spite of* the teacher or techniques used. However, we feel that the average incoming student is more passive and extrinsically motivated and needs to be initiated into a process of active learning. In that sense we agree with Sharon Parks who says that "the young do not need to be preached at; they need to be given a task" (Parks 1986, 144). We believe that lecturing should be used sparingly, and interspersed with activities that require more active participation from students where teachers can provide specific feedback on strengths and weaknesses. These include class presentations, cooperative learning formats, and the use of essay tests and papers that require syntheses of ideas and personal applications.

If we wish to foster identity formation through learning, changes to the infrastructure are also necessary. For example, if a professor wishes to free up students from obsessive note-taking for more meaningful discussion, she may need to render less mysterious the format and content of her exams. If tests may cover "anything in the book and anything I say" the student may not be able to relax the hold on her pen. She may also be conditioned to feel that only testable information is worthy of her attention. If cooperative learning is to be promoted, a more relaxed, non-competitive classroom atmosphere must be established. We believe that adding such elements as more discussion, explicit testing procedures, and cooperative learning need *not* be at the expense of course or discipline integrity.

Structural changes extend beyond the classroom as well. More emphasis on informal mentoring, and greater reliance of essay tests, papers, and projects requiring individualized feedback is not likely with several classes of 40 or 50 students, or in institutions where "tenure-driven" research and writing are piled on top of a full-time schedule of teaching, advising, and committee work. If our general education programs are to be an integral part of learning for personal growth, then these must not be "front-loaded" and casually mentioned by advisors as requirements which one needs to "get out of the way." Although faculty need to spend time introducing students to their respective disciplines, they also need to break down artificial dividers to enable students to pursue real world issues across disciplinary boundaries. This would be assisted by at least some interdisciplinary team-teaching and coordinated curricula.

If Astin is right that much of the personal development to accrue from the learning process if mediated by peers, we would do well to break down barriers that exist between faculty and students -- not to mention those that can exist between teaching and nonteaching faculty. By way of illustration, Belenky et al. (1986) claim that teachers who rely upon polished lectures and syllabi tend to hide from students a very real part of the learning process. They cite an interesting passage in which a university professor perceptively notes that

> the form of many communications in academia, both written and verbal, is such as to not only obscure the influence of the personal or subjective but also to give the impression of divine origin -- a mystification composed of syballine statements -- from beings supposedly emptied of the "dross" of the self. (Rich 1979, 144)

We have heard good things about special programs such as the Oregon Extension, Houghton's Highlander Experience, Wheaton's HNGR (Human Needs & Global Resources) program, Messiah's Service Learning Project, to mention a few, where disciplinary and faculty-student barriers are broken down in the service of meaningful learning.

We may also need to restructure education to set the stage for personal growth from the very outset of the college experience. Freshmen orientation courses can be valuable for a number of reasons: 1) they introduce students to the value of liberal arts education; 2) they identity helpful resources for students; 3) they involve mentoring relationships; 4) they often involve faculty and student development personnel working together; and 5) they tend to provide small group activities which challenge the student, within an intimate context, to explore and to apply new ways of thinking and acting.

Case studies such as those of Brian and Danielle help to raise a number of questions and issues for consideration. For example, what factors were responsible for moving Danielle from diffusion to identity achievement? With her international background, challenge began for Danielle when she first set foot on the college campus. She instantly felt a pressure to be what she was not, an informed representative of African and missionary perspectives. Her coursework set ideas "racing through her mind" that good, long talks with her mother and a few close friends helped to clarify. Her friends would "convince her with good arguments." Her experience awaiting trial for her arrests at local abortion rallies induced reflection that extended beyond the abortion issue. This self-acclaimed critical incident became a catalyst for thinking about issues of morality and law, and of faith and life. Once one area of inquiry had been opened, how could others be left closed? We see much affirmation of the value of co-curricular and extra-curricular education in Danielle's story.

Danielle's story is not uniformly one of success. She seemed to be under pressure to declare a major and her reasons for choosing music were not altogether sound. Eventually her deliberations over four different majors would result in a one-year graduation delay. Is there anything that her college educators neglected to do that would have assisted her, or did she need to reach a certain level of maturity in order to take advantage of excellent opportunities that were there in abundance?

We wonder why diversity of background, such as that which Danielle illustrates, is a challenge for one student to grow and a frustration for another student to endure? For example, we can recall one charismatic, inner-city, working class, female, business major from a broken home of mixed racial background. Although her faith was an important reason for her choice of a Christian college, she confessed to having put her religious beliefs "more or less on a shelf" for the duration of her college stay. When asked if she had engaged in many, informal religious discussions with her peers, her response was "not if I could help it."

There is much talk at present about the need for greater diversity on our rather homogeneous college campuses -- and rightly so. However, our conclusion based upon hours of videotaped interviews, is that we are often unprepared to use elements of diversity in ways that are productive to student growth. In order for a college community to balance the challenge elements of diversity with community harmony, we may need more of what Mouw (1992) refers to as *convicted civility*. One the one hand, one does not value diversity if one expects accommodation or suppression of differences. On the other hand, differences with the weight of *conviction* may require a measure of civility or good manners if a college community is to be characterized by an atmosphere of psychological safety and open communication.

Brian's background is anything but diverse. His home, private school, and church background were so similar to his college milieu that, in and of itself, it would offer him little in the way of challenge. Nevertheless, Brian appears to have come to college with a steadfast purpose of establishing and affirming choices he made before he ever came to college. He didn't appear receptive to new ideas and alternatives in occupation, religion, or politics. He seemed intent on avoiding arenas of diversity because "someone will end up hurt or offended." It apparently never dawned on Brian that college could open his eyes to new ways of thinking, deciding, and acting. Was there more that Brian's professors could have done to broaden his vision? Are we obliged to help students like Brian to reach "the simplicity on the other side of complexity" when they come all set to affirm choices which are nearly indistinguishable from the prevailing milieu?

With respect to identity foreclosure, we should keep in mind that it is rather common for a student upon entering college to be foreclosed on parental goals and ideologies. The danger appears to be for those who do not relinguish this pattern of uncritical identification. The longer it remains in place, the greater the likelihood that it will become a *terminal* as opposed to *transitory* designation. If Parks (1986) is correct in asserting that young adulthood is a window of opportunity for identity formation, then those who fail to resolve basic identity issues during the college years are missing a major opportunity to do so. Life circumstances may not be as accommodating in the years that follow. Surely the blame for squandered opportunities does not rest solely with the student. College educators have a ongoing responsibility to know the educational process and their clientele well enough to improve the educational environment for everyone.

Endnotes

1. In both of these case studies, fictitious names were used and a few facts were altered to protect the confidentiality of our research subjects.

2. Funds to offset the cost of this research effort were provided by the Teaching Values Project of the Christian College Consortium underwritten by a grant from the Pew Charitable Trust of Philadelphia. Over the past five years, no fewer than ten faculty colleagues and twenty-five undergraduate students representing five different Christian liberal arts colleges, offered invaluable assistance in various phases of this research effort.

3. Pascarella and Terenzini (1991) review studies which examine associations between p-scores and age and formal education. These include Coder (1975), Crowder (1976), and Menkowski and Strait (1983).

4. In an unpublished study by Van Wicklin (1993) of a representative sample of 95 seniors, identity foreclosed students also received significantly lower LCQ scores in comparison with identity moratoriums ($p < .03$).

5. This external and internal authority shift can be seen in the moral reasoning theories of Kohlberg (1984) and Gilligan (1982), the cognitive style stages of Perry (1970), Parks (1986), and Belenky et al. (1986), the faith development theory of Fowler (1981) and the identity development theories of Erikson (1968) and Marcia (1980).

Reference List

Adams, G. and S. Fitch. 1982. Ego stage and identity status development: A cross-sectional analysis. *Journal of Personality and Social Psychology* 43:547-83.

Astin, A. W. 1993. *What matters in college: Four critical years revisited.* San Francisco: Jossey-Bass.

Belenky, M., B. Clinchy, N. Goldberger, and J. Tarule. 1986. *Women's ways of knowing: The development of self, voice, and mind.* New York: Basic Books.

Bourne, E. 1978a. The state of research on ego identity: A review and appraisal. Part I. *Journal of Youth and Adolescence* 7:223-51.

_____. 1978b. The state of research on ego identity: A review and appraisal. Part II. *Journal of Youth and Adolescence* 7:371-92.

Chickering, A. W. 1969. *Education and identity.* San Francisco: Jossey-Bass.

Coder, R. 1975. Moral judgment in adults. Ph.D. diss., University of Minnesota.

Crowder, J. 1976. The defining issues test and correlates of moral judgment. Master's thesis. University of Maryland, College Park.

Cushing, D. 1971. Identity status: A developmental model as related to parental behavior. Ph.D. diss., State University of Buffalo.

Erikson, E. 1968. *Identity: Youth and crisis.* New York: Norton.

Fowler, J. 1981. *Stages of faith.* San Francisco: Harper & Row.

Fuhrmann, B. and R. Armour. 1993. Liberal learning as the responsibility of educators in the professions. Paper presented at 8th Annual AAHE Conference on Assessment in Higher Education, June, Chicago, Illinois.

Gilligan, C. 1982. *In a different voice: Psychological theory and women's development.* Cambridge, MA.: Harvard University Press.

Griffith, J. V. and D. W. Chapman. 1982. The learning context questionnaire. Davidson College, Davidson, NC.

Jordan, D. 1971. Parental antecedents and personality characteristics of ego identity status. Ph.D. diss., State University of New York at Buffalo.

Kohlberg, L. 1984. *The psychology of moral development.* New York: Harper & Row.

Kroger,`J. 1989. *Identity in adolescence: The balance between self and other.* New York: Routledge.

Kroger, J. and S. Haslett. 1988. Separation-individuation and ego identity status in late adolescents: A two-year longitudinal study. *Journal of Youth and Adolescence* 17:59-81.

Levinson, D. 1979. *The seasons of a man's life.* New York: Ballantine.

Marcia, J. 1979. Identity status in late adolescence: Descriptive and clinical applications. Identity Development Symposium, Groningen, The Netherlands.

_____. 1980. Ego identity development. In *Handbook of adolescent psychology,* ed. J. Adelson, 159-87. New York: John Wiley.

Meilman, P. 1979. Cross-sectional age changes in identity status during adolescence. *Developmental Psychology* 15:230-31.

Mentkowski, M., and M. Strait. 1983. A longitudinal study of student change in cognitive development, learning style, and generic abilities in an outcome-based liberal arts curriculum. Final report to the National Institute of Education, Research Report No. 6. Milwaukee, WI: Alverno College, Office of Research and Evaluation.

Mouw, R. J. 1992. *Uncommon decency: Christian civility in an uncivil world.* Downer's Grove, IL: InterVarsity Press.

Muuss, R. 1988. *Theories of adolescence.* 5th ed. New York: Random House.

Orlofsky, J., J. Marcia, and I. Lesser. 1973. Ego identity status and the intimacy versus isolation crisis of young adulthood. *Journal of Personality and Social Psychology* 27:211-19.

Pace, C.R. 1975. *Higher education measurement and evaluation kit*. Los Angeles, CA: Laboratory for Research on Higher Education.

Pargament, K. 1988. Religion and the problem-solving process. *Journal for the Scientific Study of Religion* 27:90-104.

Parks, S. 1986. *The critical years*. San Francisco: Harper Collins.

Pascarella, E. T., and P. R. Terenzini. 1991. *How college affects students*. San Francisco: Jossey-Bass.

Perry, W. 1970. *Forms of intellectual and ethical development in the college years*. New York: Holt, Rinehart, and Winston.

Rest, J. R. 1979. *Development in judging moral issues*. Minneapolis: University of Minnesota Press.

Rest, J. R., M. Davison, and S. Robbins. 1978. Age trends in judging moral issues: A review of cross-sectional, longitudinal, and sequential studies of the defining issues test. *Child Development* 49:263-79.

Rich, A. 1979. *On lies, secrets, and silence: Selected prose -- 1966-1978*. New York: Norton.

Rokeach, M. 1975. *The nature of human values*. New York: Free Press.

Sagan, C. 1979. *Broca's brain*. New York: Random House.

Shaver, D. 1985. A longitudinal study of moral development at a conservative, religious, liberal arts college. *Journal of College Student Personnel* 28:211-18.

Taylor, D. 1992. *The myth of certainty*. Grand Rapids: Zondervan.

Van Wicklin, J., K. Adlhock, and E. Carpenter. 1993. Using identity crisis as an educational impact variable. Paper presented at the Annual Conference of the Association for Christians in Student Development, Houghton College, Houghton, New York.

Waterman, A. S. and J. A. Goldman. 1976. A longitudinal study of ego identity development at a liberal arts college. *Journal of Youth and Adolescence* 5(4):361-69.

Waterman, A. S. 1982. Identity development from adolescence to adulthood: An extension of theory and a review of research. *Developmental Psychology* 18:341-58.

6. Memories and Assessments of A Christian College: A Longitudinal Study

D. John Lee and Paula Smalligan Foster[1]

The purpose of this study was to investigate the influence of a Church-related college on its students' education and development. Previous chapters have already reviewed the literature on the need for, definition of, and process of assessment in Christian higher education. We affirm the perspective that does not separate evaluation from innovation (e.g. Light 1990). We prefer assessment programs which simultaneously incorporate measures and innovations to evaluate and take action towards achieving the mission of the institution.

The variety of approaches to college assessment matches the variety of colleges and higher education programs that exist in America. Criteria used to evaluate a college cannot be separated from the purposes or goals of the institution and/or program. Some colleges and courses of study have clear, definable, and easily measured objectives which lend themselves to performance-based assessments. Other courses of study can reliably and accurately be evaluated through standardized testing. However, the assessment of most higher education goals requires judgment calls on abstract ideals. For example, general education programs in our colleges are often justified as providing a "Christian liberal arts" core of study. Deciding what knowledge and actual abilities a student should have after a Christian higher education has been a matter of much debate (Carpenter and Shipps 1987). But, what will prove to be just as controversial is how to assess whether or not our Christian college curriculums have been successful.

When attempting to assess very abstract outcomes, it has been suggested that a variety of methods be applied simultaneously (Hanson 1982; Marchese 1987). Marchese (1987) noted that one of the commonalities among successful assessment programs has been the use of "multiple methods (written exams, orals, portfolio analysis, interviews, tests, demonstrations, etc.) in a variety of settings over a period of time as a condition of judgment" (19). A critical message that we must convey to our constituencies, the general public, legislators, and accreditation agencies is that college assessment should not be reduced to a single standardized test score. Test scores have their place, but they are only part of the picture in research on educational outcomes. State or agency mandates for assessment do not necessarily imply that colleges must start "teaching for a test." Qualitative assessments, like interviews and simulation performances, are just as important in the evaluation. In the case of a Christian liberal arts education, qualitative descriptors are a necessary complement to traditional standardized test scores. Thus, while our study uses qualitative descriptors, we recognize the need for other procedures and measures to assess a Christian college education.

We had three reasons for taking up this project. One, the first author wanted to extend his dissertation research on autobiographical memory to include a review of memory content as well as process. Second, we wanted to contribute to the assessment dialogue at Christian colleges, particularly in the area of thinking about and measuring our goal of Christian maturity. Third, we wanted to explore the application of a narrative root metaphor (Sarbin 1986) to the discussion of faith development both in terms of theory and method.

Next, we describe our method or research design. Following that, we review our results in two sections: memories and assessments of college. We conclude with a summary of our recommendations.

Method

Our project is a college assessment study which combined methodology used in autobiographical memory research with interviews reviewing students' college experience. In the jargon of a methodologist, our study is a cross-sectional longitudinal design using two cohorts over a three year period. (A cohort is a group of students who all started college in the same year.) The advantage of such a design is the ability to compare two different cohorts at the same and different periods of their development. Such comparisons enable the researchers to discern what results are found for both groups and what results are unique to a group or are cohort-specific. The limitation of this methodology (like any other method which takes some form of measurement) is the possibility that the results do not generalize to current or future populations. That is, what our method revealed to us about the Classes of 1988 and 1991 may or may not be applicable or true of future graduating classes.

Procedure

During the fall semester of 1987 a group of Calvin College first-year students kept "diaries" of unique events (defined later) in their lives. At the end of the semester, various measures were taken to test their memories for the events they had recorded. Then, during the spring semester of 1988, another group of first-year students kept diaries for two months. At the end of their semester, these students were interviewed to see what they remembered from their first year or to assess the impact of their first year of college on their lives. Arrangements were then made to contact the students when they were seniors (1990-91) to do more memory testing and to assess their entire college experience.

In addition to the two groups of first-year students, a third group of seniors were interviewed during the spring semester of 1988. Since these students had not kept diaries, no memory testing was done with them. An outline of the research design is presented in Table 6.1.

Table 6.1 Memories and Assessments of a Christian College Research Design

	Fall 1987	Spring 1988	Spring 1991
Group 1 Class of 1991	diary keeping & memory testing (n=20)	____	memory testing & college assess. (n=8)
Group 2 Class of 1991	____	diary keeping & 1st yr. assess. (n=30)	memory testing & college assess. (n=18)
Group 3 Class of 1988	____	college assess. (n=20)	college assess. (n-16)

The memory testing involved asking students to recall portions of an event that they recorded in their diaries as well as rate their memory for the event and estimate when it may have occurred. The kind of results these measures produced are reported in Lee (1987) and Thompson, Skowronski and Lee (1988a; 1988b).

The college assessments were three types of interviews which varied in their procedure and primary purpose.[2] Each interview began with a description of the purpose of the research and an explanation of how confidentiality would be maintained. While still respecting their privacy, the participants were encouraged to be as honest as possible. The interviews were audiotaped and later transcribed for review and analysis.

The *salient memory* assessment proceeded by asking the student to describe "the first memory that comes to mind" from each semester and summer of their college years.[3] The purpose of this interview was to see if there was a relationship between the kind of memories recalled and the different periods of a college student's life.

The *topical* college assessment interview was a qualitative measure. We invited the student to review their college years by focusing on a series of topics (e.g. housing, academics, co-curricular activities, significant others, dating, faith, etc.). This type of interview is often used by developmental psychologists, although the focus is usually on only one aspect of the subject's life: e.g. moral reasoning or faith development. The college assessor's "exit interview" is similar, but again, there is usually a clear expectation and focus. Our procedure was broad and sacrificed detail, but we attempted to minimize the problems that can occur in focused interviews, (e.g. social desirability). This assessment was undertaken to explore what kind of experiences facilitate or inhibit the qualitative changes which a Christian liberal arts college hopes to see in the lives of its students.

The *undirected* college assessment provided both autobiographical memory and qualitative assessment data. In this procedure, students were asked to describe their college experience. The interviewer simply said to the person, "Please describe the last four years of your life." The interviewer tried to minimize his or her interaction with the student, interrupting only to ask for clarifications. This assessment allowed the students to determine their own topics as they reviewed their college years. What is contained in these college narratives is what the students chose to describe and not necessarily what we wanted to hear.[4] Besides the assessment data these college stories provided, they also provided some interesting data on how people remember a segment of their life. That is, in this procedure, we were interested in both the content and the process of remembering. It was our expectation that students would "narrativize" their experience. We expected that the process of remembering in this context would be through various narrative forms or structures (Gergen and Gergen 1983). Simply put, we thought that students would tell us stories.

Participants

As indicated in Table 6.1, seventy (70) students began the study in 1987-88. Unfortunately, only forty-two (42) participants returned for the follow-up memory testing and/or college interviews. Most of the attrition from Group 1 was probably because their experience in 1987 with the memory testing had been tedious. In support of this interpretation, more than half of Groups 2 and 3 came back in 1991, many of whom expressed how enjoyable the first interview was and how they had looked forward to doing it again. Participants from the first two groups were volunteers from the first author's introductory psychology course. The students from the third group were volunteers from a random sampling of the entire 1988 graduating class.

Of the twenty-six students in Groups 1 and 2 who completed the study, eighteen were female and eight were male. There were a variety of majors represented in these two groups: education (5), nursing (3), English/literature (3), history (2), psychology (2), business (2), social sciences (2), sociology, social work, political science, recreation, biology, and communications. The median grade point average (GPA) of these graduates was 3.16 with a high of 3.90 and a low of 2.24. The majority were born in 1969, and thus, were 22 years when we did our final assessments. One person was six years older than the others and was attending college part-time. A third of the students had grown up in West Michigan, another third in other areas of Michigan, and the remaining third in other parts of North America. When asked about their religious affiliation, three-quarters of the students identified with the Christian Reformed (CRC) or the Reformed Church in America (RCA) while the others named other Protestant denominations. One person did not identify with any religious group or faith community. Apart from the low numbers of males these demographics are very close to overall statistics for the class of 1991.

There were an equal number of males and females in Group 3. Again, a variety of majors were represented; English/literature (2), communications (2), psychology (2), art (2), education, history, art history, philosophy, mathematics, biology, computer science and nursing. The median GPA was 3.09 with a high of 3.93 and low of 2.22. The majority of these students were 25 years old at our follow-up assessment. However, one person was 29 and another 32 in 1991, both of whom had been full-time students but had started college at a later age. Six of these graduates had been raised in Grand Rapids, four in other areas of Michigan, and eight in Illinois, Wisconsin, New Jersey, California, Washington state and Ontario, Canada. In terms of religious identification, ten students named the Christian Reformed Church, two were Presbyterians, and four identified with non-denominational Christian churches. Even with this very small sample, these demographics are representative of the entire class of 1988.

In terms of their larger cultural context, most of the participants were North American urban or suburban dwellers who identified their socio-economic status as "middle class." Some news or public events which happened during Group 3's college years (1984-88) were the famine in Ethiopia, the Chernobyl nuclear plant disaster, the Challenger explosion, the Iran-Contra controversy, the New York stock market collapse, the television evangelist scandals, Madonna's song "Like a Virgin," and the Vietnam war was often the topic of Hollywood movies and documentaries. Some of the events which occurred during the first two groups' college years (1987-91) were the Seoul Olympics, the Exxon's Valdez oil disaster, the San Francisco earthquake, the U.S. invasion of Panama, Lithuanian independence, the fall of the Berlin Wall, the Gulf War, and rap music made its mark on popular culture.

Results

Our methodology yielded an enormous amount of data. Although the results are all related, we have decided to present them in two sections. The first deals primarily with the college memories of our participants and how they remembered events from their college years. The second section focuses on the results of our college assessment interviews.

Section One: Memories of College

This section is divided into three parts. The first briefly describes the results of our memory testing. The second reviews the content of the diaries kept by Groups 1 and 2 during their first year of college. The results of our salient memory assessment interview and a short discussion on what implications our memory data has for assessment research are presented in the third section.

1. Memory Testing

The participants were told that they would have their memories tested for events entered into their diary. To avoid rehearsal, the students handed in their diary entries each week for the two month recording period. They were not given the details of the memory measurements but were assured that their performance would not effect their course grade. The memory test involved three components: 1) a recall task, 2) a memory rating, and 3) a dating estimate.

The first component of the memory test, a recall task, was tested in this way: for a sample of 32 diary entries (4 per week), we first read the entry back to the participant leaving out one of three details (WHAT, WHO, or WHERE) and asked him or her to recall the missing detail. At the first testing, participants were able to recall the missing detail on the average 90% of the time. As expected, three years later, this average falls to 50% correct recall. The age of the events could not predict the errors, but there were more errors when the WHAT information was omitted than with the WHO or WHERE cues. That is, WHAT a person did appears to be more important to this kind of recall than WHO they did it with and WHERE it occurred (Burt 1992; Wagenaar 1986).

Memory rating, the second component of the memory test was to ask the participants to rate their memory for the event. Herrmann and Neisser's (1978) 7-point anchored scale was used which ranged from "not at all" (1) to "perfectly" (7) which was defined as an exceptionally clear and vivid memory. The results from the first testing replicated what we had found earlier. The average memory ratings when charted over age of the event produces a classic "forgetting curve" where older events are not rated as high as more recent events. However, at the second testing three years later, our participants rated their memory for the events either very high or very low. They either remembered the event very well or barely at all. That is, the three year delay disabled our scale from its ability to make discriminations on the basis of the age of the event.

Finally, a dating estimate was collected by providing students with a calendar of the semester in which they kept their diaries and asking them to estimate when the event occurred. Again, the results from the first testing were not different from what we had found before. The average dating error increased as the age of the event increased and participants were quite accurate in locating when an event occurred if there was a reference point they could use in making their determination: e.g. "I know that happened the day before our Thanksgiving break." During the second testing, the only events that were dated with any accuracy were those which could easily be located because of reference information: e.g. "That obviously occurred on Valentine's day." Thus, when participants tried to estimate when an event occurred three years later, they guessed most of the time.

These results are not different from those reported in previous research (Lee 1987; Thompson, Skowronski, and Lee 1988a; 1988b). It should be noted that the relevance of autobiographical memory research has been extensively debated (Banaji and Crowder 1989; Loftus 1991). We believe that systematic inquiries into memories for naturally-occurring events can have a variety of applications, one of which is college assessment research.

2. Diary Content

Keeping a "diary" consisted of recording one unique event every day for eight weeks. A "unique event" was defined as an event which the person did not expect to occur more than once during the semester. For example, "Today, I broke up with my boyfriend from high school" was a unique event.

In contrast, students were instructed not to record events such as "I went shopping at the mall today," which, in most cases, would not be a unique event. Table 6.2 summarizes the type of unique events the participants entered into their diaries. Using the work of David Pillemer and his associates (1986), the first author wrote coding rules for the three typologies. The second author and another assistant coded the diary entries. The average intercoder agreement for the three categories was almost 90%.

Table 6.2 Diary Content

A. Event Structure

	Specific	General	Mixed	Missing Value
Mean %	90	1	1	8

B. Dominant Theme

	Academic	Housing	Romantic	Recreation/ Leisure	Missing Value
Mean %	10	5	10	65	10

C. Social Orientation

	Individual	Interpersonal	Missing Value
Mean %	20	70	10

The average number of entries per participant was 50. The *Missing Value* category represents the average percentage of entries which were left blank in diaries OR did not fit into the categories.

Event structure refers to the form or type of experience that the participants recorded in their diaries. Ninety (90) percent of the entries were *specific* or "one-moment-in-time" events. For example, "I dropped my lunch tray today in the cafeteria. It was so embarrassing," was categorized as a specific event. A *general* entry did not pin down a specific episode or event: e.g. "My roommate and I went to the beach today and met two of his friends from high school. We had a good time." A *mixed* event contained both specific and general components. The prevalence of specific events (see

Table 6.2A) is certainly due to the instructions to record only "unique" events.

The diary entries were also coded into six content or dominant theme categories. *Academic* entries focused on scholastic activities such as exams, grades, or studying: e.g. "I took my first college midterm today in history. I was really nervous but it was not as difficult as I expected." The *Housing* category encompassed moving in or out and events involving the participants living situation: e.g. "My roommate finally moved out today. What a relief!" *Romance* events described explicit romantic intentions or interactions: e.g. "I had dinner tonight with Pat for the first time. I sure hope this is not a unique event!" *Recreation* events involved entertainment, pleasure-seeking, or free-time activities (except for romance): "Jane and I went to see the new Star Trek movie at the Showcase Theaters. It was terrific!"

The distribution of average percentages presented in Table 6.2B is not surprising and is consistent with those found by David Pillemer who used a questionnaire method to elicit memories from the first year of college (Pillemer et al. 1986). Our diary method, with its demands for unique events, biases the recording towards recreational events and away from academic events which are usually not unique. And, in spite of the assurance that their diaries would be kept confidential, most participants recorded events which were safe or socially acceptable. Interestingly, the average percentage of romance events for females (12%) was twice that for males (8%). This difference could be due to a variety of factors (e.g. cultural norms around keeping diaries) but also could reflect a female peer system which places a high priority on attractiveness and romance (Holland and Eisenhart 1990).

The *social orientation* of the diary entries was discerned by asking the question, "Are other people a central component of the memory?" Almost all of the events recorded included other people besides the participant and thus were classified as interpersonal (see Table 6.2C). In sum, the majority of the diary entries were specific recreational events involving friends or relatives.

3. Salient Memory Assessment

Eleven students (7 women and 4 men) participated in this assessment interview, once in 1988 and again in 1991. The results of asking them to describe the "first memory that comes to mind" from each semester and summer of their college years are summarized in Table 6.3. For these seven students who had kept diaries, 25% of their salient memories had been ones they had recorded. About half of the events reported on the second interview were the same as the first and, therefore, were only counted once. We coded the memories independently and agreed appoximately 90% of the time on the structure, theme, and social orientation of an event.

To elicit salient college memories we cued the participants with the built-in time periods of a college education: i.e. semesters and summers. In

TABLE 6.3 Salient Memory Assessment

A. Memory Structure			
Specific	General	Mixed	Missing Value
Mean % 30	5	60	5

B. Dominant Theme				
Academic	Housing	Romantic	Off-Campus Activities	Missing Value
Mean % 15	20	10	50	5

C. Social Orientation		
Individual	Interpersonal	Missing Value
Mean % 35	60	5

The average number of memories per participant was 30.

most cases, these cues stimulated the students to think about "where" they lived and/or with "whom" or "what" they were involved in during that time period. For example, "I moved to the campus apartments that semester." The importance of "place" in organizing memories has been found in another study looking at oral histories of college (Pillemer et al. 1991). Sometimes participants would begin by describing how they "felt" or the emotional tone of the time period in question and then proceed to recount a specific event: e.g. "I was really lonely that semester (my best friend was in Spain). I remember pulling my first all nighter that spring" or "We had a great time that semester. We pulled off a prank you wouldn't believe." Given this kind of remembering process, an average of sixty percent of the memories reported proceeded in general fashion and then moved to a description of a specific episode. An average of thirty percent of the salient college memories were immediately specific in their structure: e.g. "That was the interim I met my fiancé. I remember meeting her the first day but not really being interested in getting to know her. She told me later that she didn't take much notice of me either."

It was no surprise that the salient memory interview yielded a majority of mixed structure memories. The conversational norms of an interview probably beg the students to provide some background for their memories, thus increasing the general mixed type responses. Pillemer and his colleagues

(1991) found that remembering events from college orally yielded more general memories than when they were asked to write down their memories. Likewise, our diary method was framed to elicit specific events with very little concern for the context of those events. The different methods of memory sampling can lead to slightly different types of memories.

There was no consistent relationship between the kind of memories and the four years of college. However, two-thirds of the memories recalled from the first semester of college were descriptions of events which occurred on the very first day. The following quotation exemplifies the vividness and intense emotions often associated with these memories:

> I remember arriving on campus all by myself. I didn't know anyone. I was scared and excited at the same time. I can still picture walking into my dorm room, seeing my roommate sitting at his desk and wondering if there would be any room for my stuff.

Pillemer et al. (1986; 1988; 1991) also found that some of the most vivid episodic memories from the first year of college occurred in September -- the point of entrance and a period of life transition. These findings support the research of retention consultants who argue that "first impressions" can weigh heavily into a student's decision to remain at a particular college.

Echoing the diary content, female participants described twice as many romantic memories than the male students. Again, this difference could be due to a variety of factors (e.g. willingness to share such memories), but it could also reflect a greater salience of this life dimension for women within the college subculture.

As Table 6.3B indicates, fifty percent of the salient memories recalled involved activities which occurred off campus. These memories can be divided into three types. The first type is *recreational* and was usually about what the participants did for Spring Break: e.g. "Five of my friends and I packed ourselves into one car and headed for Florida that year. Besides having a great time together, we really grew closer together." The second type of off campus memories were about *work experiences*, either full-time jobs over the summer months or part-time employment during the school year: e.g. "I left Pietro's that fall and started working at Snickers. That was a real mistake."

The third type could have been categorized as academic memories since they were part of the college curriculum or co-curriculum. However, to remain consistent with Pillemer's research and our diary content, we categorized them with the other activities which occurred off-campus. These memories, which we will refer to as *off-campus learning*, were from semesters spent abroad or in other parts of the U.S., travel interims to other countries, and internship or volunteer experiences: e. g. "I spent that semester at the Oregon Extension. It was pretty intense but I learned more in that semester than I had in the previous two." Or, as another student said, "That interim we did some volunteer work with organizations which help the homeless. I realized that I couldn't easily explain poverty by blaming the victims." In most cases, the participants went beyond describing a single memory and elaborated on these off-campus learning experiences as being extremely significant to their personal growth and career development.

Implications for assessment research

It is appropriate at this point to reflect upon what implications our memory data might have for assessment research. First of all, the content of the diaries and the salient memories remind us that there is much more affecting a student's education and development besides those aspects directly targeted by a college curriculum. It is too easy, especially for faculty, to forget that for many students, taking college courses is only one part of their lives. Most students are also working, volunteering, and involved in familial and/or dating relationships, both of which can be intense during the college years. One participant, almost apologetically, made the following comment which is representative of our sample:

> Boy, most of my memories have nothing to do with Calvin. Most of my memories revolve around people more than classes. I can't even remember what classes I was taking.

Of course, we have to be careful how to explain this phenomena. It could be that our memories are organized around people and events while our knowledge is structured in some other fashion. The objective of most college classes is to provide knowledge or build competence, not necessarily to be "memorable." For example, we both know that the capital of Canada is Ottawa, but we don't remember the circumstances in which we learned this fact. However, we both know how to conduct an analysis of variance and we both remember who taught us this and the process we went through in order to learn this skill.[5] What we remember is not always a reflection of what we know, but what we remember can reflect what has had an impact or influence on our lives. That is, we think it is accurate to say that our data suggests that there are several other dimensions of a student's life which are at least *equally important* as the curriculum.

It may be embarrassing to some that there were so few salient memories which were academic in nature. To others, it may be a surprise that there were any academic memories at all! We were embarrassed that participants recalled so few academic type memories, and that half of their salient memories were from off-campus activities. But again, it would be a mistake to suggest on the basis of these findings that what goes on off-campus is more important than what goes on in the classroom. What our data does suggest is that what happens outside of the classroom is often more memorable than what occurs in the classroom.

But now, we must ask ourselves the obvious question: "Why isn't what occurs in the classroom just as memorable as off-campus learning experiences?" The few salient academic memories that our participants did have provide testimony that calculus can be engaging, biology can be sobering, literature can be moving, history can be revealing, philosophy can be enlightening, art can be liberating, and so on. Perhaps it is not so much what is being taught in the classroom that makes it less memorable but how it is being taught. Maybe it is the pedagogy most frequently employed that makes the curriculum less memorable than the co-curriculum. For example, Kintsch and Bates (1977) found that listeners seem to remember the lecturer's irrelevant asides better than his or her text. It was not surprising (but certainly humbling) that two-thirds of the sample took introductory psychology from the first author and no one described a salient memory from that class.

Section Two: Assessment of College

The bulk of our data focused on assessing the impact Calvin College had on a student's education and development. As described earlier, we employed two types of interviews to make our assessments. One of which asked the students to review their college years using various topics as prompts or catalysts: e.g. "Please review for me your academic life during college" or "Please describe for me what you consider to be your faith now and is this any different than four years ago?" The other interview was undirected in that we simply asked the participant to "Please describe the last four years of your life." Before looking at the content of these interviews, we will make some brief comments on the structure and process of these interviews.

On Structure and Process

The *topical* college assessment interview took a traditional "question-answer" format. The students were given as much time as they wanted to respond and they usually proceeded in a chronological fashion focusing on whatever topic they had been given to review. For example,

On Housing: The first two years I lived in the
                               dorms. The last two years I lived
                               off-campus in a rental with
                               Sharon, Kim, and Christi.

On Academics: I started off as an engineering
                               major, but quickly found out that

> I probably wouldn't make it
> through the prerequisites so I
> switched to business.

Interestingly, this kind of format was adopted by almost all of the participants of the *undirected* interview as well. They would begin talking about some dimension of their college experience and recount what happened throughout their four years. The metaphor of memory being a "re-membering" process was reaffirmed since roommates or significant relationships most frequently served as the first peg from which the participants began hanging their college experiences. Then, after exhausting what they had to say about that topic, they would consider something else and begin another narrative. Pillemer et al. (1991) described this process as "chapterizing" where an oral history is divided up into "memory chapters."

Often times one narrative would act as a catalyst for another. The following quote exemplifies how a person's "academic story" easily slides into her "faith story":

> I took pretty much all core courses during my first two years. During my sophomore year I took this religion class which really made me think about my faith. Up to that point, I pretty much just believed what I had been told growing up. But that professor challenged us to defend our beliefs and I realized that I didn't have much to back up what I believed. Since then, I've started to own my faith.

This person continued to talk about her faith up to the time of the interview and then returned to finish what she wanted to say about her academic journey. This connection and interaction of stories suggests that a participant really only has a single story. But, because of the several facets and dimensions of that story, telling it demanded breaking it up into different themes or topics. In contrast, a couple of participants spent the entire hour talking about a single topic as if that theme framed their entire college experience. For example, one person, in both the 1988 and 1991 interviews, talked about her college years as a journey of faith, trying to figure out what it meant to be a Christian in the modern world.

Several of the participants who returned to tell their college stories three years after graduation began, without us asking, updating us on what had happened since our last meeting. Since we had not seen these people for three years, this could easily be explained as a polite conversational expectation. However, it could also support the notion that recalling the past is through the present. The "present" had changed for these people and perhaps they felt compelled to update us before they went over their college years again. Also, for some of these graduates, some very significant events had occurred in their life since college: events which had changed their view of what had happened in college and what they were willing to share. These changes offer support for Bruner's (1987) contention of "how our way of telling about ourselves changes."[6]

A few of the *undirected* assessment interviews did not proceed in the nicely connected narrative fashion. On these occasions, we had to do a lot of prompting and encouraging without treating the session like a topical interview. These exceptions reminded us that autobiographical memory is not always organized or retrieved chronologically or narratively (Friedman 1993). Using time or a theme to organize one's memories are two possibilities, but they are not the only ways to remember events from one's life.

Although we can argue that there was some chronological and narrative consistency in the structure and process of these assessment interviews, it is much more difficult for us to reduce the content down to a few categories or a single developmental scheme. *The remainder of this chapter is written from the perspective of the first author. I shift voice to match the theoretical umbrella I used to interpret the content of our assessment interviews.*

On Content

It has been two years since I completed collecting the data for this project. Besides the long process of analyzing the data and transcribing interviews, I wrestled with how I was going to interpret over eighty college stories. Initially, I planned on using James Fowler's (1981; 1984) and Sharon Parks' (1986) faith development theories since they had done such a fine job of integrating the work of Jean Piaget, Erik Erikson, Lawrence Kolhberg, William Perry, and Carol Gilligan. Then, after reading the work of my colleagues John Van Wicklin, Richard Butman, and Ron Burwell, I considered using James Marcia's (1980) typology of identity development. However, I found myself agreeing with most of the criticism of the structural-developmental theories. Stages of development are abstracted from general trends, masking the uniqueness of individuals, and misrepresenting the fluid, and sometimes paradoxical, nature of human experience and growth (Oosterhuis 1989). Also, I wanted to avoid the tendency for people to use stages as diagnostic labels to rank students on a hierarchy. Further, I dislike the propensity of stage theorists to hide their ethics and values behind secular psychological language. Most critiques of Fowler and company strip away the psychological jargon or secularity and challenge their theological and ethical presuppositions (Dykstra and Parks 1986). When scrutinized, most developmental stage theories reveal a European American rationalistic-individualism hidden beneath the guise of social science (Broughton 1986; Dueck 1979).

As I began writing it became obvious to me that I could not squeeze the people I had come to know into some developmental theory or script. I could not reduce the experience of my participants into another person's story. I wanted to find a way to respect the uniqueness of each of our participants' lives but at the same time offer my own interpretations. It became clear to me that the only person's story that I could use to interpret the stories I had collected was my own. I confess that my assumptions and values are weaved throughout this study. I designed the interviews and conducted most of them. My assumptions, values, and expectations are reflected not only in the interview questions but also within the conversational (verbal and non-verbal) context in which the interview occurred. What I have selected to focus on and how I frame it also expresses my story, my development.

There were three edges that I was growing on while reviewing our college assessment interviews. First of all, I was wrestling with what multiculturalism might mean to the Calvin and Christian Reformed community as I conducted this research. This edge is expressed in my decision to focus on the ethnic identification and experience of our participants. The second growth edge I have lived on for the last couple of years is how I approach teaching and learning. My passion for teaching has been renewed as I have shifted my pedagogy away from monologue to dialogue. Sharing the testimony of our participants to the importance of experiential learning reveals my commitment to reforming my teaching. Thirdly, and most importantly, I was trying to reconcile the tension I felt in respecting the differences between the participants without judging or implying that one person was more "mature" than another. I have resolved this struggle by affirming the authority of Jesus Christ and reforming my view of time.

I believe that my admission of my agendas does not negate the validity of my research, it simply provides the hermeneutical context in which I present my findings (Kvale 1983). One implication of my confession is to relativize (in the good sense of that word) my perceptions. That is, the data we have collected is extremely rich and open to a variety of interpretations and uses.

Calvin College Ethnicity

In 1991, Rodger Rice and I argued that ethnic identification and salience were important variables to consider in Calvin's movement towards becoming an "authentic multicultural Christian academic community." Building on the experience of other multiculturalism policies and practices, we demonstrated that if the ethnic majority did not see themselves as being members of an ethnic group, any attempts to become "multicultural" would be met with resistance or superficial tolerance. Using questionnaires, we measured the ethnic identification and salience of almost 200 Calvin College students. We found that two-thirds of our sample did not consider themselves to be members of any ethnic group and, thus, did not think that ethnicity had any significant influence on their lives. The students who did say they were members of an ethnic group identified themselves as "Dutch" or "Dutch-CRC." As we expected, the ethnic-religious "Dutch-CRC" label yielded the highest ethnic-salience scores. A few students used race terms such as "white" or "anglo-saxon," but these labels were not associated with high ethnic salience scores (Lee and Rice 1991).

To continue this exploration, I included some questions in the demographic section of our college assessment interviews. We asked our participants, "Do you consider yourself to be a member of an ethnic group?" If the answer was "No," we moved on to the next question. If the answer was "Yes," we asked the students to identify their ethnic group and to describe the degree of influence they thought their ethnicity had on their lives.   The results in 1988 and 1991 were almost identical to our questionnaire study. Sixty percent of our sample did not consider themselves to be members of an ethnic group, thirty percent identified themselves as "Dutch" or Dutch-CRC" and the remainder used race terms (e.g. "white"). Our results are not surprising given that the majority of our participants were from the same cohort as our questionnaire sample. However, the consistency does offer some validity to our pen and pencil measure since our interviews were conducted with the assurance of confidentiality and encouragements to be forthright.

The responses to our ethnic identification and ethnic salience questions revealed some of the dynamics of ethnicity and ethnic interaction within Calvin's community. Members of the ethnic majority have a difficult time being aware of their ethnicity since their particular way of life is the norm. Fish do not know that they are wet. The majority of Calvin's student body have grown up in a subculture with very little interaction with people from other ethnic groups. Going to Calvin, for some, may be their first exposure to people who are not members of a Dutch-American Christian Reformed Church and did not attend Christian schools.   This was the case for the following first year student:

> I'm Dutch. I really didn't think of it before I came here. One of my friends here isn't Dutch and I never really thought about it until she was discussing her un-Dutchness.

For most others, attending Calvin was not sufficient to spark their awareness of their ethnicity and the influence it had over their lives. Their college experience continued to insulate them from ethnic diversity. It took a physical relocation for Charles to become aware of the pervasiveness of the subculture in which he grew up.

> Dutch, but only when I left Calvin and Grand Rapids three years ago. I grew up in this Dutch subculture, a lot of which is insular and closed-in. You don't see too much outside of it since so much of it is directed towards itself and building off of itself. Same sort of thing with economic class. When you

are middle-class you are not aware of anything else. Even when you give to
the poor and so on you are rarely in touch with the people who are really in
need. I've come to realize that my Dutch middle-class subculture defined my
life from K-through-Calvin.

This "K-through-Calvin" experience is not unusual for members of the
CRC which is deeply committed to Christian education. If one thinks about
ethnic influence in narrative terms, it is like having a "life script" which
offers security to its actors. Sharon and Ralph captured the scripted nature
of their traditional subculture.

The reason I decided to go to Calvin was because it was a family tradition.
My sister had gone, my dad had gone, it was more or less expected so I
didn't explore too many options.

I came to Calvin primarily because my parents wanted me to. I didn't want
to. I went to Grand Rapids Christian High School and everybody there goes
to Calvin, its sort of this white middle-class mamma's boy goes to Calvin,
marries this nice little Dutch girl, settles down, gets a picket fence and forces
his kids to do the exact same thing.

Perhaps Ralph's cynicism is because he did not get married after Calvin, but,
having been raised in the CRC, he certainly was not alone in his awareness
of what was expected of him. The majority of our sample said they had
decided to attend Calvin because some member of their family was attending
or was an alumnus of the college. For many, however, the security of this
script quickly disappeared when they entered the workplace. Amanda
continues:

Calvin is a very homogenous society. It is not a situation where students are
encouraged to explore other options. We are all expected to think and act in
the Reformed way. It has been a real experience for me leaving that and
having to deal with people who are Jews, Catholics, Muslims, atheists, and
so on.

The "Dutch-CRC" ethnic label testifies to the religious aspects of Calvin's
ethnic tradition as its most salient dimension. Nadine, who used the term
"Dutch" as a first-year student, changed to "Dutch-CRC" as a senior three
years later. She explained that the change represented her recognition of the
religious diversity among Dutch people and the different ethnic groups within
the CRC. Reba's comments on ethnic-religiosity were very acute for a first
year student, but not unusual for a "missionary kid."

As a missionary kid, you see things totally different because you go from one
culture to the next. I'd never heard of the CRC before I came here. I found

it interesting how the culture could influence Christianity. I saw Roman
Catholicism in Spanish people but I thought it was more geographical. You
come here and you see Americans with their own cultural expression of their
religion.

It was not too long ago in North America that if someone said they were
Polish, Irish, or Italian, it would automatically be assumed that they were
Catholic as well. This kind of assumption is often legitimate for the
Dutch-Americans at Calvin College. Catherine, in her first year, identified
her ethnic group as "Dutch" but was quick to point out that the influence was
significant "in the sense of religion, but not in the sense of Dutch practices."
Her qualification reveals the difficulty in being able to separate religiosity
from ethnicity. Religion is packaged in cultural wrappings. A religious
tradition cannot be understood or expressed without it being framed in cultural
forms (Lee and Rice 1991). As Christian colleges move towards becoming
more multicultural, one of the first tasks is to discern the nature of the college
culture and train the ethnic-majority to be better prepared to interact with
people from other traditions.

It is most often the people on the margins of a culture or ethnic group
who can articulate the group norms or what the group consider to be
"normal." A few of the participants shared their "insider -- outsider"
perspective on Calvin's ethnic-religious tradition. Kyle, whose mother is
"Dutch-CRC" but whose father is not, said,

> I grew up in a Dutch-CRC community but never really felt a part of it
> because we didn't follow all the rituals and practices. I feel like I have some
> of it, but I don't feel like I belong to it.

Another participant, Rachel was not Dutch but had attended the Dutch-CRC
Christian schools, was more critical in her response.

> I sometimes think of myself as non-Dutch. I have dark hair and tan real
> easily. I have always stuck out among the kids with blonde hair and blue
> eyes. I see a lot of contradictions in the Dutch-CRC community. It is
> supposed to be transforming society, but it is so closed-off from the rest of
> the world. To the outside community we are a scary college. I think people
> think that we are just a bunch of Dutch-CRC people who want to learn about
> Calvin and its true and wonderful but we are more than that too.

Frank, a complete stranger to the CRC and Calvin was the most direct in his
critique of Calvin's ethnic-religiosity:

> It was at Calvin that I started to see the conflict between cultural Christianity
> and conversion Christianity. At Calvin there are people who were born and

raised in a conservative Christian environment who have no idea of what it is like not to be a Christian. I became troubled by the people who talked Christianity but who had no particular lifestyle distinctives that evidenced Christ.

Certainly this call for Christian integrity or distinctives could be made to any Christian group, but the pleas was also made by an insider who was also concerned about the continued reformation of Christianity in the Dutch-American CRC ethnicity.

If you've been in a Dutch-CRC background your whole life -- Christian grade school, high school, and college -- it means you've spent your whole life surrounded by a certain type of people and something weird happens. I'm very suspicious of our Christian rituals and traditions. It has to be our everyday actions because I've know people who have done profession of faith and the next day they are out smoking dope and telling people to f-off.

Being the "salt of the earth" has never been an easy task for Christians, especially when Christian traditions have become more tradition than Christian.

As evidenced by the labels used, ethnicity was sometimes confused with race which led the students to talk about their experiences of racism and sexism. For example, Laura said,

I do not usually think of myself as being a member of an ethnic group, but I guess I am white. I think that has a great deal of influence on my life, probably more than it should. I think there are a lot of preconceptions about people based on their skin color.

In a similar vein, Martha and Paul continue:

I didn't realize how it was an advantage to be white until I moved to the South. But I've also realized it's not an advantage to be a woman in the South, it really makes me mad!

I am a white male. During the last few years I have become aware of the white male oppression of other ethnic groups and how other ethnic groups and women view me because of the way I look. Three years ago, I think I said "Dutch" but when you get away from Calvin it doesn't matter. In the South, you are either white or black, that's it!

Interestingly, all three of these voices are from Calvin alumni, people who have lived for three years outside of their nest in other ethnic or cultural environments. Ethnic-majority group members are usually not aware of their ethnocentricity, racism, or sexism until they themselves become victims of these social diseases.

For the one-third of our sample who chose to identify themselves with some ethnic label, I heard several examples of how members of an ethnic-religious tradition wrestle with what it means to be Christian in a multicultural but racist and sexist society. Also, I see a common thread between those participants who perceived themselves as being members of some ethnic group. There was either a condition which kept them on the margins of their group (e.g. Rachel's dark hair of Kyle's non-Dutch CRC father) or an experience which took them outside of their ethnic familiarities (e.g. Nadine making a friend who was not Dutch-CRC or Charles' move to another city). These "fish-out-of-water" experiences revealed themselves as critical learning experiences for many students.

Experiential Learning

As described earlier, off-campus learning experiences were often described as salient and educationally significant memories. Tricia's comments describe how these events can be like "conversion" experiences, where every aspect of the person's life (i.e. faith, identity, career, etc.) is in some way affected.

> My interim in Kenya was a turning point for me. Being away from the luxuries really challenged me. The people there didn't have all the distractions of what they looked like, how they dressed, and they were really alive for Christ -- focused. I didn't have to worry about my hair, make-up, etc. And, in the hospitals, we could actually pray with the patients! This experience solidified my career decision to go into medicine and to devote some of my life to serving people in the Third World.

Similarly, Harold's interim in England "was a watershed" for him. Up to that point, he had been a communications major, but his experiences and the "heart-to-heart" discussions he had during this month made him realize that he "didn't want to spend the rest of my life in theater." As a result, when Bernice returned from her interim in Europe, she said, "I had the attitude that America is the most materialistic, awful, self-centered place there is in the world! I had to re-think what my Christian faith was all about." Visiting another culture also had a "shipwrecking" effect on Laura's faith:

> My semester in Spain really made me aware of the rest of the world. I had travelled abroad before but this was the first time I became immersed in another culture and realized that there was another way of thinking besides the way I had been brought up. I really was a fish out of water. When I came back, I realized how little we really know about Christianity and God.

Learning to be "amphibious" is not an easy process for fish and fortunately most students survive and learn from these cross-cultural experiences.

However, positive transformations do not always happen when students participate in off-campus learning experiences. Florence's internship in New York was "a waste" because she ended up having three different supervisors "and to top it off, I was robbed one day!" Along the same vein, Vivian got homesick during her interim in the Dominican Republic and described the experience as "boring."

> I wanted to come home real bad. The reason was because we were so removed from the culture, staying in a hotel. The purpose of the course was to use our Spanish, but when we were together in the hotel, we spoke English.

What this suggests is that learning does not automatically occur when a student goes off-campus or visits another culture. The critical factor for the learning to occur is not "where" the student goes, but what the student "does" when they are there. Vivian's case supports this conclusion when she described her second cross-cultural interim.

> My senior interim was to Costa Rica. There we lived with families for four weeks. Because I was immersed into the culture, I learned so much there that nobody could ever teach me. I didn't want to leave them. I'm sure my maturation had something to do with it, but I also think the nature of the experiences in another culture matters too.

Learning experiences which contain active participation usually involve some sort of risk (or at least the discomfort of admitting one's ignorance). Off-campus activities, which often demand adjusting to new circumstances and relationships, have great potential to become educational.

What happens when a person re-enters their native culture can also be decisive with regard to how much learning occurs from these off-campus experiences. Ann stated that "It was more of a culture shock to come home than to leave and go to Russia! There was so much poverty there and we have so much and throw so much away!" In her junior year, Patricia spent a semester in London and said this about her return:

> It was a real culture shock coming back to Grand Rapids from London. My dearest and closest friends were developed from this experience. We became a community and it was hard to adjust when we got back. Very few people asked me about it and the college did not integrate the experience for us at all.

Adequate preparation and active participation are essential ingredients that go into making an off-campus activity a valuable learning experience. However, individual reflection and communal assessment, during and after the experience, are also critical (Kolb 1984).

For a variety of reasons, many students cannot afford to take a travel interim or a semester abroad. But, since it is what happens and not necessarily where it happens which makes an experience a learning one, we heard examples of significant educational experiences which occurred within five miles of the campus. Some students had served as volunteers during their college years with local social service agencies and mentioned how important this was to their overall education. In some cases, their learning experiences occurred almost by accident. For example, Corrine recalled going out with some international students to a Chinese restaurant.

> I remember sitting there and realizing that I was the only American. They were all talking about when they had been in India and ate food there, when they had been in Europe and ate food, etc. I remember thinking that I hadn't even left the country. It may seem trivial, but that experience was another important factor in why I started evaluating who I was and what I believed. With no experience with other cultures, I just couldn't write-off them as being all wrong.

And, of course, experiential learning can occur on-campus as well. Several students commented on how their involvement in co-curricular activities (i.e. residence halls, student associations, government, athletics, etc.) was central to their college experience and personal development. Such was the case for Larry who got heavily involved in a student organization. His case is extreme but it does demonstrate what can happen when students are given responsibility for their own learning.

> I was the Executive Director my senior year and was consumed by our programming. I lived, ate, and drank that organization. It was my mistress, my wife, my child, and my hope for the future. However, I learned a lot that year about myself and the career direction I wanted to pursue.

During his junior year, Stanley and his roommates held a weekly Bible study which he described as "really formative in my Christian thinking and just how a Christian should act. We talked about everything and were completely honest with one another." Having control of the agenda in a peer atmosphere was common to these on-campus learning experiences.

Three years after graduation, Wendy had this to say about her college education:

> I think I have to say that my most significant learning experiences were the ones I shared with my friends and not the wonderful coursework. Although I think I received a good education, I would not say it was my formal coursework that got me to where I am today. I would say it was the interaction I had with friends, growing emotionally and spiritually more so than academically. And especially looking back now, I have learned more in the last three years of my life than I have in the previous twelve as far as things that are going to take me forward.

Wendy's conclusion does not negate the role of coursework in her education, but it certainly emphasizes that there is more to a college education than what happens in the classroom. Tom Peters, a management consultant, once said that "some of the most important people in an organization are the least respected." I think it is appropriate to conclude from our data that "some of the most significant educational experiences in college are some of the least respected."

Although most of the learning experiences that our sample reported occurred outside of the classroom, there were a few students who commented on how important a particular course had been to them. Interestingly, when students described what had made these courses significant, they usually mentioned the professor's style or how the course deviated from classes which relied on a textbook and lectures. This supports our earlier suggestion that pedagogy is primarily responsible for what makes salient academic memories.

Regardless of where they occur, those learning experiences remembered from college involve the students in some meaningful activity where they must take responsibility for their own learning. The pedagogical metaphor is active dialogue or interaction rather than passive monologue and information transfer. David's comments testify to this distinction:

> I really didn't learn much in most of my courses here. I was just regurgitating information. I really appreciated the fact that we didn't have a textbook in your Intro Psych class and you made us think about the issues Christians have to deal with in response to psychology. I think more of the core classes should be like interim courses which involve group discussions, engaging interactions rather than lectures, and so on. Core courses should not be treated as the first course in a major.

In a special issue of *Theory into Practice* entitled "Metaphors we learn by," Tobin (1990) pointed out that changing our metaphors and beliefs can operate as a "master switch for teaching." Lakoff and Johnson (1980) argued that most theories of learning are rooted in a "computer" metaphor where information is transferred from one place to another through some conduit. In contrast, Palmer (1983) has encouraged educators to re-think our assumptions about truth and knowledge, and adopt a more relational, communal, and participatory approach to teaching and learning. Our research on salient college memories and significant learning experiences supports Palmer's call for a pedagogical revolution in higher education. It is my hope that, as assessment becomes more of a part of our everyday lives as college and university teachers, we will also see widespread pedagogical reform.

Diversity and Unity

As pointed out earlier, there was a wide range of opinions within our sample. The students' reviews of their first year display this diversity of experience. For example, note the contrast between these four participants' comments:

> I hated my freshman year. I hated the whole thing. I didn't like the course work or my roommate. (Nancy)
> During my first year, we didn't study much. Mostly social events and dorm activities. (Lillian)
> I went potluck and my roommate and I hit it off really well. My first year classes were not difficult. (Betty)
> My freshman year was an academic turn-on. I really became interested in learning. I did outside reading and everything. (Bob)

This extreme range of experience probably continues through the college years as symbolized by these memories of graduation.

> I was so excited to graduate! I was so glad to have finished my courses, get out, and be involved in the real world. (Sherry)
> Graduation was the worst day of my life. I was leaving a secure environment and moving towards something I wasn't totally sure about at all. (Gary)

This diversity of experience is not surprising given the enormous number of factors which can influence a person's college experience. But, diversity and complexity cannot be used as excuses not to evaluate whether or not we are achieving our goals as Christian educators. I think the presence of diversity and complexity forces us to consider how we make our assessments and under what theoretical umbrella they occur.

Careful evaluation of our theories and methods is especially appropriate when considering students's definitions and stories of faith (Basinger 1990; Van Wicklin 1990). Here are few images of faith our participants shared with us:

> I believe in God, the Trinity, that Jesus died for my sins, and all that stuff. It really hasn't changed much over these years although I haven't gone to church as much as I should have. (Eric)

I have come a long way as a Christian being able to tell people I am a Christian and not having a problem with it. In my Christ and Culture class, I didn't like the professor but s/he made me think. We never agreed on anything. We were always arguing. I started to question the "rightness" of the CRC community. I just don't accept it at face value anymore. I started owning my beliefs rather than what Mom and Dad taught. I've made friends from a lot of different denominations, and have formed my own set of Christian beliefs and practices. Sharing the gospel is trying to redeem both individuals and society. I still have the idealism of wanting to change the world in my profession, of transforming the world, but I'm in an internship now and I'm finding out how difficult that is. (Bernice)

Four years ago I would have give a nice little Christian Reformed catechism answer. Now it's more but I am still trying to find my faith. I have come to college and interacted with different faiths. I even dated someone who was a Muslim for awhile. He asked me questions I thought I knew the answers to and I realized that I am still looking. It bothers me that I am still looking, I feel like I should be strong and I am not. From day one I have been taught that Jesus came, died, rose from the dead, born of a virgin, all that stuff. Sometimes I wonder if it really happened? Is this the right faith? Am I believing this just because I have been told it all my life. I want to know if I really believe it. I do believe there is a heaven and hell. I certainly want to go to heaven. I heard in a religion class that you are picked from day one to go to heaven or hell. I believe it, but is it just because it has always been told to me? That is my big worry. (Three years later) I'm still not settled on what or why I believe what I do. When I do go to church now I definitely choose a more active and lively worship service. (Florence)

I realize that these statements could be interpreted to support some faith and/or identity development theory. Using Marcia's (1980) typology, Eric's identity appears to be "foreclosed," Bernice seems to have "achieved" a Christian identity, and Florence's comments reflect an "identity moratorium." But again, I do not want to squeeze the experience of these students into someone else's developmental theory or story. I simply wish to point out that we heard different images of faith and avoid making the judgment that one expression is more "mature" than another. I believe that these statements represent a sincere attempt to relate to God given the experiences, decisions, and conditions of each of the participants. How then can I, in a Christian fashion, interpret and respond to these faith narratives?

Developmental Theory and the Christian Story

I have, in two other publications, told the story of how I have come to adopt a narrative root metaphor for doing psychology (Lee 1993a; 1994). Quite simply, in order to understand human behavior and experience, I use the metaphor that life is a story and people are storytellers. Applied to this research, I tried to view the content of our interviews as segments or chapters in the participants' life stories. For each person, there was a setting and a plot to her or his comments. There were primary and secondary characters making choices which reflected their values and dreams, sometimes behaving unexpectedly, but always moving the narrative towards some end point. These narrative metaphors are especially applicable to developmental studies and Mary and Ken Gergen (1986) have pointed out that most theories in developmental psychology have an implicit narrative structure.

James Fowler has openly admitted the narrative nature of his research. He is always worth quoting, but most appropriately here:

> Theorist of adult development have begun to play the role in our society that storytellers and mythmakers once played in primitive and classical cultures. Using the organic root metaphor of development in a variety of ways, their research and theories aim to provide empirically grounded chartings of predictable patterns and turning in human life cycles. (Fowler 1984, 15)

Fowler goes on to admit that he, and others like him, are offering contemporary versions of what 17th Century scholastic theologians called *ordo salutis* -- the path or steps to salvation, wholeness, completion. Developmental psychologists have provided the normative stories for modern men and women, or what he calls "myths of becoming." Couched within very formal and abstract language are their prescriptions of the telos or goals of human life. I especially like Fowler's reference to himself and other developmental theorists as "gossips," not just because their writings make extensive use of the stories of others, but because the root meaning (god and sib) implies "one who has contracted spiritual affinity with another by acting as a sponsor at baptism." That is, Fowler is offering to his readers "spiritual direction." To extend the metaphor, he is the priest listening to the confessions of his research subjects and sharing his "myth of becoming" with his parish, the students of faith development theory.

Claiming the authority modern people have given to the academy and science, most faith development theorists are extending and providing evidence for their own theological philosophy. Phrased narratively, they are using the stories of others to understand and support their own faith story. Then, as gossips, they are providing a normative story to which other faith stories can be compared and evaluated.[7] If faith development theories are essentially normative narratives then shouldn't a Christian faith development theory be based on *the* Christian story?

Paul Vitz (1992a; 1992b) proposed that there are four archetypes of human experiences based upon Frye's (1957) literary categories of comedy, romance, tragedy, and irony. Mary and Ken Gergen (1986) have also used literary forms to represent narratives of the self. Figure 6.1 presents their graphic representations of tragedy, comedy-melodrama, happily-ever-after, and romance narratives. Vitz argued that as Christians we are to see our lives in a comic mode. That is, he believes that the Christian narrative structure is:

> ...a blend of romance and comedy. No matter how unfulfilled or how great the suffering is in this world, we must get past present tragedy or irony. Our ultimate hope of union with God and of eternal life means that no matter what our separation, sorrow, and anxiety in this life, ultimately we are living in a comedy in which "all's well that ends well." (Vitz 1992a, 16).

However, this progressive linear depiction of the Christian narrative is not unlike the faith developmental theories I criticized earlier for not taking the diversity of Christian experience seriously. I agree with Vitz's conclusion, but I also believe that the Christian narrative also contains tragedy and irony. I need to explain further.

The Alpha and the Omega

Ever since my college days, the first chapter of the apostle John's gospel has served me as a starting point for doing Christian scholarship. The "Word became flesh" is central to my theology of culture which I use to address the issues of ethnic and cultural diversity in evangelical Christian colleges (Lee 1991). In this context, the opening verses are the cornerstone of my thoughts concerning a conception of Christian development and growth.

> In the beginning was the Word, and the Word was with God and the Word was God. Through the Word, all things have been made. Without the Word nothing has been made, is made or will be made. (John 1:1-2 paraphrased)

There are two important ideas in these verses which are important to my argument. First, what I hear in these verses is the timelessness of Jesus. Jesus is not bound to our experience of time. To use another metaphor from the Apostle John, Jesus is the "Alpha and the Omega" (Rev. 1:8). Second, these verses claim the dependence of all of creation -- past, present, and future -- on Jesus. Jesus is simultaneously the Beginning, the End, and the Way (John 14:6). Within these metaphors is a view of time which is not linear, a view of experience which is not bound to the past, present, and future. It is a perspective which makes Jesus' incarnation, death, and resurrection timeless events -- above time, or extending from creation to eternity. This is certainly not to imply that Jesus' story did not actually happen, but rather that it occurred, is occurring, and will occur. Jesus' story was, is, and will be.

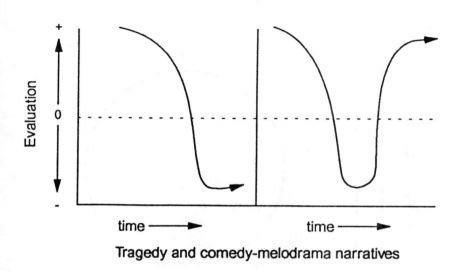

Tragedy and comedy-melodrama narratives

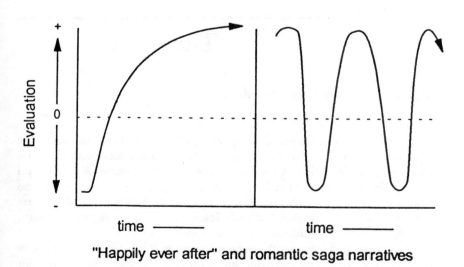

"Happily ever after" and romantic saga narratives

Figure 6.1 Gergens' Narrative Forms (1993)[8]

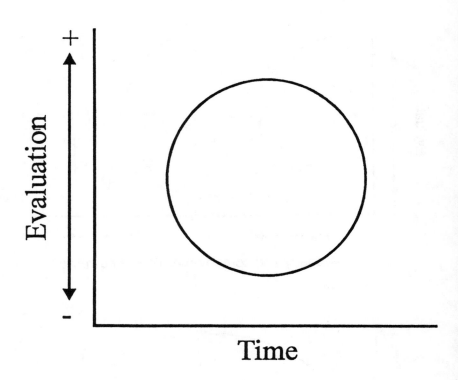

Figure 6.2 The Alpha and the Omega

Another way to illustrate these metaphors for Jesus is to make use of the graphic story structures of the Gergens. How should Jesus' story structure be represented if he is not limited by time but the Creator of it? May I suggest that we think of the Jesus story as a circle -- a line which has no beginning or end, or alternatively, a line whose beginning and end are indistinguishable. Figure 6.2 depicts Jesus' story where tragedy, comedy, happily-ever-after, and romance simultaneously co-exist.

It is possible to interpret this representation as Vitz' (1992a) archetype of irony, where skepticism and cynicism might reign because "there is nothing new under the sun." But, the ultimate triumph of the death and resurrection of Jesus is only possible if such an event is not bound to our limited linear experience of time. I suppose there is a certain irony in my belief that what was is and what will be has already happened.   I cannot completely understand God's time but I can respond to God's Word (Ecclesiastes).

My conception of *the* Christian story attempts to simultaneously respect the diversity of Christian experience and the unity of Jesus Christ. It tries to capture both the variety of narratives that Christians have lived, are living, and will live and the oneness that each life shares in Jesus Christ.   This metaphor also disarms any Christian person from making the claim that his or her story is *the* normative Christian journey.   To describe and explain differences in Christian experience along a single narrative comes very close to setting up a "graven image." Cultures or ethnic groups which have been Christian for more than one generation have a tendency to make idols out of their traditions (see Larson 1991). The iconoclast of this idolatry, like the challenge to faith development theories, is diversity: the presence of different cultures, ethnic groups, and individuals does not allow any group or anyone to claim Jesus' position of judge and "Author and Finisher of our faith" (Heb. 12:2).

I believe that the unity in our diversity is found in Jesus Christ. But, it is through our differences that we experience Christ's unity. Through the communal process of being "Christ's Body" we discern direction, both individually and corporately. Speaking narratively, at any one time within a group of people living in relationship with Jesus there would be tragedy, irony, comedy, and romance. Or, using the language of stage theorists, "Christian community needs all of the stages all of the time." Robert Sears once said about his stages of faith development or spiritual maturity, "God is present in all the stages and God's presence is known through all the stages" (Sears 1989; 1983).   Finally, as the apostle Paul stated almost 2000 years ago,

> ...speaking the truth in love, we will in all things grow up into him who is the Head, that is, Christ. From him the whole body, joined and held together by every supporting ligament, grows and builds itself up in love, as each part does its work. (Eph. 4:15-16; see also 1 Corinthians 12)

By being present to one another we realize the presence of God to bring healing to our relationships and growth to our body. We realize our unity by respecting and honoring our diversity.

I believe that each one of our participants is a unique creation of God. As ridiculous as this may sound, I also believe that I am not God, nor have I been given the authority to pass judgments on a person's standing before God and his or her path towards salvation or wholeness. What I can offer is my own story of faith and invite students to a process of dialogue where in the presence of one another, God's presence can be known. This "spirituality of education" is not bound to a particular pedagogy but is reflected in the nature of relationships within our learning communities (Palmer 1983).

Please note that this Alpha and Omega argument does not mean we cannot or should not try to measure or evaluate faith development or Christian growth. My argument just means that we cannot reify or deify any one particular conception or measure of Christian development. (This conclusion can be extended to all types of measurement -- including ethnic identification and salience!). In pointing out the limitations of assessing faith development, I have emphasized that measurements and evaluations are not ends in themselves, but means to our goals. Perhaps it is our North American preoccupation with progress which leads us to focus more on the goal (and who gets there first) than on the process it takes to reach that goal. We have a tendency to view assessment only in terms of evaluating how we have done. Assessment is primarily to facilitate learning, not to reify the process of learning. Fowler's faith development theory was primarily to facilitate Christian growth, not to reify the dynamic nature of faith.

Scripture provides us with some clear images of what Christian maturity should look like: "love, joy, peace, patience, kindness, goodness, faithfulness, gentleness, and self-control" (Galatians 5:22-23). I believe we can measure these fruits, but I also believe that because these are the fruits of the Spirit of God, they can never be reified or captured by some words or scale. Thus, we are challenged to be constantly reforming our conceptions and measurements. These fruits of the Spirit are interpersonal in nature and may therefore require interpersonal or communal discernment. In addition to the measures currently available (Bassett et al. 1991; Butman 1990), which are based on individual self-report and late 20th century Euro-American conceptions of growth and maturity, we should consider developing ways to assess Christian maturity which are communal and multicultural in nature. For example, we might consider having cohorts of students assess each other on some yardsticks of love, joy, peace, patience, etc. We might consider developing ways to assess a community's Christian maturity perhaps through the use of stories and other forms of narrative (Vitz 1990). We might consider inviting women and people from other Christian ethnic and cultural traditions to critique our definitions and assessments of Christian maturity. Finally, for accreditation agencies, we should make it clear that part of our institutional mission is to teach the process of Christian growth (i.e. truthing it in love) and then present evidence and curricular/pedagogical innovations which demonstrate success and commitment to that objective.

This project embodied, and to some extent realized, my ideal of assessment research being both evaluative and innovative. I remember the feelings I experienced after a day of conducting some college assessment interviews. I felt rich beyond measure. I felt privileged that two or three individuals had just shared some very significant, and sometimes painful, parts of their lives with me. Within the context of confidentiality, students "spoke the truth" or "trothed" with me. I considered their memories and stories not as raw data but as gifts offered to me to use for the improvement of their college. Over the last two years, I have been learning how to invite students to enter dialogue with one another, to "story" themselves in a risk-free (i.e. not tied to grades) confidential environment for the purpose of learning. My role as a researcher encouraged, informed, and complemented my role as a teacher.

Summary

Our longitudinal study of a Christian college education yielded a wide variety of memories and assessments. Certainly, what is remembered from college does not necessarily reflect what is learned, but the college memories we collected forced us to reconsider our priorities and learning strategies. Some of the most significant learning at a Christian college occurs outside of the classroom. This finding can be interpreted in a variety of ways but one suggestion we have is that the co-curriculum receive greater respect -- which implies larger budgets and more accountability. Experiences where students take responsibility for their own learning can occur anywhere but it seems that most effective ones are those which are carefully designed and involve dialogue and collaboration. In closing, we hope that our research will have three effects: (1) to push Christian colleges further towards the multicultural reality of the world and Christ's body; (2) to add fuel to the pedagogical reform occurring in higher education; and (3) to encourage a continual review of our theories and assessments of Christian maturity.

Endnotes

1. We would like to recognize Chris Van Wingerden, Terri Postma, and Justin Barrett for their contribution to this research. Also, this project was made possible, in part, by the support of a Calvin Alumni Association Faculty Research Grant, a Calvin Research Fellowship, and the Calvin Psychology Department.

2. These three college assessment interviews were piloted in 1990 with Tabor College students who had kept diaries during the 1986-87 academic year.

3. The first salient memory assessment for Group 2 used each month of their first year as the memory prompts.

4. As interviewers, we certainly had some degree of influence on what and how the person told their story but we deliberately tried to minimize our responses and even our non-verbal interaction.

5. Our distinctions here have been discussed by memory researchers. Tulving (1983) distinguishes between episodic and semantic memory and J. R. Anderson (1983) has described a difference between declarative and procedural memory.

6. Bruner (1987) also suggested that "we become the autobiographical narratives by which we tell about our lives." Unfortunately, we did not explore to what extent the students' first-time accounts had influenced their lives. Also, we did not inspect our data for the differences Bruner suggested existed between men and women when telling their self-narrative.

7. In his 1984 book, Fowler did something that most of the other structural-developmental stage theorists have not -- he took off his mask. He admitted that his theory of faith development, rooted in the theology of H. Richard Niebuhr, was a modern form of mythmaking. Further, in recognizing the function or role his theory of faith development plays for modern folk, he also confessed his Christian beliefs and commitments.

8. From Gergen, K. J. and Gergen, M.M. (1983), "Narratives of the self." In T.R. Sarbin and K.E. Scheibe (Eds.), *Studies in social identity*, 254-73. New York: Praeger.

Reference List

Anderson, J. R. 1983. *The architecture of cognition*. Cambridge, MA: Harvard University Press.

Banaji, M. R. and R. G. Crowder. 1989. The bankruptcy of everyday memory. *American Psychologist* 44(9):1185-93.

Basinger, D. 1990. The measurement of religiousness: Some philosophical concerns. *Journal of Psychology and Christianity* 9(2):5-13.

Bassett, R.L., W. Camplin, D. Humphrey, C. Dorr, S. Biggs, R. Distaffen, I. Doxtator, M. Flaherty, P. Hunsberger, R. Poage, & H. Thompson. 1991. Measuring Christian maturity: A comparison of several scales. *Journal of Psychology and Theology* 19(1):84-93.

Burt, C. D. 1992. Retrieval characteristics of autobiographical memories: Event and date information. *Applied Cognitive Psychology* 6:389-404.

Butman, R. E. 1990. The assessment of religious development: Some possible options. *Journal of Psychology and Christianity* 9(2):14-26.

Broughton, J. M. 1986. The political psychology of faith development theory. In *Faith development and Fowler*, eds. C. Dykstra and S. Parks, 90-114. Birmingham, AL: Religious Education Press.

Bruner, J. S. 1987. Life as narrative. *Social Research* 54:11-32.

Carpenter, J. A. and K. W. Shipps, eds. 1987. *Making higher education Christian: The history and mission of evangelical colleges in America*. Grand Rapids: W.B. Eerdmans.

Dueck, A. 1979. Religion and morality: An evaluation of Kohlberg's theory of moral development. Paper presented at the Christian Association for Psychological Studies Annual Meeting.

Dykstra, C. and S. Parks. 1986. *Faith development and Fowler*. Birmingham, AL: Religious Education Press.

Fowler, J. W. 1981. *Stages of faith: The psychology of human development and the quest for meaning*. San Francisco: Harper & Row.

_____. 1984. *Becoming adult, becoming Christian: Adult development and the Chrisitan Faith*. San Francisco: Harper & Row.

Friedman, W. J. 1993. Memory for the time of past events. *Psychological Bulletin* 113(1):44-66.

Frye, N. 1957. *Anatomy of criticism.* Princeton, NJ: Princeton University Press.

Gergen, K.J., and M. M. Gergen. 1983. Narratives of the self. In *Studies in social idendity,* eds. T.R. Sarbin and K.E. Scheibe, 254-73. New York: Praeger.

_____. 1986. Narrative form and the construction of psychological science. In *Narrative psychology,* ed. T.R. Sarbin, 22-44. New York: Praeger.

Hanson, G. R., ed. 1982. *Measuring student development.* New Directions for Student Services, No. 20. San Francisco: Jossey-Bass.

Herrmann, D. J., and U. Neisser. 1978. An inventory of everyday memory experiences. In *Practical aspects of memory,* eds. M. M. Gruneberg, P.E. Morris, and R.N. Sykes, 35-51. New York: Academic Press.

Holland, D.C. and M. A. Eisenhart. 1990. *Educated in romance: Women, achievement, and college culture.* Chicago: University of Chicago Press.

Kintsch, W. and E. Bates. 1977. Recognition memory for statements from a classroom lecture. *Journal of Experimental Psychology: Human Learning and Memory* 3:150-59.

Kolb, D. 1984. *Experiential learning: Experience as the source of learning and development.* Englewood Cliffs, NJ: Prentice-Hall.

Kvale, S. 1983. The qualitative research interview: A phenomenological and hermeneutical mode of understanding. *Journal of Phenomenological Psychology* 14:171-96.

Lakoff, G. and M. Johnson. 1980. *Metaphors we live by.* Chicago: University of Chicago Press.

Larson, D. N. 1991. Evangelical tribalism at Christian colleges. In *Ethnic-minorities and evangelical Christian colleges,* eds. D.J. Lee, A.L. Nieves, and H.L. Allen, 159-202. Lanham, MD: University Press of America.

Lee, D. J. 1987. Memory for naturally-occurring events: Experienced versus reported events and telescoping in dating estimation. Ph.D. diss. Kansas State University.

_____. 1991. Ethnic-minorities and evangelical Christian colleges: Basic issues and assumptions. In *Ethnic-minorities and evangelical Christian colleges,* eds.

D.J. Lee, A.L. Nieves, and H.L. Allen, 1-46. Lanham, MD: University Press of America.

_____, ed. 1993a. *Storying ourselves: A narrative perspective on Christians in psychology.* Grand Rapids: Baker Books.

_____, ed. 1994. *Life and story: Autobiographies for a narrative psychology.* Westport, CT: Praeger.

_____. Lee, D. J. and R. R. Rice. 1991. Multiculturalism and ethnic identity: Concepts, history, research and policy. In *Ethnic-minorities and evangelical Christian colleges*, eds. D.J. Lee, A.L. Nieves, and H.L. Allen, 65-143. Lanham, MD: University Press of America.

Light, R. J. 1990. *Harvard Assessment Seminars.* Cambridge, MA: Harvard University Graduate School of Education and Kennedy School of Government.

Loftus, E. F. 1991. The glitter of everyday memory and the gold. *American Psychologist* 46(1):16-18.

Marchese, T. J. 1987. Third down, ten years to go. *AAHE Bulletin* 40:3-8.

_____. 1988. The uses of assessment. *Liberal Education* 74(13):23-27.

Marcia, J. E. 1980. Ego identity development. In *Handbook of adolescent psychology*, ed. J. Adelson, 159-87. New York: John Wiley.

Oosterhuis, A. 1989. On de-staging our relationships. *Journal of Psychology and Theology* 17(1):16-20.

Palmer, P. 1983. *To know as we are known: A spirituality of education.* San Francisco: Harper & Row.

Parks, S. 1986. *The critical years: The young adult search for a faith to live by.* New York: Harper & Row.

Pillemer, D. B., E. D. Rinehart, and S. H. White. 1986. Memories of life transitions: The first year in college. *Human Learning* 5:109-23.

Pillemer, D. B., L. R. Goldsmith, A. T. Panter, and S. H. White. 1988. Very long-term memories of the first year of college. *Journal of Experimental Pyschology: Learning, Memory, & Cognition* 14(4):709-15.

Pillemer, D. B., L. Krensky, S. Kleiman, L. R. Goldsmith, and S. H. White. 1991. Chapters in narratives: Evidence from oral histories of the first year of college. *Journal of Narrative and Life History* 1(1):3-14.

Sarbin, T. R., ed. 1986. *Narrative psychology: The storied nature of human conduct.* New York: Praeger.

Sears, R. T. 1983. Healing and family spiritual/emotional systems. *Journal of Christian Healing* 5(1):10-23.

_____. 1989. Personal communication with the author.

Thompson, C. P., J. J. Skowronski, and D. J. Lee. 1988a. Telescoping in dating naturally-occurring events. *Memory & Cognition* 16(5):461-68.

Thompson, C. P., J. J. Skowronski, and D. J. Lee. 1988b. Reconstructing the date of a personal event. In *Practical aspects of memory: Current research and issues,* vol. 1, eds. M. M. Gruneberg, P.E. Morris, and R. N. Sykes, 241-46. New York: John Wiley and Sons.

Tobin, K. 1990. Changing metaphors and beliefs: A master switch for teaching. *Theory into practice* 29(2):122-27.

Tulving, E. 1983. *Elements of episodic memory.* London: Oxford University Press.

Van Wicklin, J. F. 1990. Conceiving and measuring ways of being religious. *Journal of Psychology and Chrisitanity* 9(2): 27-40.

Vitz, P. C. 1990. The use of stories in moral development: New psychological reasons for an old education method. *American Psychologist* 45(6):709-20.

_____. 1992a. Narratives and counseling, Part 1: From analysis of the past to stories about it. *Journal of Psychology and Theology* 20(1):11-19.

_____. 1992b. Narratives and counseling, Part 2: From stories of the past to stories of the future. *Journal of Psychology and Theology* 20(1):20-27.

Wagenaar, W. A. 1986. My memory: A study of autobiographical memory over six years. *Cognitive Psychology* 18:225-52.

7. The Role of Learner Characteristics in Higher Education Assessment

Steven R. Timmermans

It is curious that assessment in higher education is a new topic of great currency on many campuses. One would think that colleges and universities representing both honored and proven traditions of the past as well as empirically-derived findings for the future would have long histories of proven institutional effectiveness -- including well-established methodologies for assessing effectiveness. Certainly, we would not exclude Christian colleges or universities from this expectation. For, as Stronks has recently stated, our unique perspectives on education include a specific responsibility:

> If we claim that we are developing the talents of our students and we are teaching students to think and to react to life's problems from a Christian perspective, it is important to do all that we can to show that our claims are justified. (Stronks 1991, 104)

It is unfair to suggest, however, that Christian and secular colleges and universities have not been engaged in assessment. Certainly, the professor studying the outcomes of student learning in her class, the director of admissions analyzing admission standards in relationship to retention, and the registrar tracking graduation rates have all been involved in assessment. However, what is often missing is the overall plan for assessment that connects various assessment activities and relates them to ultimate outcomes.

Assessment Components

When an institution begins to justify its claims in a holistic way, it is reasonable to suspect that there are a number of steps involved. Although the order may vary, one step is that of defining *what* it is the institution wishes its students to learn. The institution may develop a list of objectives and in the process will recall that there is a difference, for example, between expecting that "the graduate will be able to *explain* existentialism, naturalism, and theism" and expecting that "the graduate will be able to *distinguish* among various worldviews operant in contemporary cultural expressions." So then, the differing levels of objectives will be rediscovered as Bloom (1976) is "dusted-off" and re-opened.

There is another step as well. There will be a discussion about the purposes of assessment, particularly as plans are made to respond to assessment findings. Astin suggests that "although a great deal of assessment activity goes on in America's college and universities, much of it is of very little benefit to either students, faculty, administrators, or institutions" (Astin 1991, ix). Thus, the institution will clarify its expectations for assessment. A group of colleagues at Alverno College suggests that "we expect assessment -- carried out by and for an institution -- will improve educational practice and student learning" (Mentkowski et al. 1991, 1). Similarly, a group at Calvin College proposes that "our assessment program should be concerned with matters that directly relate to student learning and development" (Stronks et al. 1993).

Careful planning for the second step or phase leads to a third step, that of defining what is meant by student learning. Mayer's recent review (1992) is helpful as he describes, by way of metaphor, the evolution of ideas about learning over the course of this century. The first theory of learning could be understood as *learning as response acquisition* and rested primarily upon behavioral understandings of learning. For example, teaching that emphasizes drill and, relatedly, teacher-provided reinforcments is based on the belief that the learning situation must be structured in such a way to increase the number or degree of correct learner behaviors. The next metaphor was that of *learning as knowledge acquisition* and was the result of cognitive information-processing theory. Here, the goal is that the learner acquires an ever-increasing body of knowledge provided by the teacher. The metaphor currently most appropriate is that of *learning as knowledge construction*. Using this metaphor, Mayer describes the learner in the following way.

As a result, the view of the learner changed from that of recipient of knowledge to that of a constructor of knowledge, an autonomous learner with metacognitive skills for controlling his or her cognitive processes

during learning.   Learning involves selecting relevant information and
interpreting it through one's existing knowledge. (Mayer 1992, 407)

The sense of responsibility given the learner is evident in Mayer's description.
When coupled with the idea that truth exists in God's world, learning can be
defined as the personal responsibility of constructing meaning from God's
revelation.   Note that the responsibility is held by the person: the
responsibility is, before God, to engage in the task of constructing (analyzing,
fitting, comparing, acting-upon and even "nailing-down") for oneself that
which God has made known.   Teaching expands the responsibility to the
horizontal plane of interdependence and leads the learner to conclusions others
have discerned and to hypotheses yet unproven.

When learning is considered as knowledge construction and the learner
is believed to have been created in the image of God, the great variability in
learners cannot be ignored. Despite the goals of instruction, why does one
student, for instance, remain at the comprehension level of learning while
another student moves to a level of analysis? Relatedly, how do we determine
whether or not instruction has been effective?

The Importance of Learner Charateristics

To answer these questions, the dimension of *learner characteristics* must
be addressed.   The skills, styles, and abilities that are individually expressed
and influence learning are learner characteristics.   The origins of this
definition can be found in I Corinthians 12.

Metacognition

Continuing to use the metaphor of learning as knowledge construction,
two salient learner characteristics deserve scrutiny.   First is the degree to
which the learner is aware, both dynamically and statically, of her own
learning.   Those in psychology or education refer to this as *metacognition*
(Hagen, Barclay, and Newman 1982).   For instance, it is important for a
college student to understand relatively constant characteristics about his
learning (e.g., I find objective tests confusing, or I understand professors in
the lecture hall, but later on, my notes don't bring me to that same level of
understanding). This knowledge one has about self as a learner is the static
or rather constant component of metacognition. Also needed, however, is a
dynamic dimension, an in-process component, of metacognition (e.g., I didn't
understand what I just read so I should re-read it).   Not only must the learner
have an (accurate) assessment of self as learner, but she must also have an
on-going monitoring and evaluative system that assesses self (and the task)
while learning so as to most effectively construct meaning.   While

metacognition has greatly enriched our understanding of reading instruction and other curricula of elementary and secondary schooling, it has not yet greatly influenced pedagogy in higher education except in an isolated area explored later.

Background Knowledge

The second learner characteristic suggested by Mayer's understanding of learning is the knowledge base of the learner. As Mayer explains, if learning is construction, the existing foundation or structure of knowledge is critical. Whether Piaget's notion of the process of adaptation by means of accommodation or assimilation is used or Vygotsky's understanding of the zone of proximal development is called upon, what is already *known* is integrally involved in new learning. Although background knowledge may not be immediately considered as a learner characteristic, when rather typical standardized measures used in higher education are made available, they may be used as a way to gauge background knowledge. For example, the ACT is often considered a measure of student preparedness to profit from postsecondary education (The American College Testing Program 1988). Without going into a thorough theoretical analysis, it is appropriate to assume that the test measures the knowledge and skills the student presently knows in order to predict college performance. Thus, a necessary measure becomes a suitable way to understand learner characteristics with respect to background knowledge.

The exception to this conclusion is, of course, the questionable validity of measures such as the ACT for certain students. Jones and Watson suggest the following:

> Educators are quite familiar with the debate regarding the validity of SAT and ACT scores for minorities, females, and the disadvantaged. It is also generally accepted that, for these groups, grades are a more accurate predictor of academic performance than aptitude test scores. (Jones and Watson 1990, 72)

Thus, when measures such as ACT scores are used in higher education assessment as an indicator of background knowledge, there are some inherent limits to the conclusions drawn.

Learner Characteristics in Higher Education Assessment

Although there are others, metacognitive abilities and background knowledge are significant learner characteristics that must be considered in higher education assessment efforts. Consider, for example, this possible scenario in higher education. A professional program within the college or university has been debating the merits of a new model of professional preparation. Because the department cannot reach consensus as to whether they should shift to the new model or stay with the old model, a number of colleagues propose an experiment. The current-year group of students entering the program are randomly divided into two groups, an experimental group and a control group. The experimental group will receive the new method of professional training, the control group, the existing method. Pre- and post-testing will be arranged using an evaluation form based upon observational analysis of professional skills and qualities. At the conclusion of the professional training period, statistical analysis will be completed, and the department will be able to determine whether there is a significant difference between the two approaches.

Most often, a classic, experimental approach such as this is neither possible nor practical in higher education. If it were, though, the accompanying statistical analyses might indicate that the within-group differences may be more important and pertinent for professional training than the between-group differences. The range of student abilities and characteristics in the control group as well as the range of student abilities and characteristics in the experimental group may have a greater impact on outcome than the difference between the two groups in method. In other words, learner characteristics may be important considerations when considering whether student learning has occurred.

This lesson of paying attention to learner characteristics has significant implications for higher education assessment in any form, be it a classic experimental design or in any other form of descriptive analysis. For the characteristics of the learners are as significant a consideration as are the methods and the curriculum used with those learners. Although it is difficult to conceive of any higher education assessment endeavor which would exclude considering differences in learners, it happens frequently in a time when the diversity in college classrooms is increasing.

Consider another scenario. Suppose that a college, in an effort to bolster sagging enrollments or in a desire to reach new markets, begins to include a significant number of adult students by means of evening courses in its various programs of study, the same courses that are filled with traditional students in its daytime offerings. The two groups of students represent an extreme example of differences in learners. Perhaps the nontraditional students have more extensive background knowledge than traditional students, but they may not possess a depth of knowledge necessary for academia. They may be more aware of themselves as learners, yet they may lack the specific skills necessary for self-monitoring while learning. Just as there is a need to differentiate between these two groups of students in instruction, there is also a need to differentiate between the two groups in the analysis of assessment findings.

Although this example may be an extreme case, there are other situations which demand attention to learner characteristics. Many times, in a desire to be considered sufficiently rigorous and different from the image of inferiority that today's culture holds for Christianity, the Christian college will seek to limit admission to only those at a select level of ability and preparation. The initial conclusion may be that because of a restricted range of abilities, learner characteristics are unimportant. Nevertheless, learner characteristics must be considered, for even within such intellectual homogeneity, gender and ethnic differences in learning must be addressed. Probably more prevalent in many Christian colleges, however, is the temptation to include in the student body those whose abilities and preparation for college leave them at-risk for making sufficient academic progress. This temptation is particularly alluring when a potential applicant's sincere desire seemingly fits with the college's mission, and when, one could reason, that the smaller size of the college would allow for significant "individual attention."

Learner Characteristics and the College Mission Statement

Diversity in the college classroom should not be, however, the most compelling rationale for including the dimension of learner characteristics in an assessment program. Rather, the place to begin this consideration of learner characteristics in assessment is the college mission or purpose in education. Clarity in describing the types of students the college wishes to serve is necessary. One Christian college begins with this statement: "Given its mission, the college seeks to serve any student interested in higher education that is shaped by the Christian faith" (Calvin College 1992, 15). However, the mission statement from this college brings a further sense of definition to this claim:

> ...the college seeks to serve students from a variety of socioeconomic backgrounds, from a range of intellectual abilities, and those with disabilities that do not prevent them from the task of learning. Not only does this honor our commitment to being a diverse community, it also recognizes the diverse educational needs that the body of Christ must meet and the diverse ways in which leadership in society occurs. Our academic programs should enable people with different intellectual abilities, socioeconomic backgrounds, and gifts prepare for positions of leadership and lives of service. (Calvin College 1992, 15)

As companion to these goals, that same college has maintained admission criteria that allow the college to achieve its mission with respect to gathering a diverse group of students.

One subset from its diverse student body is that of students admitted into its alternative-entry program, the Access Program. Student applicants are screened by a committee when they fail to meet one or more admission standards and may be offered admission by means of this program. This program provides special advising, skills placement tests, possible review courses, and mandatory enrollment in a study strategies course. The goal is to assist these "at-risk" students in their development as learners, thus giving rise to the name of *developmental education* for the category of programs such as these. If the goal of development is accomplished, such students will be able to more fully benefit from their college education, and the mission of the college will be realized.

The two learner characteristics offered by Mayer can be readily identified in this program. First, with respect to the metacognitive dimension, the mandatory enrollment in a study strategies course is a key component of the program, for the goal of the course is to make the learner better aware of self (both dynamically and statically) and the tasks of learning. Thus, developmental programs such as the Access Program are the exception to metacognitive implications for learning not having yet made a significant impact on pedagogy within higher education.

Second, the ACT score (without ignoring its limitations) serves as a measure of background knowledge when decisions are made about student acceptance into this developmental program. A certain level of background knowledge is necessary if the student is to construct meaning in college courses she encounters while she simultaneously becomes more cognizant of her role as learner. If development is to occur, awareness alone will not suffice if there is a paucity of background and preparation.

Using data from the Access Program, two examples of assessment efforts follow. In presenting outcome data that differentiates among learner characteristics, it is the intent to demonstrate that our claims of mission are justified and the potential exists for the improvement of educational practice and student learning.

Example One

Although sequential courses are common place in higher education, this example provides data about a particular form of sequential course pairings, that of a pre-college grammar and composition review course paired with a basic college written rhetoric course. The students enrolled in the course pairings were all Access Program students which implies completion of the mandatory study strategies course. The purpose of college assessment in this case was to determine whether the review course is effective in preparing at-risk students for the basic written rhetoric course; in addition, the role of learner characteristics in this preparation is of particular interest.

As expected, an experimental design is neither appropriate nor possible for this assessment. Rather, an alternative form of assessment is used. This form involves the two steps of setting a standard and evaluating whether that standard has been met. In setting the standard for determining whether sufficient preparation is accomplished by means of the review course, two factors are considered. First, because a grade of "C" or better in the written rhetoric course is required of all students to demonstrate competency, one aspect of the standard relates to the grade of "C." Second, because the group of students are known to be at-risk, the standard also must be realistic with respect to the goal. Therefore, in this assessment the goal is that 67% of the students taking the review course will attain a grade of "C" or better in the subsequent written rhetoric course.

With this standard, the performance of 48 students was analyzed after they completed the written rhetoric course immediately following completion of the review course. Of these 48 students, 27 of the 48, or 56%, obtained a grade of "C" or better. Thus, at this initial level of analysis one conclusion is that the review course is not reaching its goal of developing and preparing a sufficient number of at-risk students for the written rhetoric course. However, before curriculum revision begins, further analysis is necessary.

First, these 48 are a subset of a larger group of 86 Access Program students who completed English 100 despite being identified at-risk. The remaining 38 were not asked to take the review course for they had performed reasonably well on a locally developed and administered English placement test. They were, however, required to complete the study strategies course. Examining the performance of these 38 in English 100 provides us a context in which to ask whether the 67% standard is reasonable. Indeed, 26, or 68%, of these students who were not required to take the review course obtained a grade of "C" or better in the written rhetoric course.

After determining reasonability, the next step is to determine whether the 48 students were all similar with respect to learner characteristics or if the range of learner characteristics is related to outcome. With respect to the metacognitive dimension, similarity among the learners is not assumed. However, having all participated in the study strategies course, it would be fruitless to determine whether there were differences in self-perceived metacognitive abilities. Because all students had completed the study strategies course, it is conceivable that they would all report using the metacognitive skills that they *ought* to use instead of the skills they actually use.

The second area, then, is the area of learner characteristics more available for analysis. Using the ACT as a measure of background knowledge, the following information provides the necessary context for drawing conclusions.

The mean English ACT score of these 48 students was 18.48 (range: 13-23). Dividing the range into thirds allows for tracing effectiveness at three different levels of English ACT scores. Table 7.1 provides the results of this analysis.

Table 7.1 ACT English Score As Related To The GPA Goal

	Grade < "C" n	Grade of "C" or > n
ACT of 13-16	7	4
ACT of 17-20	7	17
ACT of 21-23	7	6

This analysis suggests that for the mid range of students (ACT scores of 17 to 20), the preparatory course meets the goal, for 70.8% of these students received a grade of "C" or better in the subsequent written rhetoric course. More puzzling are the other two groups of students. Those with the lowest ACT scores (13 to 16) have a probability of less than 50% for reaching the goal. The third group (ACT scores of 21 to 23) are closer to a 50% probability of reaching the goal. The results from the lowest group may be explained by insufficient background in grammar and composition. This inadequate background makes it exceedingly difficult for these students to develop to a level at which they can be successful. The highest group is more puzzling. It may be that despite adequate or nearly adequate background, other factors (non-cognitive) may interfere with their development as learners.

How could these results be used to improve educational practice and student learning? A number of options are possible. With respect to the lowest group of students, it may be necessary to identify them at the beginning of the two-course sequence and design supplemental learning activities to bolster their preparation or to increase the intentionality of the metacognitive aspect of the program. The latter could be accomplished, for example, by extensive use of student tutors modeling a metacognitive approach to writing. The alternative to these approaches is to deny admission to students with these scores; such a decision would need to be made in light of the college mission.

With respect to the highest group of students, the assumption that other-than-cognitive factors may be implicated is a place to begin. Here a "post-mortem" analysis may be necessary.

Table 7.2 Completion Rates Of Access Program Students

Year of Entry	Entering Students	Graduated $\underline{n}$ (%)	In-Progress $\underline{n}$ (%)	Total $\underline{n}$ (%)
1982-83	102	22 (21.59)	0 (0)	22 (22.59)
1983-84	128	38 (29.69)	0 (0)	38 (29.69)
1984-85	133	41 (30.83)	0 (0)	41 (30.83)
1985-86	116	46 (39.66)	0 (0)	46 (39.66)
1986-87	129	47 (36.43)	1 (0.8)	48 (37.21)
1987-88	133	44 (33.08)	1 (0.8)	45 (33.83)
1988-89	139	25 (17.99)	29 (20.9)	54 (38.84)

In conclusion, this example illustrates that assessment failing to consider differences in learner characteristics may lead to premature and simplistic conclusions. When characteristics are included, more reasoned and valid conclusions may be drawn that will contribute to the improvement of educational practice and student learning.

Example Two

The Access Program has tracked the retention of its students by semester over a period of ten years. Thus, a number of analyses are possible by which assessment findings can be converted into improvement of educational practice and student learning.

Completion Rate

One way to assess the effects of the Access Program is to review the persistence of its student participants in college to the point of graduation.

Table 7.2 provides these data. These data suggest that the program reached
its most effective level with the group of students entering in 1985-86. Since
that time, the percentage of those graduating has not dipped below 30% in
contrast to the first two years.

Of interest is the degree to which learner characteristics impact Access
student success and failure. For instance, one might hypothesize that those
with lower ACT scores would be more prone to discontinue and that those
with higher ACT scores would be more likely to persist and graduate.

Examining only those students who began in 1987-88 (omitting the one
student still in-progress), the first step is to ascertain the range of ACT
composite scores. Of this group of 132 students, the ACT scores ranged
from 9 to 26. Table 7.3 provides the frequency of each ACT score.

Table 7.3 Frequency Count Of ACT Composite Scores

ACT	n	(% of total)	ACT	n	(% of total)
9	1	(0.76)	18	15	(11.36)
10	2	(1.51)	19	13	(9.86)
11	5	(3.79)	20	11	(8.33)
12	6	(4.54)	21	10	(7.58)
13	8	(6.06)	22	1	(0.76)
14	11	(8.33)	23	4	(3.03)
15	18	(13.64)	24	2	(1.51)
16	10	(7.58)	25	1	(0.76)
17	12	(9.09)	26	2	(1.51)

Next, these groups can be divided into four groups based on ACT and
their completion rate examined. As Table 7.4 indicates, there does not appear
to be a relationship between participants' ACT composite and graduation. In
particular, the 25.6% for those with ACT composites of 18 to 20 is
unexpected, given the 40% or better rate for those immediately below and
above that range. This may be due to the overall restricted range of ACT
scores, or more importantly, selection into the Access Program as the result
of committee scrutiny. For instance, those with low ACT scores may have
been selected into the Access Program because of a more promising high
school GPA, an alternative measure of background knowledge.

Table 7.4 Completion Rates By ACT Composite Score

ACT Composite of Students	Discontinued n	Graduated n	(% of n)
9,10,11,12,13,14	24	9	(27.3)
15,16,17	24	16	(40.0)
18,19,20	29	10	(25.6)
21,22,23,24,25,26	11	9	(45.0)

Probably more helpful for improving educational practice is to determine *when* students discontinued. Figure 7.1 provides these data and demonstrates that the greatest loss of students occurs between the conclusion of the second semester and the conclusion of the third semester. The question is whether information about learner characteristics, i.e., the ACT composite, provides an explanation as to what happens at this seemingly crucial time.

Of those students who discontinued at this crucial time, 67% had ACT composites below 18. In terms of those who started college, only 58% had ACT composites below 18; in terms of those who finished college, only 57% had ACT composites below 18. Thus, a disproportionate number of those with lower ACT scores discontinue between the second and third semester. One conclusion is that the developmental approach may not be as immediately effective with those students with lower ACT scores. If they manage to survive beyond this crucial time, then they are able to develop and persist. But they are most at-risk early in their college careers.

Can educational practice be improved by means of this knowledge? Certainly an alternative-entry program such as the Access Program could be extended beyond the first semester so that these students are followed into the second year. However, it may also be the case that the need is greater than monitoring. Background knowledge is deficient, and so, as these students continue on in college coursework, new information continues to "accumulate" and may place "unreasonable" demands on their insufficient knowledge bases.

Percent of Students

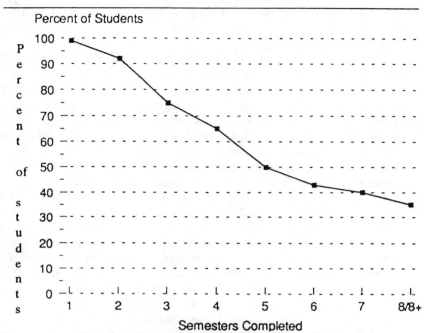

Figure 7.1 Retention Statistics Of 1987-88 Access Students By Semester

A concluding question is unavoidable. Could longitudinal assessment data, particularly if it included considerable sophistication with respect to learner characteristics, allow a college or university to develop and use a predictive model on which to base admission decisions for borderline students? These models are available and are called expert-systems models. Such a model is a computer simulation which "analyzes previous decisions about admissions and then makes new decisions based on the logic and/or illogic of past decisions" (Jones and Watson, 72). These authors caution, however, that such consistency in decision-making could be a "short-coming of the model, because profiles of high-risk students are such that qualitative, subjective decision making must sometimes take precedence over logic" (Jones and Watson, 72).

Metacognitive Changes

After focusing on the background knowledge component of learner characteristics, it is also possible to focus on metacognitive components of these Access Program students. As discussed earlier, all of these students participated in a study strategies course built upon metacognitive principles. The most recent three groups of entering first-year students (those who entered in 1990, 1991, and 1992) participated in this study strategies course which had a significant change in practice from earlier years.

During the earlier years, the students were required to be concurrently enrolled in any reading-lecture course. Theoretically, it was possible that in a given study strategies section, each student would be in a different reading-lecture course. Therefore, the study strategies instructor was powerless to explicitly point to the learning tasks facing each student. Rather, the instructor could only provide models and examples, trusting that the students would transfer the approach to their studies. In terms of metacognition, the students were *directly* taught self-monitoring; they were *indirectly* taught analysis of the learning task as part of a metacognitive strategy.

During the more recent years, the students were required to be concurrently enrolled in a reading-lecture course. Furthermore, the specific reading-lecture course in which they enrolled was controlled. The result was that in any given study strategies course, only four targeted reading-lecture courses would be represented; every student was in either one of the four. The study skills instructor, therefore, was able to minimally "shadow" the course by following each of the four course texts and syllabi. Then, when analysis of the learning task was necessary, rather than using a model or an example, the instructor was able to refer the students to a learning task in each of the four target courses. In this way, instruction in the study strategies course began to promote metacognitive skill development in terms of both knowledge of self and of task.

Assessment data provide the number of students attaining academic good standing at the conclusion of their first semester of enrollment. If the targeted course enhancement of the last three years truly allowed for more complete development of metacognitive skills, then it is reasonable to expect that these students would have attained higher GPAs than a similar group of students who had begun during the three years prior to the course enhancement. Table 7.5 provides these data.

Since a number of sources of variability are possible (e.g., perhaps the students selected for the Access Program for the second set of years were intellectually more capable than those of the previous three years, or perhaps the study strategies course instructors "improved" over time), no causal conclusion may be reached. Nevertheless, a trend appears to be evident. Moreover, the importance of this illustration is that a theory about learner characteristics led to a change in educational practice. The assessment data suggests that there may be a relationship, although not causal, between the teaching method and student learning. In other words, educational practice has been examined by means of student learning outcomes.

Table 7.5 Academic Status at the Conclusion of the First Semester

	% of Access Students Reaching Academic Good Standing	% of Access Students Failing to Reach Academic Good Standing
Without a Target Course:		
1987-88	80.9	19.1
1988-89	76.2	23.8
1989-90	67.1	32.9
With a Target Course:		
1990-91	73.2	26.8
1991-92	81.3	18.7
1992-93	90.5	9.5

In conclusion, this example demonstrates, as did the previous examples, that assessment data is necessary to improve educational practice and ultimately student learning in higher education. Although the controlled, experimental studies of the true empiricist may not be readily available for assessment in higher education, much can be accomplished particularly when the college mission becomes the context for assessment that includes salient, theory-based learner characteristics.

Reference List

American College Testing Program. 1988. *Content of the tests in the ACT assessment.* Iowa City: American College Testing Program.

Astin, A. W. 1991. *Assessment for excellence: The philosophy and practice of assessment and evaluation in higher education.* New York: Macmillan.

Bloom, B. S. 1976. *Human characteristics and school learning.* New York: McGraw-Hill.

Calvin College. 1992. *The expanded statement of the mission of Calvin College.* Grand Rapids: Office of the Provost.

Hagen, J. W., C. R. Barclay, and R. S. Newman. 1982. Metacognition, self-knowledge, and learning disabilities: Some thoughts on knowing and doing. *Topics in Learning and Learning Disabilities* 2(1):19-26.

Jones, D. and Watson, B.C. 1990. *High-risk students and higher education: Future Trends.* ASHE-ERIC Higher Education Report No. 3. Washington D.C.: The George Washington University, School of Education and Human Development.

Mayer, R. E. 1992. Cognition and instruction: Their historic meeting within educational psychology. *Journal of Educational Psychology* 84(4):405-12.

Mentkowski, M., G. Rogers, D. Deemer, T. Ben-Ur, J. Reisetter, W. Rickards, and M. Talbott. 1991. *Understanding abilities, learning, and development through college outcome studies: What can we expect from higher education assessment?* Symposium presented at the annual meeting of the American Educational Research Association, Chicago, Illinois, April.

Stronks, G. 1991. Assessing outcomes in Christian higher education. *Faculty Dialogue* 14:91-105.

Stronks, G., D. Guthrie, D. Laverell, R. Rice, A. Shoemaker, and D. Ward. 1993. *Educational assessment at Calvin College.* Gloria Stronks, Calvin College Education Department, Grand Rapids.

8. Staying on Course or Straying Off Course? Final Examinations and the Missions of a Christian College

Harold Faw and Harro Van Brummelen

The primary purpose of student assessment and evaluation is to furnish evidence of learners' progress toward certain explicit and implicit goals. Instructors design their assessment and evaluation procedures to measure student achievement in their courses. Thus, evaluation practices often make concrete and explicit the goals of a course.

Research at the secondary school level shows that the nature, structure and emphases of assessment methods directly affect the nature, structure and emphases of both course content and methodology (Anderson et al. 1990). More specifically, what instructors measure in their examinations quickly becomes the de facto curriculum and predisposes how students approach the task of learning in their courses (Bateson 1992). Students' grade point averages affect the likelihood of entry into professional and graduate programs and, to a lesser extent, employment prospects. Therefore, it is reasonable to expect that the nature and design of final exams in post-secondary institutions similarly influence in substantial ways what students learn from the planned curriculum.

Student assessment at Christian post-secondary education institutions has traditionally followed the main modes used in their public counterparts.

Typically, professors base the final grade on several smaller assignments or a major paper, a one-hour midterm test (especially at lower levels), and a two-to-three hour final examination. Some instructors also evaluate class participation or require an oral class presentation. Except for specific feedback on term papers and assignments, professors (and students) focus on summative evaluation. In other words, instructors emphasize ranking students so that "appropriate" proportions of students receive As, Bs, Cs, Ds and Fs.

Student assessment and evaluation at Trinity Western University usually reflect such a pattern. It is an explicit institutional policy that final examinations count for at least thirty percent of students' final course grades. They must also cover the full semester of course content. This means that both students and faculty members take the exams seriously. The university accentuates the importance of these exams by allowing instructors to administer them only at specified times during a ten-day period after regular classes are over. Such recognition means that the exams play a substantial role in the students' educational growth.

A question that therefore arises is whether the format and scope of such examinations supports or detracts from the mission of the university. This mission is "to develop godly Christian leaders: positive, goal-oriented university graduates with thoroughly Christian minds; growing disciples of Jesus Christ who glorify God through fulfilling The Great Commission, serving God and people in the various marketplaces of life." Does the nature and use of final exams help to develop "godly Christian leaders," or does an emphasis on recall of information produce unthinking followers who simply conform? What proportion of exam questions -- and therefore how much student preparation for them -- involves Christian worldview thinking that would cultivate "thoroughly Christian minds?" Answers to these questions may shed some light on what role, if any, exams play in encouraging students to be "growing disciples" who thoughtfully use their God-ordained gifts to serve Christ as Lord over every nook and cranny of life.

This paper reports the results of our analyses of both the content and the types of questions found in a broad sample of final exams administered by Trinity Western instructors in April, 1992. A central focus of our analysis was the extent to which these final exams encouraged (or discouraged) students from developing "thoroughly Christian minds" and helped (or hindered) students' preparation for Christian leadership, both key aspects of Trinity Western's official mission. Since final exams do not reflect the total assessment picture in a liberal arts institution, we also investigated how professors planned other course components as they relate to mission attainment. Our interpretation of the results leads, finally, to recommendations for assessment procedures that, in our view, would encourage the development of Christian thought and leadership.

Design of the Study and Data Collection Procedures

Our starting point was to identify a sample of courses that represented the whole university curriculum. We chose 48 courses from those listed in the Spring 1992 timetable of Trinity Western University. We selected them to represent all four faculties (academic groupings) and all 24 disciplines in which the university offers at least a minor (eight 3-semester-hour courses). The Faculty of Arts and Religious Studies includes art, communications, drama, English, French, music, philosophy and religious studies. The Faculty of Business and Economics encompasses aviation, business and economics. The Faculty of Natural and Applied Sciences contains biology, chemistry, computing, mathematics and physics. Finally, the Faculty of Social Sciences and Education comprises geography, history, physical education, political science, psychology, recreation, sociology and teacher education.

Several considerations, all intended to ensure a representative sample, guided our choice of specific courses. We represented all four undergraduate years equally, and each discipline in proportion to its number of academic courses. We omitted applied music and physical education activity courses normally worth only one semester hour of credit and involving a predominantly applied flavor. We included a suitable mix of both required and elective courses. Also, we chose our sample to include a proportional representation of courses taught by both full-time and part-time instructors. Finally, we included only one course taught by any specific individual. Thus our sample comprised twelve courses at each of the 100-, 200-, 300-, and 400- levels. It included approximately 28 percent of the courses taught during that particular semester, and comprised a broad cross-section of all academic courses offered at the university.

Having identified this group of 48 target courses, we then requested from the appropriate instructor a copy of the final exam used in each. (In two cases, due to the course not being offered this semester, we obtained the most recent exam available.) In addition, we obtained copies of the syllabi for all 48 courses in order to review both the instructors' formal objectives and other required projects and assignments.

Following our analysis of the content of the final examinations and our inspection of the course syllabi, we selected a sub-sample of ten courses and arranged for a brief interview with each instructor. We again chose this smaller set of courses to represent all faculties and year levels. Included in this subset of ten courses were some in which a Christian perspective was very evident in the final exam and others in which it was missing or unclear.

The purpose of this follow-up contact was to understand better how and to what extent professors incorporated a Christian worldview in the course, how they evaluated student progress in grasping such a perspective, and the degree to which they addressed the theme of leadership.   To help the instructors, we invited them to give some thought before our meeting to four questions we planned to ask: How do you teach this course differently than you would at a public institution?   How does your course contribute to developing a "Christian mind?" Do you evaluate your students' growth in their understanding of a Christian worldview in ways other than the final examination? Do you find it possible to incorporate the development of Christian leadership in your course, either in content or in structure?   We took notes during each 20-30 minute interview. All instructors were co-operative and eager to help us by clarifying the way they went about teaching their courses.

The analysis of the information we gathered proved to be challenging! No obviously appropriate set of guidelines or statistical procedures was evident to us from the outset. Our strategy evolved as we perused the examinations, looked for patterns, and brainstormed together what our observations might mean.   Our guiding objective was to explore the relationship between the content and requirements of the courses (especially the final exams, but to some extent other elements as well) and the university's mission of developing "godly Christian leaders" and graduates with "thoroughly Christian minds."

We based our analysis of the examinations mainly on two distinct sets of judgements. First, we assumed that if examinations were to contribute to leadership development, they should require students to formulate their own views as they critically examine course issues. Therefore, as we considered each exam, we assessed the proportion of different types of exam questions. Also, we judged the percentage of the total exam that required use of each of three levels of thinking skills (recall and comprehension, simple interpretation and direct application, and higher level analysis).   Second, we judged the presence and extent of any explicit reference to Christian worldview thinking or biblical perspectives in the exam questions. We categorized the component in each case as substantial, minor, or completely absent.

In surveying the course syllabi, we paid particular attention to how instructors stated their objectives and whether they made any specific reference to Christian perspectives. We also noted other major aspects of assessment besides the final examination, and whether or not these aspects appeared to include a Christian world view component. We used the comments instructors provided during our interviews as well as the results of student course evaluations to interpret our other findings. From them, we also determined the extent to which Christian views and values were an important part of the course, whether or not they were evident in course objectives, projects or exams.

In the next section we will consider evidence indicating whether professors take into account the development of leadership characteristics in their final examinations.   Thereafter, we reviewed how the exams may nurture the

Christian mind and biblical vision. In a final section before our conclusion, we explored how other course components relate to the attainment of Trinity Western's mission.

Final Examination Questions and Leadership Characteristics

Leadership is a complex phenomenon, one that involves a diverse array of personal attributes functioning in particular cultural and social settings. The constraints of the structure of final examinations do not give students the opportunity to develop or demonstrate all such leadership ingredients. Yet final exams can contribute to some essential aspects of leadership. In particular, Christian leadership stems from a thoughtful perspective that uses the mind to interpret, evaluate, and set out directions within the contours of God-given guidelines.

This section, then, documents the extent to and the ways in which final examination questions supported basic aspects of leadership development. Leadership, we believe, can only be fostered in a context of thoughtfulness and discernment. This requires a learning context where students do not just name things by, for instance, memorizing and recalling factual information. Rather, they also must be expected to analyze problems, ask incisive questions, examine issues, evaluate different approaches, affirm and apply values and principles in new ways and settings, and justify and communicate their views effectively (Webb and Grant 1992). This is as true for final exam questions as it is for in-class discussions and student assignments.

Our age is often described as the "information age." Acceptance of this metaphor often also embraces the assumption that information and factual data provide the basis of thought and action. At the same time, the need for understanding rooted in our cultural heritage and for discerning analysis and vision based on moral guidelines and spiritual significance is often implicitly downplayed (Bowers 1992). We believe, however, that examinations which foster leadership will go beyond the "information age" metaphor. They will, for instance, require responses in which students demonstrate higher level thinking and the ability to communicate the results of their thinking effectively and creatively.

We therefore analyzed the type of questions asked on our sample of final examinations in two different ways. First, we determined what percentage of the marks assigned to questions were in each of four categories: (1) true/false, matching, or questions requiring one or two word answers; (2) multiple choice questions with a choice of a "best" answer from four or five alternatives; (3) questions for which students have to formulate answers (one to three sentences or one to six lines in length); and (4) essay questions more extensive than those required in #3. Table 8.1 shows the percentage of each type of question in final exams at each of the four undergraduate levels (in

162 Staying on Course or Straying Off Course?

terms of the point value assigned by the instructor to the questions rather than the number of questions). Table 8.2 does so for each of the four faculties at Trinity Western University.

Table 8.1 Percent of Questions of Different Types for Final Examinations at the Four Undergraduate Years

Question types--> Year	T/F, matching, blanks	Multiple choice	Up to 3 sentences	Essay questions
First year courses	19	33	14	33
Second year courses	19	7	28	46
Third year courses	6	18	16	61
Fourth year courses	1	0	12	87
TOTAL	**11**	**14**	**18**	**57**

Table 8.2 Percent of Questions of Different Types for Final Examinations in the Four Faculties

Question types---> Faculty	T/F, matching, blanks	Multiple choice	Up to 3 sentences	Essay questions
Arts & Religious St	16	8	10	66
Business & Econ	8	12	14	66
Natural Sciences	0	7	40	54
Soc. Sc. & Educa.	12	26	17	45
TOTAL	**11**	**14**	**18**	**57**

We based our second categorization of the final examination questions on a simplified version of Bloom's taxonomy of educational objectives (Bloom 1956). We specified three levels. A basic level consisted of recall and comprehension. All true/false, matching, fill-in-the-blank and most multiple choice questions fell into this category, as did questions instructing students to define, describe, list, name, identify, select, or state. A middle level included interpretation and simple application. Exam questions that asked students to explain, give examples, compute, convert, illustrate, interpret, predict, rearrange, paraphrase, outline, relate, or demonstrate were normally of this type. This category included some multiple choice questions, most short essay and some long essay questions. Finally, higher level questions required students to perform more difficult application, problem solving and higher level critical thinking. Instructors here asked students to analyze, differentiate, appraise, compose, criticize, relate, solve, critique, evaluate, compare, contrast, justify, or construct.

Sometimes it was difficult to decide where a question fit (e.g., with a vague instruction such as "discuss"). However, two separate analyses several weeks apart showed very high consistency in our categorization. If we judged an answer to a question to require more than one level of response, we assigned the question to the higher level. This was often the case, for instance, in essay questions where higher-level analysis and evaluation could not take place without the students recalling and interpreting facts and concepts. If a question consisted of different parts, we analyzed each part separately to determine its categorization. Table 8.3 shows the percentage of each level of question in examinations at each undergraduate level (again, in terms of the worth assigned by each instructor to the questions rather than the number of questions). Table 8.4 does so for each faculty at Trinity Western University.

Table 8.3 Percent of Questions Representing Different Intellectual Levels for Final Exams at the Four Undergraduate Years

Intellectual Level--- > Year	Basic level	Middle level	Higher level
First year courses	58	18	23
Second year courses	38	30	32
Third year courses	44	21	31
Fourth year courses	7	14	79
TOTAL	37	21	42

These data reveal clear trends, at least within our sample of final examinations. First, while instructors assigned more than half the marks on the exams to longer essay-type questions, the proportion increased from one-third in the first year to almost 90% in the fourth. There was a noticeable shift from multiple choice questions in first year exams (33%) to shorter essay questions in second year (28%) to longer essay questions in third and fourth year (61% and 87% respectively).

Table 8.4 Percent of Questions Representing Different Intellectual Levels for Final Examinations in the Four Faculties

Intellectual level---> Faculty	Basic level	Middle level	Higher level
Arts & Religious St.	29	14	58
Business & Econ.	37	29	34
Natural Sciences	27	29	44
Soc. Sc. & Education	51	22	27
TOTAL	**37**	**21**	**42**

When categorized by faculties, patterns were not as striking. Instructors in the Faculty of Social Sciences and Education did use more multiple choice items than any other faculty (26% vs. an average of 9% in the three other faculties). Moreover, the Faculty of Natural Sciences gave more shorter essay questions including ones showing the steps of solving a problem (40% vs. an average of 14% in the remaining faculties). Instructors in the faculties of Arts and Religious Studies and Business and Economics gave somewhat more long essay questions than the other two faculties (66% vs. 47%).

Tables 8.3 and 8.4 show that second and third year examinations differed little in the level of thinking required. Instructors gave first-year students, however, a majority of recall and comprehension questions (almost 60%). They more than doubled the proportion of questions requiring more higher level thinking between third and fourth year (from 34% to 79%). The Faculty of Social Sciences and Education put much more emphasis on recall and comprehension than the other faculties (51% vs. an average of 30% for the other three). On the other hand, the Faculty of Arts and Religious Studies required more difficult application and higher level thinking (58% of the total marks assigned compared with only 33% in the other faculties).

Within these overall patterns, examinations differed a great deal. Three exams at the first year level consisted exclusively of multiple choice and/or true-false factual recall questions. Multiple choice items formed seventy percent of two other exams, one each at the first and second year levels. The other thirty percent consisted of essay questions also requiring mainly factual recall. One second year exam consisted exclusively of essay questions, thus requiring students to organize and formulate their knowledge. Nevertheless, the questions focused almost exclusively on describing factual recall, with students not asked for any interpretation or evaluation of what they had learned.

On the other hand, most examinations beyond the first year and especially those in the fourth year demanded some higher level thinking. Typical instructions for such questions, in disciplines as diverse as English, economics, mathematics and education were the following:

Compare and contrast . . . .
Set forth the . . . position. Then argue for or against it.
State your agreement or disagreement with one of these theories and tell why. Be as persuasive as you can.
What are the advantages and disadvantages [or strengths and weaknesses] of . . . ? In your view which is the most effective means, and why?
Discuss the origins and impact of . . . and assess the validity of concerns raised by opponents of this process.
Give a brief account of the pertinent issues involved, state the main views you have encountered, and defend your own position.

The above questions usually asked students to analyze certain theories, views and developments discussed in class and then defend their own evaluation or position. Other questions asked students to assess, based on what they had learned during the course, current issues as well as statements or articles that were new to them:

Explain and critically assess the following statement: . . . .
Comment on the strategic implications of the [attached] article.
List ways . . . can respond to women's issues and concerns in the urban environment.
Examine the negative consequences of stereotyped female roles in . . . .
To what extent, if at all, do you believe the Canadian government should protect Canadian culture from American domination?

Eight professors (none in the first year courses) asked students to deal with hypothetical situations that they might face as leaders in particular disciplines. The most common type was the analysis of particular case studies based on theories and principles taken up in class. One business examination consisted of a detailed analysis of a single complex case. Other exams required students to write a letter or a news release explaining their position on key issues in the discipline. Two instructors asked students to imagine that they had entered a certain career and to develop and defend their personal approaches to specified situations or problems. One of them was a take-home exam personalized for each student based on their anticipated career situation.

Leadership, as we pointed out earlier, has essential moral and spiritual dimensions. While in the next section we will discuss in more detail the Christian worldview components of the examinations, we do want to note here that several exam questions directly linked the ethical dimensions of the discipline to leadership concerns:

> What are the ethical and strategic areas where North America needs to respond to Japan and in what fashion?
> List and discuss some of the prominent ethical issues in . . . and describe the role the practitioner plays in dealing with them.

Our analysis indicated that a significant proportion of final examinations, including most of those at the fourth year level, contributed to the development of certain leadership characteristics. Professors asked questions that called for probing analyses of current issues and for applying discerning understanding of our cultural and Christian heritage. They required them to evaluate different points of view and apply what they had learned in the course in resourceful ways. Especially in fourth year courses, instructors expected students to be able to compose and communicate the results of their thinking effectively. Trinity Western University often assigns a course to third-year or fourth-year level somewhat arbitrarily. Our sample of exams surprised us, therefore, in that a sizable difference existed between instructors' expectations at third- and fourth-year levels.

For first-year examinations in general and for selected ones at other levels, the proportion of required higher level thinking was disappointingly meager. More than half the questions at first-year level were of the "objective" type, including true-false questions whose reliability is suspect. While multiple choice questions can in theory assess higher level thinking, the vast majority of these items in our sample tested factual recall. Only a few scattered ones involved interpretation or simple application.

We were disappointed that almost sixty percent of the first-year final examination questions involved nothing more than factual recall and comprehension. No doubt part of the reason was that many disciplines had first-year class sizes of fifty to sixty-five students. Further, some Trinity Western University professors have expressed their belief that their first year courses need to lay a solid factual basis for further study in a discipline. Nevertheless, on many first-year exams, professors asked students to do tasks that required less higher level thinking than that often demanded at the senior high school level.

If our sample of Trinity Western University's first-year final examinations accurately reflected the level of work expected in the corresponding courses, then such courses contributed little to the leadership component of its mission. A biblical conception of knowledge involves personal response and commitment. Thoughtful understanding and perceptive use of knowledge is an essential base for effective leadership. Moreover, learning for recent high school graduates at this age needs to emphasize the complex process of causal chains and networks and the search for truth. Students also need to develop, evaluate, and apply general theories and ideologies (Egan 1990, 176-179). Yet many first year final exams in our sample emphasized fragmented pieces of informational recall. They provided little opportunity for students to display and apply personal insights, something that would help prepare them for leadership roles.

Final Examination Questions and the Christian Mind

Trinity Western University's mission statement makes explicit reference to the goal of developing graduates with "thoroughly Christian minds." This phrase echoes an emphasis discussed in Harry Blamires' book entitled *The Christian Mind* (1963). It also represents a recurrent theme in the writing of Arthur Holmes (1985; 1987). Fostering the growth of Christian minds is generally thought to be the unique challenge of Christian higher education.

This focus has implications for the total curriculum of Christian liberal arts colleges and universities (e.g., core and interdisciplinary courses). Further, for the content and thrust of specific courses, it demands that all concepts, theories and systems of thought be studied from a Christian perspective. This in no way implies that secular views and philosophies are excluded. It does mean, however, that professors and students examine them in the light of such biblical themes as creation, fall and redemption, humanness, and accountable stewardship. The foundational assumptions used to examine a range of perspectives must be compatible with, if not derived from, a biblical understanding of life and knowledge.

We expect those involved in Christian higher education to pay more than lip service to the goal of developing "Christian minds" in our graduates. Thus, it seems inescapable that students must be accountable for both understanding and applying Christian perspectives in their academic work. We reasoned that assessment of these insights and capacities should be represented in the influential final course examinations. Therefore, the second major component of our final exam analysis explored the extent to which Christian worldview (CWV) understanding appeared necessary for acceptable answers.

In assessing the presence of this component, we watched for key words such as "truth," "biblical perspective," "Christian view," etc. We reasoned that biblical understanding would be evidenced in ability to compare Christian and secular views, to trace theological themes such as salvation, guilt and responsibility, to apply disciplinary concepts in Christian contexts, or to evaluate ideas and concepts based on biblical perspectives. As in the leadership section, we also held that demonstrating a Christian understanding must involve more than recall of information. Again, students should be able to use higher level thinking skills of analysis and evaluation. Hence to some degree we considered both the content and the level of questions.

Although we recognized that in-class instruction might lead students to interpret a question as inviting CWV thinking, we were able to assess only explicit CWV components. In general, we proceeded by judging whether a given question seemed suitable for an examination in a comparable course taught at a secular institution. The specific wording used to evaluate the presence of a "Christian mind" in students varied widely. Questions drawn from a variety of discipline areas contained the following expressions:

> Compare sacramental and Reformed attitudes . . . to faith and art.
> Define cognitive dissonance and apply it to Christians.
> Discuss divine involvement in . . . the Aeneid.
> How will Christianity affect each area of education?
> How do mathematics and theology affect one another?
> Take into account a biblical view of knowledge . . . .

We were fairly confident in judging the explicit requirement for Christian thinking in the examinations and categorizing it as absent, minor (weighting of 5 percent or less), or substantial (weighting of more than 5 percent). This method, of course, likely somewhat underestimates the CWV component. We have summarized the quantitative results of this analysis in Tables 8.5 and 8.6. Table 8.5 presents this data according to undergraduate year level, and Table 8.6 according to the four faculties at Trinity Western University.

Since the data in Tables 8.5 and 8.6 are based on frequencies and since the maximum values are small (12 in Table 8.5 and between 7 and 18 in Table 8.6), the patterns evident here require cautious interpretation. Still, an explicit CWV component in exams was most often totally absent (in 63 percent of all exams). When represented (in 37 percent of the exams), it was usually substantial. Representation across the four year levels showed no clear pattern. Comparisons across faculties revealed that a CWV component was most frequently present in Arts and Religious Studies courses (56 percent of exams), and less common elsewhere (20 percent of exams).

Making judgments of the exact proportion of a given examination that reflected Christian worldview thinking proved difficult. We noted, however, that when this element was overtly present, it was often a very major component. For example, one communications exam consisted of 25 marks on matching of terms, 15 marks on short definitions, and the remaining 60

Table 8.5 Number (and Percent) of Cases in which the Explicit Christian World View Component in Final Examinations was Substantial, Minor, or Absent in Each of the Four Undergraduate Years

CWV component---> Year	Substan- tial	Minor	Absent	Total cases
First year courses	2 /17%	2 /17%	8 /67%	12
Second year courses	5 /42%	0 / 0%	7 /58%	12
Third year courses	2 /17%	0 / 0%	10 /83%	12
Fourth year courses	7 /58%	0 / 0%	5 /42%	12
TOTAL	16 /33%	2 / 4%	30 /63%	48

Table 8.6 Number (and Percent) of Cases in which the Explicit Christian Worldview Component in Final Examinations was Substantial, Minor, or Absent in Each Faculty

CWV component--->> Faculty	Substan- tial	Minor	Absent	Total cases
Arts & Religion St.	10 /56%	0 / 0%	8 /44%	18
Business & Econ.	1 /14%	0 / 0%	6 /86%	7
Natural & Appl. Science	1 /14%	0 / 0%	6 / 86%	7
Soc. Sc. & Educ.	4 /25%	2 /13%	10 /63%	16
TOTAL	16 /33%	2 / 4%	30 /63%	48

marks on longer essays. In the essay part, the instructor asked students to answer two of five questions. One of these questions asked students to describe what they would say to a group of high school students on the topic of "a Christian understanding of the media." Another question asked how the topic of "evaluating and choosing role models" would be addressed in light of their knowledge of the media. Both questions included substantial CWV components. Another final exam (a 400-level psychology course) asked students to answer five long essay questions chosen from a larger set of eleven items. Several of these had clear Christian worldview elements. An example of one such question was, "Should Christians use knowledge of psychological processes to encourage conversion, healing, worship, etc.?"

It is evident from the foregoing that final exams varied markedly in Christian worldview emphasis. Much creativity was evident in some exams, with instructors challenging students to apply their Christian perspective in worthwhile, important, and inventive ways. Those instructors who included such a component usually required both a deeper level of understanding and a range of applications. On the other hand, in many exams no CWV component was evident. For those, it was impossible to identify any evidence that students would need to bring a Christian perspective to these exams.

The content and objectives of different courses vary widely. Therefore, the inclusion of CWV components is more difficult in certain discipline areas. Nevertheless, if Christian liberal arts institutions intend their courses to be distinctly different from those at public ones, such distinctives should be evident in components as important and influential as final examinations. In the next section, we consider the additional information provided in syllabi, student evaluations, and direct contact with a sample of instructors in order to interpret correctly the patterns we have already noted.

Exploration of Other Course Components

A final examination is very important both as a means of assessment and as a powerful influence on student learning. However, it is only one of

Table 8.7 Number (and Percent) of Cases with Christian Worldview Explicitly Addressed in Various Components of the Course During Each of the Four Undergraduate Years

CWV component--> Year	Objec- tives only	Exams & project only	Both obj. & exams/pr	No CWV evident	Total cases
First year courses	4/33%	1/ 8%	4 /33%	3 /25%	12
Second year courses	2/17%	2/17%	3 /25%	5 /42%	12
Third year courses	3/25%	1 /8%	1 / 8%	7 /58%	12
Fourth year courses	2 /17%	3/25%	4 /33%	3 /25%	12
TOTAL (no./ %)	11/23%	7/15%	12 /25%	18/37%	48

Table 8.8 Number (and Percent) of Cases with Christian World View Explicitly Addressed in Various Components of the Course in Each Faculty

CWV component--> Faculty	Objectives only	Exams & project only	Both obj. & exam/pr	No CWV evident	Total cases
Arts & Religion St.	3 /17%	4/22%	7/39%	4/22%	18
Business & Econ.	2 /29%	1/14%	0/ 0%	4/57%	7
Nat. & Applied Sci.	2 /29%	1/14%	0/ 0%	4/57%	7
Soc. Sc. & Educ.	4 /25%	1/ 6%	5/31%	6/38%	16
TOTAL (no./%)	**11/23%**	**7/15%**	**12/25%**	**18/37%**	**48**

several elements that need to be considered. Therefore, we also sought to discover how the university's mission related to other course components by examining syllabi and course projects, and by talking directly with several instructors. We give a summary of the evidence of explicit CWV components in the syllabi and final examinations in Tables 8.7 and 8.8.

Stated course objectives are important. They guide instructors in their planning and direct students as to what they should focus on in the course. In perusing the objectives for each of the 48 courses in our sample, several patterns emerged. In the vast majority of cases (44 out of 48), instructors stated specific objectives clearly either in a numbered list or in paragraph form. For syllabi including written objectives, professors made explicit reference to the goal of providing biblical or Christian perspectives in the course in just over 50 percent of the cases (23 of 44). They expressed their intention in a variety of ways, including the following:

--   to describe a Christian perspective of media use and responsibility
--   to introduce scriptural principles to solving practical business problems
--   to open the eyes of students to the tremendous order . . . of creation, and thus contribute to an appreciation of how great God is
--   to aid students in developing a Christian philosophy of recreational leadership
--   to show how...literary arts...disclose truths about God, humanity, and the world

These samples indicate commitment to providing biblical perspectives. We were disturbed, however, to discover that this intention translated into explicit attempts to assess students' grasp of such a perspective in barely 40 percent of all the courses. In other words, in 60 percent of the courses we examined, professors did not indicate the inclusion of a Christian perspective in any test, assignment or project. Evidently, in some cases, the link between objectives and assessment procedures is weak. Since exams and assignments control student study activity to a significant extent, in these cases we suspect that students may absorb and retain little of the intended perspective.

In order to obtain an independent check on our judgments regarding the CWV component in the examinations and the courses in our sample, we consulted data obtained from the course evaluations that Trinity Western's students complete each semester. One item on these evaluation forms asks students to indicate their agreement or disagreement with the following statement: "Given the nature and content of this course, the instructor has attempted to conduct it from a Christian perspective." The students respond on a four-point scale ranging from "strongly agree" (1) to "strongly disagree" (4). Mean student ratings on this item were available for 38 of the 48 courses in our sample. In 24 of these courses, our estimate of the CWV component in the exam was zero, and the corresponding mean student rating of the CWV component was 1.62. In the remaining 14 courses, our estimate of the CWV component of exams was 27 percent, and the mean student rating was 1.29. Both results reflect student perception that the courses included a Christian perspective, but the lower value indicates a stronger CWV element. Analyzing the same information in a different way, the correlation between our estimates and student ratings was -0.47, indicating a substantial degree of consistency between student perception and our judgements of the CWV component in the courses.

We also correlated these same student ratings with an index of the number of course elements incorporating a definite CWV component. This index ranged from zero to three, reflecting the presence or absence of explicitly stated Chrisitan elements in each of (1) course objectives, (2) the final exams, and (3) the other course assignments. The correlation value was -0.58, once again indicating that student perceptions correspond to a substantial extent with our estimates based on examinations and course syllabi.

Our interviews with course instructors yielded a more encouraging picture than our foregoing analyses. The instructors' comments were both varied and illuminating. A sample of their thoughts will help to put the remainder of our analyses in perspective.

We first asked the instructors the question, "How do you teach this course differently than you would at a public institution?" Some mentioned that they commonly open class with prayer. Others indicated that they adopt a "whole person" view, or that they refer to the spiritual dimension of life. Still others identified specific discussion of worldviews or reference to biblical themes, passages, or values as the most distinctive aspect of their course. In one or two cases, it was evident to us that a course would be taught totally differently if at all in a secular setting.

Our next question was, "Does your course contribute to developing a 'Christian mind'? If so, how?" In response to this question, several referred to the importance of a correct understanding of human nature and of helping students think about what it means to be truly human. Others mentioned stressing the value of community or of appreciation for our religious heritage. Still others felt that they helped students develop Christian minds by analyzing ideas from theological or philosophical perspectives. Several said they included practical biblical principles of conduct or opportunities for ministry appropriate to their discipline.

Thirdly, we asked instructors the question, "Do you evaluate your students' growth in their understanding of a Christian worldview in ways other than the final examination? If so, how?" Some instructors required that students include Christian worldview thinking in term papers. Others asked students to make oral presentations that incorporated such a view, and still others expected the same in case study reports. One instructor asked students to reflect on the material in each chapter in terms of how a Christian should respond to the information conveyed. Several admitted that they did not directly assess this perspective at all, or that it was an optional component in various course assignments.

Our last question was, "Do you find it possible to incorporate the development of Christian leadership in your course, either in content or in structure?" Responses to this question were readily grouped into those dealing with ideas covered in the course, and those related to activities expected of students. With respect to the former, instructors made reference to models of leadership in literature, the example of Christ as a leader, and the notion that we have a *calling* to make a difference in our world. Some said that they point out biblical examples and principles of leadership. For example, they stress the idea that leaders are responsible for the well-being of those they influence. Others identified the fostering of critical thought and Christian responses to ideas as their contribution to leadership development. Instructors considered activities in their classes such as oral seminars and reports, presentation of papers or workshops in class, and group discussions and debates to be part of practical leadership development. One person mentioned that the instructor's own modelling of Christian leadership was an important element.

Several conclusions seem warranted. First, there was great diversity in what professors understood "Christian leadership" or "Christian mind" to mean. Some instructors had evidently thought carefully about these matters. Others were obviously just beginning to grapple with them. Secondly, most if not all instructors made a sincere effort to incorporate something distinctive in their courses, a task clearly much more challenging in some areas than in others.   Finally, when a biblical perspective was included in a course, it usually occupied a substantial place, at least in the mind of the instructor. We concluded that most courses were either minimally different from those taught at secular institutions, or were thoroughly permeated with biblical perspectives, views and values. There seemed to be no "middle ground."

We are genuinely encouraged by the attempts instructors usually make to provide a Christian perspective. At the same time, we continue to be troubled by the obvious failure to assess student progress toward these very significant goals in many courses.   Professors have good intentions of placing the concepts they teach in a Christian context. They may not, however, actually be getting through to students and helping to "transform and renew their minds" to the extent we would deem desirable.

Conclusions

The role of final examinations in ranking students is a reality that no college or university can escape in today's society. Yet the preparation for and writing of final exams should, as much as possible, provide a meaningful learning experience for students. When setting final exams, professors need to consider that the nature of their exams affects the curricula-in-use. Even when instructors try to avoid letting their final exams influence their day-to-day planning, students will decide, on the basis of actual copies or reports of exams, what needs to be studied, how they will study, and what they will believe to be important about course content.

In several courses, we detected inconsistency between the course objectives and course assessment. This was particularly striking for a number of the final examinations. When an exam consists mainly of objective-type questions requiring factual recall, we need to ask: "What are we trying to accomplish?" Most students will soon forget these isolated bits and pieces of fragmented information. Are we separating smart students from dumb ones by rewarding those who are able to retain the facts until just after the exam? This type of question, usually multiple choice but also involving true-false, matching, and fill-in-the-blank ones, is too limited in doing justice to the mission of Christian college education.

We do not want to imply that there is no need for factual recall and comprehension. Students do need a conceptual background that provides a basis for thoughtful reflection. Our point here is that questions requiring nothing more than factual recall should comprise a strictly bounded proportion of the weight of any college-level examination. After all, questions requiring comprehension and higher level thinking also require recall of relevant factual information, even though they would likely encompass a smaller content sample.

We can think of only one reason for final examinations that require factual recall only. With the pressures of large classes, it is a way for professors to save a great deal of marking time. Such exams, however, usually do little to bolster directly the attainment of the course objectives or the institution's overall aims. They are far from ideal and Christian colleges should not be comfortable with their frequent occurrence. A significant number of exams in our sample comprised a large majority of narrow objective-type questions. These contributed directly neither to the development of Christian leadership nor to Christian worldview thinking.

For final examinations to become means of fostering both leadership characteristics and thoroughly Christian minds, we need questions where rote learning cannot provide satisfactory answers. We were impressed with instructors who included creative and thought-provoking questions that encouraged students to apply critical thinking to situations related to but not identical with ones discussed in class. Some instructors required students to solve problems where they needed to apply theories or results in new contexts. Others asked students to argue and justify a specific point of view, or to react to previously unseen statements or articles based on course work. A number requested students to compare or contrast ideas or works studied that had not previously been juxtaposed. Still others required students to analyze case studies, or to apply what they had learned during the course to new, complex situations.

Questions such as these stimulated students to weigh evidence, evaluate claims and use problem solving strategies. The students needed to posit, examine and appraise alternatives, defending their positions. Such examination questions required critical thinking similar to that expected of thoughtful leaders. Moreover, most answers to such questions would have been enhanced by students' biblical understanding of the relevant epistemological, ontological and ethical questions and principles (although this was less true for examination questions in the natural and mathematical sciences).

Some of the more unusual examinations were particularly strong in nurturing leadership skills and a Christian mind. Take-home exams forced students to analyze complex cases and apply approaches, principles, guidelines, and theories to more involved situations than students had previously encountered, while being able to use any resources that leaders would also have at their disposal. Some instructors encouraged students to think through important issues in the course before the exam by providing a list of questions requiring a much higher level thinking, with a subset of questions forming the final exam.

While our interviews indicated that instructors generally do more in their courses with respect to fostering leadership and Christian worldview thinking than is clear from their final examinations, we did identify several commonplace shortcomings. Some professors admit that Christian perspective is important and even mention it in their course description or objectives, but do not articulate it in their classes. Others have class discussions about the uniquely Christian aspects of a course but fail to include any of this in their course assessment methods. Still others expose students to Christian world view thinking, but do not ask students to apply the ideas in any assignments or on exams. In all these cases we ask whether instructors are doing enough to support the mission of the institution.

In conclusion, Christian colleges and universities aim to foster and promote leadership and Christian world view thinking, and to help students exercise these in all dimensions of life. If they are to continue to exist in this sense as unique, Christian post-secondary institutions, all aspects of their teaching-learning situation must contribute to their mission. The content we choose to teach and the ways in which we structure classrooms, for instance, either contribute to or detract from an institution's mission. As this study has shown, the nature of final examinations similarly can enhance or eclipse the realization of that mission. Often a scrutiny of the nature and effects of final exams together with the resulting reflection and discussion may well lead to revisions which stimulate students to take up the quest that Christ puts before each of us from day to day.

References

Anderson, J. O., W. Muir, D. J. Bateson, D. Blackmore, and W. T. Rogers. 1990. *The impact of provincial examinations in British Columbia.* Victoria: British Columbia Ministry of Education.

Bateson, D. 1992. Adding authenticity to sound measurement practices. *Research Forum* (Fall):5-8.

Blamires, H. 1963. *The Christian mind.* Ann Arbor, MI: Servant Books.

Bloom, B. S., ed. 1956. *Taxonomy of educational objectives: Handbook I: Cognitive domain.* New York: David McKay Company, Inc.

Bowers, C. A. 1992. Technology, culture, and the challenge of educational leadership. *Teaching Education* 5(1):21-28.

Egan, K. 1990. *Romantic understanding.* New York: Routledge, Chapman and Hall.

Holmes, A. F., ed. 1985. *The making of a Christian mind.* Downers Grove, IL: InterVarsity.

_____. 1987. *The idea of a Christian college.* Revised edition. Grand Rapids: Eerdmans.

Webb, C. and K. Grant. 1992. School leaders and thoughtfulness. *Teaching Education* 5(1):12-15.

Section C: Research Briefs

9. Assessment of Dimensions of Morality in Christian College Students

Steven P. McNeel

Christian colleges were originally founded with some form of moral education as a primary goal. In contrast to mainstream higher education which has become less explicitly concerned with moral education (Pascarella and Terenzini 1991, 335-336), evangelical higher education has maintained the commitment to teaching values, morality and ethics (Christian College Consortium 1979, 20-32). However, since it is possible for educational efforts to be ineffective or even to have negative effects, it is important for Christian colleges to assess their effectiveness in this area. The need for such assessment is suggested by empirical evidence showing that while liberal arts education is associated with a high level of moral judgment, conservative Christian commitment may be associated with a low level of moral judgment (see Rest 1979), and four years at a Bible college was associated with no growth at all in moral judgment (Shaver 1987). What then, is the effect on growth in moral judgment of a *conservative* Christian *liberal arts* education?

To answer questions such as this, several moral development assessment projects have recently been carried out at colleges of the Christian College Consortium.[1] Many of these projects also included measures of identity development and spiritual development, reflecting a recognition that moral phenomena are exceedingly complex and involve the whole person. Butman (1990) summarizes and evaluates many of the measures used and provides information on sources and costs.

Morality as a Complex Phenomenon: Assessment Implications

Adequate assessment of morality requires recognizing that morality includes many dimensions; we probably want to mean many things by moral maturity. There are a number of conceptual models which recognize this complexity. For example, Rest (1986) has suggested that four psychological components must be present in order for a person to behave morally. People must perceive the relevant moral issues (*moral sensitivity*), judge adequately what is right and just in the situation (*moral judgment*), order moral values above competing values (*moral motivation*), and perform the complex and often difficult task of carrying out the decision to behave morally (*moral character*). The complexity in moral matters is reflected in Holmes' (1991) eleven objectives for moral education in Christian colleges, objectives which detail some of the specifics of Rest's four components.

The view that morality is complex has important implications. First, each moral component provides a locus for assessment (and a focal point for pedagogy). This essay reports results relevant only to the components of *moral judgment* (longitudinal assessment across four years of college) and *moral sensitivity* (construction of a new measure for Christian college students). Other sections of this book will examine aspects of moral motivation and moral character (e.g. ego identity development, Van Wicklin, Burwell and Butman; and spiritual development). Other authors have examined how growth in moral judgment is related to factors such as taking ethics classes, contact with faculty outside of class, contact with faculty who have received special training in how students develop during college (Nevins and McNeel 1992), and college major (McNeel 1992).

A second implication is that, since there are many different components of morality, any given measure (focusing on a single component) only assesses a piece of a larger and much more complex puzzle. Growth (or lack of growth) on one measure of morality does not guarantee that there has been growth (or lack of growth) on another measure. Thus, care should be taken to interpret results from specific measures wisely, with humility, and within the much larger context. This is an important caution for those who might make too much *or* too little of results from any given moral measure.

The Defining Issues Test and its Underlying Theory

Each assessment project included the Defining Issues Test (DIT), a measure of moral judgment which consists of six moral dilemmas like the famous Heinz dilemma (see Rest 1979). In each dilemma, respondents recommend a course of action for the central character and then rate the importance in their thinking of 12 reasons which might stand behind their action recommendation. Finally, they rank in order their four most important reasons. The ranking of these reasons, not the action recommendation given, provides a measure of the level of the person's moral judgment; higher moral judgment is indexed by greater relative importance assigned to "principled reasons."

This scoring method reflects the cognitive developmental view that reasons for an action are key in determining the action's morality. It also reflects the view that some reasons are more mature than others; selfish motivation, motivation to please others important to oneself, or even motivation to obey the law are seen as less adequate or mature bases of moral judgment. The law, for example, may be inherently unjust or may have been created through unjust processes. Thus, use of higher order ethical principles such as dispassionate justice and ultimate valuing of the human person is viewed as more adequate moral reasoning. Persons characterized by such principled reasoning would be described by western philosophers as "taking the moral point of view," reflecting the belief that this way of thinking morally represents a mature moral judgment capability.

The research shows that DIT principled reasoning is a reliable measure of moral judgment and that it has a good degree of validity as well. Concerning validity, e.g., DIT principled reasoning is correlated with other tests of moral judgment, shows expected age/education trends, responds to ethics interventions in the expected manner, and is correlated as expected with behavioral measures of morality/immorality such as cheating, criminal behaviors, or various prosocial behaviors (see Rest 1979; 1986).

While the DIT as an assessment of principled reasoning may not include all that Christians want to mean by morality, it includes much which is relevant to moral *judgment*, and its central focus on cognitive aspects of moral development makes it particularly applicable for use in a Christian college setting. Further, as shown elsewhere (e.g., McNeel 1991) principled reasoning as conceptualized in Kohlberg's and Rest's theorizing reflects basic biblical emphases on love and on "the more important matters of the law -- justice, mercy and faithfulness" (Mt. 23:23). Thus, principled reasoning can be seen as an appropriate developmental goal for Christians as well as non-Christians. An implication of this view is that, in contrast with the empirical suggestion that conservative Christian commitment is associated with low levels of principled reasoning, significant growth on this measure should be expected in Christian liberal arts college students (see McNeel 1991).

Moral Judgment Growth in Christian College students

Figure 1 shows the results (solid lines) from the cooperative assessment project at Houghton, Messiah and Wheaton colleges (Burwell, Butman and

Van Wicklin 1992, N=74) and the study at Bethel College (McNeel 1992, N=261).   Comparison results are also shown (dashed lines) from two universities (Bridges and Priest 1983, N=104; Loxley and Whiteley 1986, N=95), a Catholic college (Mentkowski and Straight 1983, N-70) and a Bible college (Shaver 1987, N=54).   The results confirm the expectation that Christian liberal arts college students show significant (p<.01) and strong *longitudinal* freshman to senior growth in principled reasoning.   Further, the average growth was comparable to that shown in the available longitudinal studies done at universities and at a Catholic college.   In contrast to the lack of longitudinal growth in the comparison Bible college students, Christian liberal arts college students became progressively more capable of "taking the moral point of view" (as assessed by the DIT), reflecting greater maturity in moral judgment.

Since similar results for Christian liberal arts colleges have also been obtained in *cross-sectional* comparisons (see McNeel 1992), alternative interpretations such as selection, simple maturation or historical events seem unlikely.   It is more likely that the growth in principled reasoning is intrinsically connected with college attendance.

Finally, it is noteworthy that the growth in principled reasoning in these studies is comparable to or greater than the typical growth of college students on a variety of other liberal arts outcome measures such as quantitative or verbal communication skills and even subject matter knowledge (see McNeel 1992).   Thus, the college "effect" on principled reasoning growth is a powerful one indeed.

Assessing Moral Sensitivity in Christian College Students

One of the assessment projects involved constructing an entirely new measure of moral *sensitivity* in college students (McNeel et al. 1992).   This test focused directly on students' ability to *identify* moral issues; that is, it assesses students' ability of moral *perception* rather than the very heavily researched ability of moral *judgment*.

The project involved creating four complex and realistic 8-10 minute audio taped "radio dramas" in which a variety of ethical issues were embedded.   We created dramas based on earlier interview research which identified categories of realistic and meaningful dilemmas for Christian college students.   The four dramas focus on the following clusters of issues: 1) cheating, learning problems and racism; 2) pressure for sex, date rape, depression and codependency; 3) grieving a parent's death, autonomy and identity, career decisions, and parental pressure; and 4) alcohol abuse and its consequences, irresponsibility, and broken trust.   These dramas may sound like daytime or primetime soap operas -- a sort of Christian college 90210 -- but they have turned out to be convincing and effective stimuli.

Students take the test alone, listening to each drama and then playing the role of the central character's best friend, tape recording their verbal responses to the situation and to follow-up probe questions. Coding manuals allow transcriptions of the tapes to be scored reliably and validly for recognition of various ethical/moral issues.

A sample of results illustrates some of the important findings. First, we find a gender difference in moral sensitivity, favoring women, but only on some moral issues. Second, we find that perception of some moral issues is distressingly low, as in the case of recognizing that a date rape has happened in the pressure for sex drama: 58% of the females recognized it, but only 22% of the males did. Other findings along this line are that our students showed particular insensitivity to the issue of promise keeping, and that a large number did not address the key issue of drinking and driving in the alcohol abuse drama. A final point is that the dramas have proved valuable in generating classroom discussions as well as in assessing moral sensitivity; they are useful as educational stimuli relevant to several of Holmes' (1991) objectives of moral education in a Christian college.

Use of Results

The ultimate purpose of assessment is to generate useful evaluative information. The assessment projects reported here have accomplished this purpose well. First, the results have served a valuable *summative* evaluation function, in some cases for external use such as accreditation, and in other cases for internal use. For example, the results confirm that these Christian colleges are meeting their overall goals for students' growth in moral judgment. They show areas of weakness in students which can become targets for positive interventions, e.g. some moral insensitivity, or some lack of identity development (Van Wicklin, Burwell and Butman, this volume). Equally important, the results also have served a valuable *formative* evaluation function. Feedback of results to faculty and administrators, along with clarification of developmental models on which the measures are based, has led to a variety of positive changes. For example, it has produced better faculty understanding of where students begin, how quickly or slowly they mature, and how to design educational experiences which are more powerfully maturing in moral and value terms. Thus, the results of these assessment projects have shown a high degree of usefulness and provide a basis for planning more powerful educational opportunities for students.

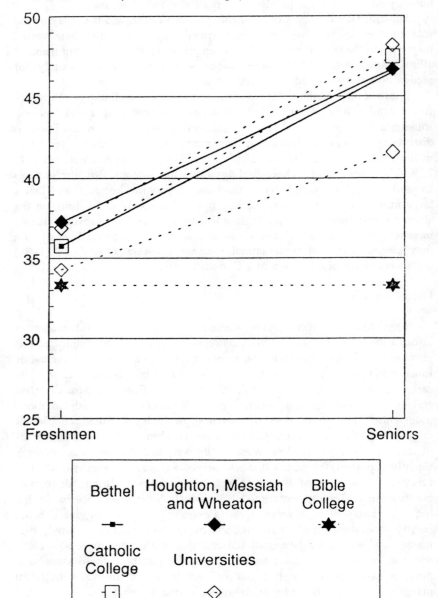

Figure 9.1 Longitudinal Mean Principled Reasoning

Endnotes

1. The college assessment projects were funded by the Pew Charitable Trusts and by the individual colleges. The author served as coordinator of the Pew Grant Assessment Team: Rich Butman and John Van Wicklin completed the team. Completed college projects: Bethel (Steve McNeel), Houghton (John Van Wicklin), Messiah (Ron Burwell), and Wheaton (Rich Butman). Ongoing longitudinal college projects: George Fox (Jim Foster), Greenville (Susan Hughey), Malone (John Koshmider), and Seattle Pacific (Ruby Englund).

Reference List

Bridges, C. and R. Priest. 1983. Development of Values and moral judgments of West Point cadets. Dialog, ERIC, ED 252566.

Burwell, R., R. Butman, and J. Van Wicklin. 1992. *Values assessment at three consortium colleges: A longitudinal followup study.* Houghton, NY: Houghton College.

Butman, R. E. 1990. Assessing ethical and moral development in young adults at Christian liberal arts colleges: Some possible options. Paper presented at The Conference on Moral Assessment, Teaching Values Project, Christian College Consortium, Bethel College. St. Paul, MN. 1 and 2 June.

Christian College Consortium. 1979. *Foundations of Christian higher education.* Arden Hills, MN: Christian College Consortium.

Holmes, A. F. 1991. *Shaping character: Moral education in the Christian college.* Grand Rapids: Eerdmans.

Loxley, J. C. and J. M Whiteley. 1986. *Character development in college students. Volume II: The curriculum and longitudinal results.* Schenectady, NY: Character Research Press.

McNeel. S. P. 1991. Christian liberal arts education and growth in moral judgment. *Journal of Psychology and Christianity* 10, no. 4:311-22.

_____. 1992. *Moral maturing in college.* Unpublished paper. St Paul, MN: Bethel College.

McNeel, S. P., Frederickson, B. Talbert, and B. Lester. 1992. Understanding difficult situations: Preliminary report of a moral sensitivity test for college students. Paper presented at the Annual Conference of the Association for Moral Education, Toronto, 12-14 November.

Mentkowski, M. and M. J. Straight. 1983. *A longitudinal study of student change in cognitive development, learning styles, and generic abilities in an outcome-centered liberal arts curriculum.* Milwaukee: Alverno College, Office of Research and Evaluation. (ERIC Document Reproduction Service No. ED 239 562).

Nevins, K. J. and S. P. McNeel. 1992. Facilitating student moral development through faculty development. *Moral Education Forum* 17, no. 4:12-18.

Pascarella, E. and T. Terenzini. 1991. *How college affects students.* San Francisco: Jossey-Bass.

Rest, J. R. 1979. *Development in judging moral issues.* Minneapolis: University of Minnesota Press.

_____. 1986. *Moral development: Advances in theory and research.* New York: Praeger.

Shaver, D. 1987. Moral development of students attending a Christian, liberal arts college and a Bible college. *Journal of College Student Personnel* 28, no. 3:211-18.

10. Learning to Read Student Culture: The Use of Qualitiative Methods

Harley Schreck, Judith Moseman, Jim Koch, Delana Gerber Brinkman, and Carolina Warner

A Christian liberal arts college is a special kind of place. It is where intellect and faith meet as faculty, administrators, staff, and students bring together the different worlds of the academy, college life, and the institutional structure and processes of the college. It is into this complex world that students move as they become part of the life of a Christian liberal arts college. This report, and the research that informs it, focuses on students at Bethel College and what their lives are like as they move into this world.

As students move onto campus they bring a lot of baggage. All one has to do is watch as the term begins in the fall. Cars, vans, and trucks roll onto campus, laden with suitcases, odd bundles of bedding, electronic gadgets of all types, and, perhaps, a few books. All of this baggage is but the tip of an iceberg. They also bring the cultures into which they have been socialized over the previous eighteen or so years. These cultures govern their actions, shape their perceptions, and will, to a great degree, define their college experience.

As students become part of campus life, howver, they encounter a whole range of new and alien cultures. Some are these of their fellow students, many of whom come from different backgrounds or other parts of the world. Others are represented by the faculty and administration. Another is the institution itself, which has a corporate culture of its own. Most importantly, students encounter a powerful and enduring Bethel student culture, which is the result of many forces, including the backgrounds and cultures brought by students, the institution, the American evangelical subculture, and the academy. Yet, a great deal of it forms on campus through the interaction and action of students themselves.

This resultant Bethel student culture is the primary context in which students live and act while they are at Bethel. If the college is to guide, teach, and serve the student effectively, it is vital that Bethel recognizes and accounts for the cultures from which students have come and the resultant culture that is created on campus. This realization prompted the research upon which this report is based. Over the past few years the professionals in the Office of Student Development at Bethel College had become increasingly aware that although they knew of the need to recognize and work with student culture, they did not have a clear idea of what this might be at Bethel. Accordingly, this project began.

In late 1991 Moseman and Koch met with Schreck to talk about research that would help them understand student culture at Bethel. A small pilot study was designed and presented to the Strategic Planning Advisory Committee (SPAC). This was approved and carried out in early 1992. On the basis of its results SPAC approved further research. Eventually, two years of intensive ethnographic research was carried out with Bethel College students. In this report we focus on the research process and how teaching and student development efforts have changed in response to its findings. Most of the attention will be given to the first year of the process. This report documents the research process, reports on its results, and suggests recommendations for action and further study.

Discovering Student Culture

This study has been concerned with student life, the culture that informs it, and the effects this has on teaching and student development efforts. American college life has been well defined since at least the eighteenth century. Horowitz argues that in the late eighteenth and early nineteenth century, "... college life taught the real lessons, and from it came the true rewards...traditional college life created an adolescent peer culture...youthful high spirits, insubordination and sexuality helped shape its forms." (Horowitz 1987, 12)

Horowitz further explains that college life, as communal experience, has eroded and is being replaced by a more fragmented, individualized experience for many students. Yet, the former continues to persist as a central reason for attending college. In a study of student culture at Rutgers University, Moffat states,

> ...college life was still very much at the heart of college as the
> undergraduates thought of it in the late twentieth century. Together with the

career credential conferred on them by their bachelor's degree, it was their most important reason for coming to college in the first place, their central pleasure while in it, and what they often remembered most fondly about college after they graduated. (Moffat 1989, 29)

If college life is of central importance to students, it often seems to be a distraction to faculty and administrators. It is clear that colleges, as institutions, hold very different definitions of the college experience than do students. To begin with, students and faculty/administration speak a different language. As Boyer states,

...we found a great separation, sometimes to the point of isolation, between academic and social life on campus. Colleges like to speak of community , and yet what is being learned in most residence halls today has little connection to the classrooms; indeed, it may undermine the educational purposes of the college. (Boyer 1987, 5)

These studies point to the importance of understanding student culture and how it shapes college life. At Bethel College, the following research questions were developed and guided the study of student culture: 1) What is the Bethel student culture? 2) How does Bethel student culture become expressed in and, in turn, shape student life at Bethel College? 3) Is Bethel a safe place? For whom? In what ways?

Research Methods and Procedures

The research is an ethnographic study of Bethel student culture. The intent was to begin with understanding Bethel student culture and then to move into a more narrow focus on the issues of individualism and community, subcultures and diversity, and the meaning of Bethel College to students and others. Throughout the entire research we were concerned with the implications of the findings for Bethel and its work with students. As such, the research flowed from a more general, broad study of the issues to narrowly focused, finely detailed questions and issues.

This process results not only from the order in which questions are addressed, but also from the very nature of ethnographic research itself. Ethnographic research is an iterative process of stating questions or hypotheses, probing and collecting data, analysis and discovery, reshaping hypotheses and restating questions, and returning to the cultural scene for more research. Thus, the narrowing focus comes from understandings gained as the research progresses with the research questions arising out of the context of the culture itself.

The research team consisted of five people. Two of these, Harley Schreck and Jim Koch, were faculty members. Three, Judith Moseman, Carolina Warner, and Delana Gerber Brinkman, were administrators. All were involved in data collection, analysis, and writing of this report.

As can be seen from Figure 1, a range of methods was used throughout the research. Participant observation ran through the entire research. Each member of the team had a unique perspective primarily due to different roles played at Bethel. As such, the team as a whole was able to pay attention to a number of areas of the life of the campus -- classroom, residence hall life,

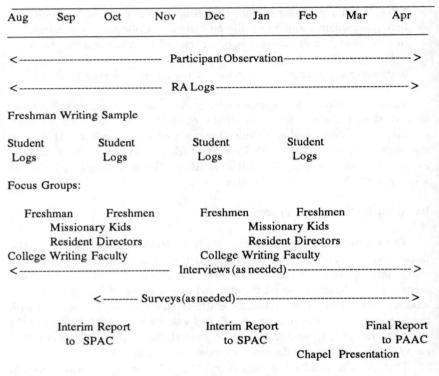

Figure 10.1 Research Design and Time Line

extracurricular activities, and informal life on campus. Members of the team participated in their normal roles and spheres of activity on campus and observed the flow of social life about them. They reported on this in team meetings and these insights were incorporated into the data that was collected in the research.

Resident Advisors play vital roles in Bethel student life. They have continuous first hand contact with students. In an effort to document the flow of normal life in the resident halls, Resident Advisors kept weekly logs on relevant events or situations that took place in the halls in which they worked. These were reviewed periodically to note trends on campus or situations that needed follow-up.

During freshmen orientation, incoming students completed a writing exercise. They were presented with a scenario in which they are asked to describe what it is like to be a young person who is coming to Bethel to a person outside the culture. They were instructed to write three paragraphs in which they were to be as descriptive as possible. Two hundred and sixty-one students participated in this. The results were subjected to content analysis to understand key themes and symbols characterizing the cultures of the students. Ten students wrote journals and kept time logs for a week at a time for each of four key periods of the college year. These were then analyzed to note key themes, time usage, and reactions to campus events that were going on at the time.

Four different types of focus groups were formed. These consisted of freshmen, missionary kids, resident directors and assistants, and college writing teachers. These were convened according to the schedule noted in Figure 1. At each meeting the focus groups were asked to enter a process of questioning and discussion around specific issues related to the research.

The research relied heavily upon interviewing. A number of types of interviews were used. Informal interviews took place throughout the research in many situations. More formal interviews, structured and unstructured, were also used, both with groups and individuals.

A number of quick, short surveys were used to probe specific areas of interest. These were distributed through campus mail. A goal of the research was to be as participatory as possible. Thus, a number of audiences were sought to provide feedback on the results. The research team reported interim results to SPAC at two different times during the year. Two groups of faculty were convened and the results were shared with them. The team also presented interim results to the College Committee of the Board of Regents, the resident directors, and student development personnel. Extensive feedback was obtained in these various sessions.

The research team worked together to write the final report. This was done in stages. First, analysis continued throughout the entire year in weekly team meetings. This involved the writing of various pieces that attempted to summarize what was known about specific topics. Some of these pieces eventually found their way into the report. Second, the principal investigator wrote an initial draft of the entire document. This was then studied in detail by each member of the research team. The team then met to work toward consensus on the report. The principal investigator then produced a common draft of the report. This was again gone over in detail by each member of the team. The team then met in a day-long session to fine tune the report and come up with a final, edited version. This was taken to final and presented to SPAC/PAAC (President's Academic Advisory Council) on April 10, 1992.

The team met with SPAC/PAAC to discuss the report and its findings. SPAC/PAAC was sufficiently impressed with the results to authorize a year long process of follow-up. This included three elements: a process whereby the larger Bethel community engage itself with the report and seek ways to implement changes based upon its findings; a further year of research on the "intersection of faculty and student cultures;" and the development of a tracking system to both understand the effects of any changes made in response to the research and continue trying to understand the changing Bethel Student Culture.

These three further steps have been completed. The President and Provost of the College now have a fairly detailed three year plan for implementing recommendations. These recommendations were made after a complex process of focus groups and brainstorming sessions where almost every "decision maker" on campus was able to work with the results of the research and provide input. The goal was wide scale participation and broad ownership. This has been achieved. The ethnography is part of the fabric of the college by now. The second year of research is complete and a tracking system is in place.

Results of the Research

The findings have profoundly affected the way Bethel looks at itself and carries out the mission of educating women and men. In our description and analysis we have addressed five themes which capture much of what is distinctive about it -- "the look," friendliness, romance, stress, and support. This is a mixed message. Bethel student culture supposedly connotes success and fun. Yet, the dark side is stress and a type of romance that entraps some people in either unhealthy relationships or feelings of inadequacy and loneliness.

Much of this is formed elsewhere and brought with students as they arrive on campus. Bethel students are children of their time. They display many cultural characteristics noted by scholars and critics of modern day life, including a new kind of privatized individualism, a heavy dose of consumerism, a fixation on romance, prolonged adolescence, and intolerance of differences. Many of these are an anathema to a Christian, liberal arts college like Bethel that stresses community and commitment, self discipline and hard work, and a rigorous form of academic and spiritual integrity.

Yet, Bethel students stand out from the larger youth culture in at least two ways. One is that they bring an expectation of a certain kind of change. All college students enter college expecting that they have reached a new stage of life. College life, for all of its elements of delayed adolescence, is also a time of experimentation, change, and growth. This is true for Bethel students. A significant difference at Bethel is that many students come expecting growth and change in their spiritual lives as well as in other areas of life. As we compared what freshmen wrote of their lives before Bethel and their expectations of what life will be like at Bethel, we find that students expected to be more involved in religious activities and spiritual disciplines then they were before coming to Bethel. They continue to see classes and homework as being a significant, if not dominant, part of their lives. They look forward to new friends, new activities, and personal growth. Yet, many have come to Bethel knowing it is a Christian place and expecting to grow in their own spiritual lives.

A second difference is that Bethel students bring a Christian heritage. Most significantly, this heritage is expressed in the widespread patterns of support we detected among Bethel students; it is a second point of distinctiveness for Bethel. Christian charity is part of Bethel Student Culture. Now, it must be said that this does not translate into active involvement in the institutional definition of community. What it does mean is that students are acting on community as they define it, with at least some as those actions being motivated and guided by a Christian set of values and understandings. These two traits, the expectations of spiritual growth and a pattern of support that is motivated by Christian values, distinguish Bethel Student Culture from the larger Youth Culture in significant ways. These are clearly linked to the Christian concepts of "call and commitment" among Bethel students, and, again, this gives us hope.

We have described college life as it is found at Bethel College. It is a clear expression of Bethel Student Culture in its style of community, role of scholarship, form of Christianity, and consideration of structure and authority. Students have created a distinct way of life. It embodies the values of individualism, a success-oriented "look," and the informality of friendliness.

Bethel students create and live in personal communities structured by networks made up by persons relatively similar to one another who are linked by multi-stranded relationships. These relationships include friendly socializing, sharing of pains or joys, sharing of information, and support of many types. They are relatively unconnected to the institutional world of Bethel and do not often include faculty, staff, or administrators. Yet, it is a community that functions for most students.

This type of community is largely divorced from the institution itself, thus faculty, staff, and administrators, there are often points of collision when college life, with its informing Bethel student culture, meets the institution and the academy. For example, when the institution speaks of integrity and trust it means adherence to a set of community values and standards. When the students speak of this they may mean Bethel is meeting their needs and allowing free expression of a privatized individuality. As another example, when the faculty see how students use their time and participate in their classes, they conclude students are lazy or incapable of serious scholarly work. The students on the other hand see the classroom as one portion of a busy and hectic life. They can not understand why the faculty thinks classes should be so all consuming. These are very different cultural worlds butting against one another -- sometimes violently.

College life as portrayed in the results, functions for the majority of the students at Bethel. Horowitz, however, talks of the outsiders to College Life. Bethel has its own outsiders. These are people who are different, defined along a number of dimensions. Bethel College students are both more diverse than they were in the past and, yet, are intolerant of this diversity. We have seen a campus where psychological safety is missing for many types of people -- students of color, Christians with variances in worship or expression, students from low income families, women with feminist viewpoints, and those espousing unconventional political or social viewpoints. For these students, much of the Bethel student population is unreachable. In a word, Bethel is not safe for them. They may find their own communities, but they are marginalized and often assume the feelings of inadequacy associated with this marginalization.

This brings us back to student culture. What we have been talking about are values, behaviors, and patterns that transcend individuals and frustrate any program that tries to change things by working with individuals. What is needed is a clear understanding of the cultural system, its strengths and its weaknesses. There is much to celebrate about Bethel, and, yet, significant challenges remain. Understanding, however, only sets the stage for change. There is little hope in transforming the cultural backgrounds students bring to Bethel. These are outside Bethel's control. Much can be done, however, while students are at Bethel. Faculty can adjust the way they teach and advise students. Student development can improve the way in which they guide and serve students. Programs and services can be designed to help students become more open to differences, form healthier relationships, attain a broader understanding of community, and have more realistic, charitable views of themselves and others. This needs to take place at the cultural level through community commitments, programs, and wide scale involvement of students, faculty, and staff.

Reference List

Boyer, E. 1987. *College: The undergraduate experience in America.* New York: Harper and Row.

Horowitz, H. 1987. *Campus life.* New York: Alfred A. Knopf.

Moffat, M. 1989. *Coming of age in New Jersey.* New Brunswick, NJ: Rutgers University Press.

_____. 1991. College life: Undergraduate culture and higher education. *Journal of Higher Education* 62(1):44-61.

11. The Christian College Freshman and the National College Student Population: Comparisons and Analysis

**Bayard O. Baylis, Ronald J. Burwell, and
Carlyle C. Dewey**

There have been many studies of the nature of the college experience and its influence on undergraduates. Many of these projects are summarized in Pascarella and Terenzini's (1991) massive review of college impact studies. One of the most significant ongoing research projects has been the Cooperative Institutional Research Project (hereafter referred to as CIRP). CIRP was initiated by the American Council on Education (ACE) in 1966 and was taken over in 1973 by the Higher Education Research Institute at the University of California, Los Angeles. For many years Alexander Astin has been associated with the CIRP research program. In his book, *What Matters in College?*, he makes this observation regarding CIRP: "It is now the largest ongoing study of the American higher education system, with longitudinal data covering some 500,000 and a national sample of more than 1,300 institutions of all types" (Astin 1993, 4).

CIRP has several components but the one of relevance to this report is the ongoing collection of data on incoming freshmen that have been conducted each year since 1966. The data are gathered using an instrument called the Student Information Form which contains over 160 items and is usually administered either during freshman orientation or very early in the fall term. Longitudinal data have been gathered by using a revised form employing essentially the same questions but administered to seniors. Hence, some

CIRP studies make use of freshman only data while others use both freshman and senior information.

There are many reasons why CIRP is an exceptional resource for studying higher education but perhaps the most important reasons have to do with the nature and quality of the sample that is used. For example, the fall of 1990 sample included data on 276,798 freshman at 574 colleges and universities (CIRP 1990). Given the magnitude of this sample it is possible to develop norms that represent the entire population of freshman entering college in a given year. In order to do this the CIRP staff have developed fairly sophisticated weighing and sampling procedures that insure representativeness.[1] Thus, the actual norms that were published in 1990 were based on a smaller, weighted sample of 194,182 freshmen at 382 institutions (CIRP 1990, 93).

Over the years a number of Christian colleges have used CIRP as part of institutional research programs. However, each institution was limited in that it could only compare itself with norms developed by CIRP that were not necessarily reflective of the unique nature of Christian colleges. In the late 1980s, Carlyle Dewey, then director of Institutional Research at Messiah College, began to work toward a cooperative venture involving the use of CIRP among members of the Christian College Coalition and other similar colleges. Eventually, he gained the approval of Alexander Astin and others at CIRP to have a subset of Christian colleges combined into a sample that would be treated as a distinct normative group. During the fall of 1990 fourteen Christian colleges administered CIRP to their incoming freshmen classes.[2] This resulted in an overall sample of 3,632 students and provides the basis for this research report.

In the following pages and tables we will present the results for the Christian college sample as well as data on two other samples: four-year private protestant colleges (this is the closest comparative group normally reported by CIRP) and the total weighted freshman sample for the fall of 1990. These samples will allow us to see where freshmen at Christian colleges might be similar or different from their counterparts at other colleges and universities. In addition, we will offer a more sophisticated analysis originally developed by Carlyle Dewey which seeks through factor analysis to identify the types of student that enter Christian colleges.

Results

Due to stringent space limitations the results for the various CIRP items are presented in Tables 11.1 - 11.5. All the results are in terms of percentages. This is similar to the way in which institutional reports are distributed to participating colleges. Thus, it will be possible for those with individual institutional reports to make comparisons with the three sample groups.

As part of a more sophisticated analysis of the data from the fourteen participating Christian colleges, a two-stage factor analysis was performed on the entire population. The purpose of this analysis was to identify groups of similar students within the total population and develop a typology of students.[3] The first stage involved the development of 36 scales which made sense in terms of their content and which were as independent of each other as possible. In the second stage of our factor analysis, we looked at all students in the data base and factor analyzed their scale scores to produce six student types. Those students who did not fit into one of the six student types which came out of the factor analysis were grouped together and called the majority.

Starting with the factor which explained the least variance and thus would have the fewest students, we selected the appropriate number of students who had the highest factor score for that group and who had not already been selected for a previously analyzed group. Because the factors were not totally independent, a few students did have high scores on more than one factor. Table 11.6 presents the six student types with associated scales, the variance explained by each factor, the percent of variance and the number of students selected for that factor.

In looking at the six student types we attempted to give them names which were descriptive. The names selected for these response patterns were (in decreasing order): Nonconformist Group; Success and Sports Group; Christian Leader Group; Confident Academic Group; Academic Liberal Group; and Creative Group. The associated scales (Table 11.6) give some indication of the characteristics associated with each type of student. Interestingly, the distribution of the six types at the fourteen colleges varied in a statistically significant fashion.

Alexander Astin has also pursued the possibility of identifying different types of students using the CIRP national data. He and others (Wingard et al. 1991) have also proposed six types of students based on factor analysis.[4] Although both Astin's types and those reported in this study were independently developed there are some striking similarities. Note the following parallels:

CIRP DATA (Christian College)	Astin (National CIRP) (Astin 1993b, 105-128)
Nonconformist	**Hedonist**
Success & Sports	**Leader**
Christian Leader	**Social Activist**
Academic Liberals	**Scholar**
Confident Academics	**Status Strivers**
Creativity	**Artist**

Although these two typologies are not exactly the same it is interesting that there are so many similarities. The major difference is in the fact that Astin assigned all the members of the sample to one or more of these six types. In other words, he did not have a "Majority" category and some students in his scheme could be classified as being more than just one type. Nevertheless, the striking convergence of findings in both studies suggests that six types like the ones proposed may be an effective way of describing the types of students not only at Christian colleges but in the national college student population.

Discussion

In reviewing the data that have been presented several observations are worthy of note. First, in comparison with the wider student population, the Christian college students come from homes where the parents report somewhat higher levels of college and graduate education compared with the total college sample. Further, the Christian students report higher grades in high school, more academic honors and some confidence in their academic abilities in contrast with their secular counterparts. Given these factors, the students are only slightly more likely than the total student sample to report plans for further graduate study. Faculty and others in positions of leadership at these colleges might wish to reflect on why this is the case. It may be that greater emphasis and encouragement should be given to these students to consider further education.

For the past decade or more, people involved in higher education have commented on how incoming students seem to be more and more interested in careers and the financial ramifications of education than other factors. This over-emphasis on career preparation is often seen as in conflict with the broader values of higher education. A second observation, then, about the Christian college students, is that while interested in career and financial issues these are not as salient as they might be for the wider university population. In other words, students at Christian colleges come with mixed motivations. On the one hand they desire a good job upon graduation but on the other hand they are also interested in the more intrinsic values of education. This should be some encouragement to those of us who have been discouraged by the seeming lack of interest in education for its own sake rather than just a means to an end. Additional encouragement comes from the fact that Christian college students are more likely to be interested in making a contribution to society, being helpful to others and participating in service activities.

Finally, the conventional wisdom is that Christian college students are quite conservative politically and in certain other ways when compared with college students in general. If one looks at the self-designation of political views this is certainly the case. The Christian college student sample is much more likely to opt for the designation "conservative" than either of the other samples. However, if one reviews the opinion items it becomes clear that on many of the issues the Christian students are not necessarily more conservative than their peers. For example, on those items dealing with the role of the Federal government one would expect conservatives to be less supportive of government actions. Yet, the Christian college students are quite like the total student population in their support of government activities in the areas of gun control, environmental protection, reducing the deficit, and consumer protection. Further, the perception is that the conservative students might differ on issues such as capital punishment, military spending, school busing and the place of women from the stereotypical more liberal, secular college and university students. Again, on each of these items the profile for the Christian college students is very much like that of the total student sample.

It is not clear, then, why students should chose the designation conservative but not necessarily consistently opt for what might be considered conservative positions on many of these social issues. One interpretation is that while students have adopted the self-designation of political conservative they have little clear understanding of the implication of that position for a variety of social issues. In other words, the designation conservative is one that is part of the world from which the students come but it is not a personally or thoughtfully appropriated position. It may function more as a code or symbolic boundary marker.

In his book, *Evangelicalism: The Coming Generation*, James Davison Hunter presented information regarding evangelical students in colleges and seminaries. Interestingly, five out of the nine colleges that Hunter used in his sample are also part of the Christian college sample reported here. Hence, it is possible to make some comments in reference to the CIRP data in comparison with Hunter's analyses.

The thrust of much of Hunter's argument is that the coming generation of evangelicals, as represented by students in evangelical colleges, is a group which has been profoundly influenced by the surrounding culture. These influences are pervasive and troubling to the extent that Hunter raises questions about the future of evangelicalism. He states: "In a word, the Protestant legacy of austerity and ascetic self-denial is virtually obsolete in the larger Evangelical culture and is nearly extinct for a large percentage of the coming generation of Evangelicals" (Hunter 1987, 73). While this is not the place for a definitive critique of Hunter's analysis it is possible to ask whether, based on the CIRP data, there are any defining differences between the Christian college students and the wider college and university student population. To some extent the CIRP data may be read both as supporting and also questioning Hunter's observations about evangelical students.

On the one hand, in support of Hunter, there are many examples of similarities such that one could argue that the Christian college sample is very much like the wider college population. For many of the items there are only trivial differences between the comparative samples. Hence, it is possible to identify the Christian college students as having "lost a binding address" (Hunter 1987, 210) and become indistinguishable from their secular counterparts. Nevertheless, this is not completely true for there are also many evidences that the Christian college students are sufficiently distinct from other students that they still bear the mark of an identifiable subcultural heritage. Both in regard to attitudes, opinions and values there is clear evidence that the Christian college students are different from the total student population. While this is clearest in regard to current moral issues debated by Christians (e.g., abortion, sexual morality) there are also differences in the more amorphous motivations for choosing a career and attending college (e.g., less emphasis on wealth and more emphasis on helpfulness and service to society). In summary, then, given a certain theoretical predilection one could argue either how similar or how dissimilar the Christian college student is to their secular counterparts. The CIRP data are a helpful source of such comparisons.

Conclusion

One of the significant things about this research is that it represents a collaborative effort of a number of Christian colleges -- that in itself is an important factor. While the plans for coordinating the CIRP data where being developed it was apparent that a number of schools saw the advantages of the project but were also fearful of the idea of collaborative research. There were several reasons for this fear. Perhaps the most prominent was apprehension that if data was collected from a number of colleges and then compared *college by college* it might reflect badly on a given institution. While this fear is understandable, it is a fear that can be defused. Having completed the study it should be apparent that it is possible to share the results without having any necessity for revealing the identity of the individual colleges. It is often useful to have the aggregate results which then can be used by each institution for comparison with its own data. Hopefully, this first step in inter-institutional cooperation should encourage future, greater collaboration among Christian colleges.

In the future, additional projects might include continuation of sharing of CIRP data as well as other types of joint ventures. One project that might be especially valuable would be to follow-up the freshmen who have been surveyed when they become seniors. By doing this important questions that might be answered by longitudinal data could be studied.

Table 11.1 Demographic Data

VARIABLE	CHRISTIAN COLLEGE SAMPLE (%) (n=3639)	PRIVATE PROTESTANT SAMPLE (%) (n=21,384)	TOTAL COLLEGE SAMPLE (%) (n=194,182)
GENDER			
Female	61.7	54.7	53.8
Male	38.3	45.3	46.2
AGE			
Traditional Age	96.8	96.7	92.7
Non-Traditional Age	3.2	3.3	7.3
RACE			
White/Caucasian	92.5	82.7	84.3
Black/African-American	1.9	13.5	9.6
Native American	1.2	0.9	1.3
Asian-American	3.2	1.8	2.9
Mexican-American/ Chicano	1.1	1.0	1.5
Puerto Rican-American	0.5	0.3	0.5
Other	2.2	1.5	1.8
MILES FROM HOME			
50 or less	24.3	27.7	40.7
51-100	15.0	16.9	18.1
101-500	39.3	37.1	30.0
More than 500	21.4	18.3	11.2
PARENTAL INCOME			
Less than $25,000	20.7	23.4	19.8
$25,000-$39,999	27.2	23.8	23.0
$40,000-$49,999	12.9	11.9	13.4
$50,000-$59,999	10.7	10.7	12.1
$60,000-$74,999	11.3	10.3	12.2
$75,000 or more	17.1	20.0	19.6
PARENTS MARITAL STATUS			
Living with each other	82.8	73.8	71.2
Divorced or separated	13.4	21.2	23.3
One or both deceased	3.8	5.0	5.4
U.S. CITIZEN	97.1	97.7	97.6
Native Speaker of English	96.4	96.6	95.6

VARIABLE	CHRISTIAN COLLEGE SAMPLE (%)	PRIVATE PROTESTANT SAMPLE (%)	TOTAL COLLEGE SAMPLE (%)
FATHER'S EDUCATION			
Less than H.S. graduate	6.8	9.2	11.2
H.S. graduate	17.8	22.6	28.0
Some post-secondary	19.4	20.7	20.2
College graduate	25.1	22.6	21.1
Graduate study	4.5	3.2	2.4
Graduate degree	26.4	21.8	17.1
MOTHER'S EDUCATION			
Less than H.S. graduate	4.0	6.7	8.8
H.S. graduate	24.8	28.2	34.4
Some post-secondary	28.1	26.5	24.5
College graduate	27.8	23.2	19.9
Graduate study	4.6	3.5	2.9
Graduate degree	10.8	12.0	9.9
FATHER'S OCCUPATION (selected)			
Businessman	27.0	28.8	27.5
Clergy/Religious worker	8.8	4.6	1.1
Educator (all levels)	9.5	6.8	5.3
Farmer	2.4	3.3	3.2
Skilled worker	7.8	8.1	10.3
MOTHER'S OCCUPATION (selected)			
Businesswoman	9.3	13.3	14.0
Clergy/Religious worker	1.1	0.5	0.1
Educator (all levels)	17.4	15.8	11.3
Homemaker	23.0	16.2	15.0
Skilled worker	1.0	2.1	2.3
RACIAL COMPOSITION OF NEIGHBORHOOD			
Mostly white or all white	88.2	80.8	83.7
RACIAL COMPOSITION OF HIGH SCHOOL			
Mostly white or all white	81.6	70.3	74.8
STUDENT'S RELIGIOUS PREFERENCE			
Baptist	24.0	28.8	18.2
Presbyterian	9.8	7.0	4.5
Methodist	6.8	11.1	9.7
Roman Catholic	3.7	14.7	32.1
other Protestant (selected)	34.3	6.1	4.6
STUDENT A BORN AGAIN CHRISTIAN?	89.1	47.9	29.3

Table 11.2 High School Activities and Experiences

VARIABLE	CHRISTIAN COLLEGE SAMPLE (%)	PRIVATE PROTESTANT SAMPLE (%)	TOTAL COLLEGE SAMPLE (%)
AVERAGE HIGH SCHOOL GRADE			
A or A+	15.0	12.6	10.2
A-	19.0	14.7	12.4
B+	22.1	22.1	18.3
B	23.9	24.6	25.3
B-	10.2	10.8	14.5
C+	6.4	6.4	12.2
C	3.2	3.1	6.7
D	0.2	0.1	0.3
HIGH SCHOOL ACCOMPLISHMENTS			
Pres. of organization	24.5	26.5	20.4
Rated high (music test)	23.5	17.7	11.7
In speech/debate contest	7.1	8.5	6.1
Major part in play	22.3	18.6	12.9
Won award in art	11.7	9.8	9.2
Edited school publication	15.7	16.1	12.4
Won award in science	4.0	5.2	4.6
Member of honor society	42.4	35.6	29.1
PERCENT WHO RATE SELVES AS ABOVE AVERAGE IN THESE AREAS:			
Academic ability	63.2	69.1	53.7
Artistic ability	29.2	31.0	25.0
Competitiveness	51.5	56.5	54.0
Cooperativeness	75.9	74.1	70.2
Drive to achieve	68.6	70.7	66.3
Emotional health	60.5	60.4	57.1
Leadership ability	56.1	56.4	50.9
Math ability	38.8	35.9	37.4
Physical health	56.2	59.0	58.5
Popularity	38.6	43.4	43.0
Popularity with opp. sex	35.3	41.2	41.2
Public speaking ability	34.8	32.8	28.4
Self-confidence (intel.)	50.6	52.8	48.3
Self-confidence (social)	43.4	46.3	44.0
Understanding of others	72.3	71.0	66.8
Writing ability	48.3	43.6	39.0

VARIABLE	CHRISTIAN COLLEGE SAMPLE (%)	PRIVATE PROTESTANT SAMPLE (%)	TOTAL COLLEGE SAMPLE (%)
PERCENT WHO REPORT THESE ACTIVITIES DURING PAST YEAR			
Was bored in class	29.6	28.2	28.6
Participated in rally	37.1	42.1	39.4
Won varsity letter (sport)	51.9	55.7	50.4
Homework not on time	70.2	70.6	67.9
Tutored another student	46.7	49.5	45.5
Did extra classwork	9.3	11.4	10.3
Studied with others	85.9	87.8	84.7
Smoked cigarettes	1.5	6.4	10.6
Drank beer	19.5	45.5	58.2
Drank wine or liquor	25.3	48.2	57.5
Studied in library	9.9	10.9	10.1
Performed volunteer work	77.1	70.6	63.1
Visited museum/gallery	59.6	57.6	52.5
Played music instrument	55.5	45.2	38.4
Checked sch. library book	28.8	25.0	26.7
Asked teacher for advice	29.4	34.6	28.5

Table 11.3 College and Career Plans/Objectives

VARIABLE	CHRISTIAN COLLEGE SAMPLE (%)	PRIVATE PROTESTANT SAMPLE (%)	TOTAL COLLEGE SAMPLE (%)
RESIDENCE PLANS			
Live on campus	94.1	89.1	70.0
Live at home	5.1	9.7	22.6
HIGHEST DEGREE PLANNED			
Bachelor's degree	29.9	26.2	29.0
Master's degree	42.2	39.1	37.2
Doctorate (all types)	20.0	23.1	18.7
REASONS NOTED FOR GOING TO COLLEGE (Very Important)			
Parents wanted me to go	35.4	37.6	35.2
Could not find a job	3.4	5.5	7.1
Wanted to get away from home	15.1	18.3	16.0
To get a better job	63.9	73.8	78.3

VARIABLE	CHRISTIAN COLLEGE SAMPLE (%)	PRIVATE PROTESTANT SAMPLE (%)	TOTAL COLLEGE SAMPLE (%)
Gain a general education	60.4	65.8	63.1
Improve study/ reading skills	38.7	45.7	43.0
Nothing better to do	2.2	2.6	2.3
Become more cultured person	39.3	44.8	39.8
Make more money	43.5	65.8	73.2
Learn more about things	71.1	72.8	73.1
Prepare for grad/ prof school	44.2	55.0	53.1

OBJECTIVES CONSIDERED TO BE
ESSENTIAL OR VERY IMPORTANT

Achieve in a performing art	14.6	13.8	10.8
Become authority in my field	49.7	63.8	65.4
Obtain recognition from others	34.6	53.0	54.9
Influence political structure	16.3	23.6	20.6
Influence social values	56.4	50.5	42.9
Raise a family	79.7	72.4	69.5
Have administrative responsibility	29.0	40.7	42.9
Be well off financially	39.1	64.7	73.7
Help others in difficulty	74.3	68.3	62.0
Contribute to science theory	9.6	16.1	17.1
Write original works	13.4	14.7	12.2
Create artistic work	11.4	12.2	12.2
Be successful in own business	25.3	40.5	43.3
Help environ. clean-up	23.4	36.4	33.9
Develop philosophy of life	46.5	47.7	43.2
Involve in community action	28.7	31.8	25.9
Promote racial understanding	36.1	44.2	38.0
Keep up-to-date on politics	43.0	47.8	42.4

PROBABLE MAJOR

Arts and Humanities	15.3	12.4	8.9
Biological sciences	4.2	5.3	3.7
Business	16.7	20.6	21.1
Education	20.3	14.1	9.9
Engineering	3.2	3.4	9.6
Physical sciences	2.9	2.8	2.4
Professional studies	10.0	11.9	15.2
Social sciences	12.0	12.9	9.6
Technical	0.7	0.9	4.0
Other	7.0	8.1	9.1
Undecided	7.5	7.9	6.6

ESSENTIAL OR VERY IMPORTANT (cont.)

VARIABLE	CHRISTIAN COLLEGE SAMPLE (%)	PRIVATE PROTESTANT SAMPLE (%)	TOTAL COLLEGE SAMPLE (%)
REASONS NOTED AS VERY IMPORTANT OR ESSENTIAL IN CAREER CHOICE			
Job openings available	57.5	65.6	70.4
Rapid advancement possible	36.6	57.6	63.8
High anticipated earnings	37.1	62.0	70.7
Well-respected job	38.7	59.6	64.9
Great deal independence	45.6	63.9	66.7
Chance of steady progress	58.2	73.8	77.7
Make contribution to society	76.9	74.8	68.4
Can avoid pressure	24.7	34.0	35.6
REASONS NOTED AS VERY IMPORTANT OR ESSENTIAL IN CAREER CHOICE			
Can work with ideas	66.6	70.5	70.1
Can be helpful to others	86.5	82.9	79.3
Able to work with people	80.6	80.4	77.3
Intrinsic interest in field	79.0	79.9	79.8
Work would be challenging	73.4	74.4	73.7
STUDENTS ESTIMATE CHANCES ARE VERY GOOD THAT THEY WILL:			
Change major field	14.4	13.2	12.4
Change career choice	14.3	12.8	11.4
Get job to pay expenses	47.2	35.5	36.0
Play varsity sports	20.5	25.8	15.4
Be elected honor society	9.8	11.2	8.1
Transfer to another college	11.2	11.3	12.8
Be satisfied with college	63.3	53.8	50.9
Find job in own field	72.3	69.2	70.6
Marry while in college	9.3	6.1	5.4
Participate in service	29.4	21.3	14.2

Table 11.4 Opinion and Attitude Questions

VARIABLE	CHRISTIAN COLLEGE SAMPLE (%)	PRIVATE PROTESTANT SAMPLE (%)	TOTAL COLLEGE SAMPLE (%)
PERCENT WHO AGREE STRONGLY OR SOMEWHAT WITH STATEMENT:			
The Federal gov't. is not doing enough to protect the consumer from faulty goods and services.	60.7	68.5	68.4
The Federal government is not doing enough to control environmental pollution.	84.5	87.6	87.9
The Federal government should raise taxes to reduce the deficit.	29.6	29.5	28.6
PERCENT WHO AGREE STRONGLY OR SOMEWHAT WITH STATEMENT:			
There is too much concern in the courts for the rights of criminals.	71.0	66.4	66.3
Federal military spending should be increased.	25.7	26.7	25.1
Abortion should be legal.	16.1	55.6	64.9
Death penalty should be abolished.	20.7	22.6	21.5
If two people really like each other, it's all right for them to have sex even if they've known each other for only a short time.	9.0	39.6	51.0
The activities of married women are best confined to home and family.	28.7	26.9	25.2
Marijuana should be legalized.	6.9	16.0	18.6
Busing is OK if it helps to achieve racial balance in the schools.	54.4	55.0	56.7

VARIABLE	CHRISTIAN COLLEGE SAMPLE (%)	PRIVATE PROTESTANT SAMPLE (%)	TOTAL COLLEGE SAMPLE (%)

PERCENT WHO AGREE
STRONGLY OR SOMEWHAT
WITH STATEMENT:

VARIABLE	CHRISTIAN COLLEGE (%)	PRIVATE PROTESTANT (%)	TOTAL COLLEGE (%)
It is important to have laws prohibiting homosexual relationships.	67.0	49.1	44.4
The chief benefit of a college education is that it increases one's earning power.	52.4	63.9	70.7
Employers should be allowed to require drug testing of employees or job applicants.	88.5	82.6	80.4
The best way to control AIDS is through widespread, mandatory testing.	58.8	63.3	66.4
Just because a man thinks that a women has "led him on" does not entitle him to have sex with her.	91.9	87.9	86.9
The Federal government should do more to control the sale of handguns.	79.2	79.4	77.1
A national health care plan is needed to cover everybody's medical costs.	65.2	71.3	73.7
Colleges would be improved if organized sports were de-emphasized.	34.2	37.8	35.8
Nuclear disarmament is attainable.	50.0	58.2	60.9
Scientists should publish their findings regardless of the possible consequences.	46.4	51.6	53.1
Faculty promotions should be based in part on student evaluations.	75.3	74.5	74.9
Racial discrimination in no longer a problem in America.	15.1	18.2	20.6

VARIABLE	CHRISTIAN COLLEGE SAMPLE (%)	PRIVATE PROTESTANT SAMPLE (%)	TOTAL COLLEGE SAMPLE (%)
HOW WOULD YOU CHARACTERIZE YOUR POLITICAL VIEWS? (PERCENT WHO SAY:)			
Far left	0.8	1.7	1.8
Liberal	12.5	22.6	22.6
Middle of the road	39.6	48.1	54.7
Conservative	44.8	26.0	19.7
Far right	2.2	1.6	1.2

Table 11.5 Additional Questions Used Only at Christian Colleges

VARIABLE	PERCENT "Frequently"	PERCENT "Occasionally"	PERCENT "Not at all"
How regularly did you engage in each of the following activities during the past year?			
Maintained daily, personal devotions.	39.7	49.2	11.0
Shared my faith with another person.	22.7	66.9	10.3
Developed a friendship with a person of a different race.	38.4	50.9	10.6
Studied the Bible or prayed in a small group.	45.4	43.6	10.8

VARIABLE	PERCENT	PERCENT	PERCENT
How important were each of the following in your decision to attend a Christian college?	"very important"	"somewhat important"	"Not at all important"
To develop competence in dealing with moral and ethical issues.	46.0	45.2	8.7

VARIABLE	PERCENT "Frequently"	PERCENT "Occasionally"	PERCENT "Not at all"
To learn how to serve others.	47.1	43.9	8.8
To develop a better understanding of different philosophies, cultures and ways of life.	43.2	48.2	8.4

Table 11.6 Factor Groups and Associated Scales

Group	Student Type	Associated Scales	Variance Explained	% of Var	No. of Students
1	Noncon- formists	Libertarian Liberalism Partying Activities in H.S. Career Concerns:Family, Helping Optimistic Grad. and Job Plans Rsn.s for Choosing C.: College Characteristics Christian Disciplines (H.S.)	2.38-9881	7.7%	273
2	Success & Sports	Athletic Involvement & Interest Car. Con.: Success & Advancement Self-Image: Popular/Social Self-Confidence Self-Image: Competitive Anti-Civil Liberties Conservatism Rsn.s for Attend College: Prof./Acad.	2.21-7310	7.2%	255
3	Christian Leaders	Self-Image: Leadership Belonging/Activism H.S. Christian Disciplines (H.S.) Rsns for Choosing C.: Altruism Social Time Use (H.S.) Career Concerns: Comm. Activism	2.00-0050	6.5%	231
4	Academic Liberals	Career Concerns: Comm. Activism Rsns for Attend C.: Gen. Educ. Academic Activities H.S. Political Disaffection Career Concerns: Altruism Self-Image: Empathetic, Achieving Traditional Political Liberalism	1.913570	6.2%	220
5	Confident Academics	Academic Success Anticipated Self-Image: Acad. Self-Confidence Career Concerns: Prof. Recognition	1.908569	6.2%	220
6	Creativity	Career Concerns: Creativity Self-Image: Creativity Scholastic Irresponsibility H.S. Drop-Out/Stop-Out Risks Rsn.s for Attend C.: Family Influence	1.600-101	5.2%	184

End Notes

1. A detailed discussion of the CIRP research methodology can be found in Appendix A of the report (1990, 93-9). The weighted sample approximates the entire population that entered college for the first time in the fall of 1990. Among other things this sample includes schools that have at least a 75% response rate from their subjects.

2. The fourteen colleges that form the Christian College sample are: Azusa Pacific University, CA; Geneva College, PA; Gordon College, MA; Grand Rapids Baptist College, MI; Huntington College, IN; The Master's College, CA; Messiah College, PA; Mt. Vernon Nazarene College, OH; North Park College, IL; Spring Arbor College, MI; Seattle Pacific University, WA; Taylor University, IN; Trevecca Nazarene College, TN; and Westmont College, CA.

3. More detailed information on the specific factor analysis methodology can be obtained from Bayard Baylis at Messiah College. Several more detailed reports on the development of the scales and student types have been prepared for distribution to the participating colleges.

4. Information on Astin's six types of student may be found in the work of Wingard, Trevino, Dey and Korn (1991) as well as Astin (1993b).

Reference List

Astin, A. W. 1993a. *What matters in college?: Four critical years revisited.* San Francisco: Jossey-Bass Publishers.

Astin, A. W. 1993b. An empirical typology of college students. *Journal of College Student Development 34*:36-46.

Astin, A. W., W. S. Korn and E. R. Berz. 1990. *The American freshman: National norms for fall 1990.* Los Angeles: Higher Education Research Institute, UCLA.

CIRP. 1990. Cooperative Institutional Research Project.

Hunter, J. D. 1987. *Evangelicalism: The coming generation.* Chicago: University of Chicago Press.

Pascarella, E. T. and P. T. Terenzini. 1991. *How college affects students: Findings and insights from twenty years of research.* San Francisco: Jossey-Bass Publishers.

Wingard, T. L., J. G. Trevino, E. L. Dey., and W. S. Korn. 1991. *The American college student, 1989: National norms for 1985 and 1987 college freshmen.* Los Angeles: Higher Education Research Institute, University of California.

Epilogue

12. Assessment As Doxology

David S. Guthrie

Michael Patton relates a curious but notable extra-biblical account of the origin of assessment as follows:

> In the beginning God created the heaven and the earth. And God saw everything that He made. "Behold," God said, "It is very good."
>
> And the evening and the morning were the sixth day.
>
> And on the seventh day God rested from all His Work. His archangel came then unto Him asking, "God, how do you know that what you have created is 'very good?' What are your criteria? On what data do you base your judgement? Aren't you a little close to the situation to make a fair and unbiased evaluation?" God thought about these questions all that day and His rest was greatly disturbed. On the eighth day God said, "Lucifer, go to hell."
>
> Thus was evaluation born in a blaze of glory. (Patton 1986, 9)

Irrespective of its beginnings, whether honorable or villainous, the call for institutional assessment has become increasingly prevalent among the nation's colleges and universities during the last decade. Many of these institutions, in response to pressures from federal and state governments as well as the public at large, have embraced assessment as a means to retain valuable financial resources, expedite accreditation, or enhance prestige. In contrast, Christian colleges have not responded as quickly to the assessment movement.

On the one hand, perhaps Christian institutions may be applauded for not rushing haphazardly and pragmatically into the assessment conversation. As one Christian college administrator puts it: "Skepticism is a healthy approach to the mandate to assess student outcomes" (Van Harn 1986, 1). Clearly, "looking before one leaps" is often a prudent act. On the other hand, however, one wonders if Christian colleges have adequately addressed their involvement in this movement, particularly since Christians seldom can be criticized for being "early birds that get the worms."

This paper is an attempt to encourage Christian colleges to embrace institutional assessment as a valuable tool by articulating what may be referred to as a "theology of assessment." Since Christian institutions ostensibly are committed to implementing programs that are based on biblically-reasoned rationales, such a theology of assessment is a necessary starting point for institutional faithfulness on this issue. Seen in another light, this paper is also an apology for assessment. I believe that Christian colleges should be assessing student learning; ultimately, I want you to believe that too and do something about it.

I suggest that assessment fundamentally is doxological activity. That is, institutional assessment brings praise to God in that it helps a Christian college come to terms with its faithfulness as an organization that is committed to a biblical view of student learning and development. Assessment glorifies God at Christian institutions because it focuses attention on acknowledging God as the convener of student learning, on reconstituting student learning in more faithful ways, and on renewing and mobilizing institutional effort to enact student learning as to the Lord.

To demonstrate the doxological nature of assessment, I rely on five doxological themes that were developed by H. O. Old (1992) in his book *Themes and Variations for a Christian Doxology.* Although Old uses these themes as a means of framing ecclesiastical worship, I believe they also provide a useful strategy for understanding assessment as doxology. Therefore, I now turn to a discussion of each doxological theme and its relevance for institutional assessment that brings praise to the Lord of our institutions.

Assessment As Epicletic Doxology

Epiclesis literally means "to call upon, to make an appeal, or to address someone." In an ecclesiastical worship context, epiclesis refers directly to the invocation. As you may know, the invocation in a worship setting is the communicants' "cry for help;" it represents the worshippers' pleas for the redeemer to take note of their individual and corporate needs and respond accordingly. Perhaps the most recognizeable examples of epiclesis, or invocation, among Christian believers are the supplications present in the Lord's Prayer that the Redeemer will consummate his Kingdom, provide daily bread, pardon sins, and protect from evil. Seen in this light, epiclesis is not mere obeisance to the divine, but must be understood as a passionate petition for God's presence in our situation; or, as Calvin, put it long ago, "[Invocation] is that habit of our mind,..., of resorting to [God's] faithfulness and help as our only support" (as quoted in Old [1992], 31).

For the Christian college, institutional assessment is an epicletic activity for two reasons. First, assessment is epicletic because it represents a tangible expression of "call[ing] upon the Lord who is worthy to be praised." A Christian college that undertakes an assessment effort demonstrates that God's faithfulness is a precondition to institutional vitality. Doing assessment reaffirms that a Christian college needs and wants God's advice and presence in constructing and delivering college education. When a Christian college assesses student learning, it is, in effect, petitioning God for assistance in creating an educational experience on campus like it is in heaven.

The second epicletic aspect of assessment is that assessment underscores the importance of accountability. When a Christian college assesses, it is confessing that it belongs to God. In the same way that a worshipper petitions God and expects response based on an existing relationship characterized by responsibility, a Christian college that embraces assessment communicates that it requires God's faithfulness to survive, desires God's direction in performing faithful education, and is willing and ready to modify existing structures and practices if it means that God will be more satisfied. Ultimately, assessment helps Christian institutions uncover what God may want for them, which, in turn, results in increased praise for God and the Kingdom.

One additional comment regarding accountability is warranted. At a national level, assessment for accountability has negative connotations. According to Hutchings and Marchese (1990), in some circles, assessment is a "dirty word" because of its perceived connection to accountability. The argument typically goes like this: assessment implies accountability; accountability implies external constraint; external constraint is undesirable; forget assessment. One hopes that such a rationale is not the explanation for the lack of assessment efforts among Christian colleges, particularly since we presumably understand the inevitability and the importance of accountability. As representatives of Christian institutions we realize that we -- as well as our institutions -- are ultimately answerable not to presidents, trustees, faculties, alumni, or donors, but to the Lord. Stated another way, since accountability is sensible within a Christian worldview, we should consider assessment a normative institutional activity. Consequently, a Christian institution which does not assess student learning is ostensibly an oxymoron.

Assessment As Kerygmatic Doxology

Kerygmatic doxology emphasizes acclamation and proclamation. In a worship context, parishioners commonly acclaim their devotion to God in both singing and speaking with characteristic simple phrases such as "Alleluia!" or "Praise the Lord!" Acclamations reflect personal acceptance of the "good news." Acclamation, however, is not without moral imperative. Those who personally acclaim God are obliged to publicly proclaim God as well; believed "good news" must also be testified "good news." Amidst the many wonderful hymns in the Christian church, Charles Wesley's are exemplary for their balanced expression of both acclamation and proclamation. Those who may sing the following Wesley hymn clearly proclaim a highly acclaimable Master:

Ye servants of God, your Master proclaim,
And publish abroad His wonderful Name;
The Name, all victorious, of Jesus extol;
His Kindgom is glorious, and rules over all.

God ruleth on high, almighty to save;
Though hid from our sight, His presence we have,
The great congregation His triumph shall sing,
Ascribing salvation to Jesus, our King.

Salvation to God who sits on the throne!
Let all cry aloud and honor the Son:
The praises of Jesus the angels proclaim,
Fall down on their faces and worship the Lamb.

Assessment is also kerygmatic in that it highlights institutional acclamations and proclamations. In fact, one might say that the business of assessment is comparing an institution's acclamations and proclamations to determine the degree to which they correspond. Every college in the nation, including Christian colleges, acclaims certain institutional beliefs concerning learning, students, and personal development in their promotional/admissions materials, mission statements, and informal conversations. Christian colleges acclaim, for example, that they exist to develop Christian leaders, cultivate students' talents in response to a divine calling, or train students for informed and principled service in all walks of life.

These same Christian colleges concomitantly make daily proclamations such as classroom lectures, policy decisions, residence hall activities, committee discussions, advising appointments, and donor solicitations. Examining the congruence between institutional self-pronouncements on the one hand and institutional enactments on the other constitutes the "basic stuff" of assessment: are students learning, by both formal and informal means, what we say they will learn? In the same way that an individual Christian seeks to harmonize personal profession (acclamation) and public performance (proclamation), Christian institutions must strive to create environments in which daily proclamations consistently reflect acclaimed presuppositions and, conversely, every proclamation can, with great sincerity, receive hearty acclamations from institutional constituents. According to the former president of Harvard University, Derek Bok (1986), failing to devote serious energies to an assessment of student learning is, irresponsible, self-serving, anti-progress, and anti-improvement. If Bok is correct, and I am inclined to believe that he is, Christian colleges must make haste to discard any existing pretense that simply being a Christian institution ensures that everything is automatically done right. Rather, Christian colleges must embrace assessment as a crucial point of departure in clarifying and reconciling their institutional acclamations and proclamations.

Assessment as Wisdom Doxology

The centrality of wisdom is clearly apparent in the Christian tradition, so then it comes as little surprise that a third dimension of assessment is wisdom. In Christian worship, the reading and preaching of the Scriptures has a primary role because the testaments reveal the nature of divine Wisdom. In turn, as worshippers attend faithfully to God's Word, which serves as the foundation of wisdom, their lives are enlightened and transformed.

In a similar way, institutional assessment produces light and potential transformational change; in short, assessment opens our institutional eyes. It not only reveals to us the works of our hands concerning student learning but, like a lighthouse beacon, assessment illumines a path for faithful institutional navigation in the future. In so doing, assessment provides responses to two fundamental questions about the educational endeavors at our institutions: What has been accomplished? and, How might it be accomplished better? (Manning 1986). Insofar as we are seeking honest answers to these two questions, I believe that we are pursuing wisdom institutionally. Clearly, an institution that deals with its affairs prudently may be described as an institution that invests itself in an assessment effort that is designed to "improve retention and recruitment strategies,...identify problems within particular curricula,... establish the need for [increased emphasis] on particular skills areas across the curriculum,... improve program articulation with primary feeder institutions and with institutions that receive graduates,... revise and evaluate particular service or support functions across the campus,... [and] focus institutional attention on its most critical activities, teaching and learning" (Ewell 1985, 2).

A word of caution is in order here. Although we typically attach positive connotations to words such as illumination and enlightenment, I suggest that they also may be challenging -- and even threatening -- words as well. As Christians we know that following the Light has costs involved. Similarly, because assessment enlightens, it also is risky.   One wonders whether Christian colleges have not rushed into the assessment movement precisely on this point.   After all, assessment may spotlight some issues that Christian colleges may not want to address. Or worse, assessment may illuminate new paths of institutional faithfulness. In short, assessment may -- God forbid -- produce change. From my perspective, we should not eschew assessment because of a preference for institutional preservation rather than institutional transformation.   Rather, our institutions are wise and God is glorified to the degree that we perform our educational task with our institutional eyes open not shut -- and assessment helps us do that.

Assessment as Prophetic Doxology

The primary focus of prophetic doxology is holiness.   In a Christian worship context, prophetic doxology is vital because creates an understanding among the communicants that the holiness of God demands the righteousness of his people. Further, God's holiness is magnified to the extent that God's people live upright lives; individual righteouness embellishes God's praise; as others see Christians' "good works" they give praise to God.

In a Christian college context, assessment functions as an effective way to monitor institutional holiness. Although the idea of institutional holiness may sound strange, I submit that institutions that take on the name Christian -- just like persons who take on the name Christian -- must seek to produce faithful testimony to their holy callings. Assessment is prophetic in that it assists Christian colleges in uncovering areas of righteousness and unrighteousness concerning their God-given mandates to help students learn. When Christian colleges, to use Astin's words, "are not really very clear about we are trying to accomplish, and...perpetuate questionable practices out of sheer habit, for convenience, or to fulfill purposes that are unrelated or at best tangential to [their] basic mission[s]" (Astin 1991, 1), I submit that they are not pursuing institutional holiness.   In turn, God's praise is muted. Assessment, however, provides Christian colleges an opportunity to take stock of institutional purposes and practices and highlight the glories and glitches of student learning. The importance of such activity, to state it again, is to realize that insofar as our institutions strive for holiness and understand the points at which they are faithful as well as unfaithful, they give praise to God and augment his own holiness.

Assessment offers more than simple summation of institutional holiness. It also may improve educational practices.   Bok observes that "the time faculties and administrators spend working together on education is devoted almost entirely to considering *what* their students should study rather than *how* they can learn more effectively or *whether* they are learning as much as they should" (Bok 1986, 20). One wonders whether the same might be said about Christian college faculty members and administrators. Whether the "shoe fits or not," assessment is a means of discovering how student learning might be improved, and may include many strategies such as rethinking the core curriculum to ensure that college objectives are more intentionally addressed, restructuring course sequences to better account for human developmental concerns, offering innovative strategies for positive faculty-student interactions, experimenting with creative pedagogies that account for diverse learning styles and maximize students' involvement in learning, providing students with more, different, and better methods of classroom feedback, creating and/or restructuring the delivery of academic and co-academic student services that better account for student needs, and modifying the larger campus environments in which learning occurs to ensure that students receive a uniform message regarding educational expectations. Again, as Christian colleges utilize assessment to improve student learning, they not only righteously fulfill their calling as institutions, but they magnify God's holiness as well.

A similar discussion is currently raging in the larger postsecondary education environment, but the fashionable words are quality and excellence rather than holiness and faithfulness. Typically the issues are these: the public is dissatisfied with higher education and is demanding a better quality product for the money; institutions must demonstrate that they are making concerted efforts to improve educational programs; state legislatures, accreditation agencies, and other interest groups use assessment as the proverbial "stick" to improve the quality of colleges and universities in response to public pressure; and, institututions are complying with external constituencies, mounting assessment efforts, and creating managerial techniques to implement assessment results -- thus the proliferation of approaches such as strategic planning, TQM, CQM, CQI, and so on. One of the overarching principles of each movement is that quality is no longer defined by the producers of education, but rather by the consumers or customers of education (Marchese 1993).

One of the most interesting aspects of this larger discussion is that, despite increased interest and initiatives about quality, many institutions retain their fundamental assumptions about excellence -- namely that the best institutions are those with reputations and resources (Astin 1991; Astin 1987; Halpern 1987). That is, the really "good" schools are those get ranked in magazines because of the SAT scores of entering students, faculty productivity measured in articles published or grants received, size of endowment, cost of tuition, worth of physical plant, beauty of physical plant, or prowess of athletic teams. Needless to say, such a situation probably comes as little surprise given the generally materialist values of American culture at large.

Before I drift too far afield, however, I wish to make two observations regarding Christian higher education and the search for excellence. First, with one notable exception (which is Robert Sandin's, *The Search for Excellence: The Christian College in an Age of Educational Competition*), discussions regarding quality in Christian higher education are scant at best. We prefer to converse with one another about the nature and preservation of institutional orthodoxy. Although "staying the course," so to speak, is a vitally important issue, I believe we have ample reading material on the subject and would do well to shift our energies to understanding and creating quality living/learning campus environments.

Second, I wonder whether the absence of a dialogue among Christian colleges regarding quality, excellence, and assessment is an indication that they are following their secular counterparts in defining "good education" in reputational or resource-related terms. Or, even worse to my mind, perhaps many Christian colleges believe quality to be a moot point. After all, so the argument may go, since we are God's colleges, how could we be anything less than the best: being Christian colleges makes us excellent colleges. To embrace such a view, whether conscious or unconscious, is to deceive ourselves and dishonor our students. Like the Israelites in Amos's day, we believe our institutions to be automatically faithful, but our educational holiness is, in reality, wanting. For us, Amos 5:21-24 may read like this:

> I hate, I despise your attempt at learning,
>   and I take no delight in your faculty meetings.
> Even though you offer me your integrated core curriculum and
>   major fields of study,
>   I will not accept them,
>   and the faculty advising, co-curricular activities, and sports teams,
>   I will not look upon.
> Take away from me the noise of your educational policy committee meetings,
>   to the melody of your alumni donors I will not listen.
> But let justice roll down like waters,
>   and righteousness like an ever-flowing stream.

The point is simply this: Christian colleges are not automatically holy. We must educate as to the Lord and work hard to pinpoint the quality of our efforts. Without assessment, identifying the quality of institutional performance in this regard is impossible. Assessment not only illuminates those educational efforts of a Christian college that are holy and bring praise to God but also reveals those efforts that mock God's holiness. In short, assessment helps Christian colleges discover and maximize institutional holiness with respect to student learning.

Assessment as Covenantal Doxology

The last aspect of doxology, covenantal doxology, represents a summation of doxological living. In an ecclesiastical context, it refers to interrelated responses from parishioners (although one Hebrew word, *yadah,* means all three): giving thanks to God for our redemption, confessing our covenantal obligation to God that we owe him our lives, and witnessing to the faithfulness of God while in the highways and byways beyond the comfort of the church walls. Insofar as those assembled in Christian fellowship unite around these three activities, God is worshipped and praised.

Assessment provides a similar experience for the participants of Christian colleges. It enhances a college's potential to offer God faithful worship institutionally by evaluating and refocusing its educational mission, by recommitting necessary energies to do education for God's own glory, and by mobilizing institutional participants around the proclamation that the institution belongs to God who will be rightly praised to the extent that faculty, staff, and students envision and execute student learning with wisdom and grace. Seen in this light, assessment may be analogous to the notion of biblical sabbath in that assessment demonstrates covenantal relationship between Christian colleges and God. That is, when a Christian college assesses student learning, it is making several important statements. First, it is stating, "Thank you, Lord, for taking care of us over the years. By your grace, much good learning has occurred in this place." Second, when a Christian college assesses, it is offering, "Lord, here's what we've been up to recently at our college. Take and look and see what you think. Because we always wish to be mindful that our institution belongs to you, please tell us what we're doing that gives you great pleasure, what we're doing that makes you sick to your anthropomorphic stomach, and how we might do better in the future." And, third, when a Christian college assesses student learning, it is saying, "Thanks for your mercy and grace, dear Lord. We enjoy your input, and look forward to putting your advice into action. After all, Lord, we want most to do education that gives you pleasure and praise. We'll be back later for more guidance. Until then, bless our efforts and please don't desert us." From this perspective, assessment is a natural feature and necessary component of institutional life precisely because it reifies the covenantal bond between a Christian college and God. Moreover, assessment gives visible expression to a Christian institution's obligation to educate for Christ alone.

Conclusion

Rossman and El-Khawas (1987) posit three primary reasons for assessment, political, economic, and educational, to which Erwin (1991) adds a fourth -- the public's right to know what to expect from higher education. To these, I would add a fifth rationale, namely that Christian colleges assess because it is right to assess; assessment is simply a natural outworking of the values of Christian colleges and reflects a biblical pattern -- God creates, then assesses; Christian colleges educate in service to God, then assess in an effort to identify new directions and strategies that will produce greater institutional faithfulness.

In a recent article, Ward suggests that Christian higher education is currently "writing its way through... an ultimate final examination" (1992, 8) that includes answers to questions about survival, interpersonal relationships, community, and mission. While I have no quarrel with the content of the article, Ward's words are incomplete. A student must study to pass and, better yet, "ace" an exam; stated in more formative terms, one must study to learn and develop. What makes us think that it is any different for our institutions? Unless we dedicate ourselves to examining and understanding what we really mean by higher education (Westling 1988) and, moreover, unless we come to terms with the extent to which we are realizing our educational goals, we may survive, but we certainly will not experience, if I may, abundant institutional life. And to go one more step, unless we honestly seek to fold our "results" back into the highways and byways of education as it finds expression on our campuses, we cease to pursue institutional sanctification. I submit that when a Christian institution neglects to assess its efforts or shrinks from utilizing the wisdom gained from assessment as a means of improving its continued efforts, even though that institution says all the "right" things in its college catalog, then its potential to praise God is truncated. Insofar as Christian colleges embrace assessment as doxology, however, I believe their educational expectations and educational performances will coalesce and improve, God will be honored, and his blessings will flow as he responds to our work with delight: Well done, good and faithful Christian colleges. Should we strive for anything less, even if our respective accreditation agencies had never mentioned assessment?

Reference List

Astin, A. W. 1987. Assessment, value-added, and educational excellence. In *Student outcomes assessment: What institutions stand to gain* (New Directions for Higher Education), ed. D. Halpern, no. 59 (Fall):89-107. San Francisco: Jossey-Bass.

————. 1991. *Assessment for excellence: The philosophy and practice of assessment and evaluation in higher education.* New York: American Council on Education and Macmillan Publishing Company.

Bok, D. 1986. Toward higher learning: The importance of assessment outcomes. *Change* (November/December):18-27.

Erwin, T. D. 1991. *Assessing student learning and development.* San Francisco: Jossey-Bass.

Ewell, P. T. 1985. Editor's notes. In *Assessing educational outcomes* (New Directions for Institutional Research), ed. P. Ewell, no. 47 (September): 1-5. San Francisco: Jossey-Bass.

Halpern, D. F. 1987. Student outcomes assessment: Introduction and overview. In *Student outcomes assessment: What institutions stand to gain* (New Directions for Higher Education), ed. D. Halpern, no. 59 (Fall): 5-8. San Francisco: Jossey-Bass.

Hutchings, P. and Marchese, T. 1990. Watching assessment: Questions, stories, prospects. *Change* (September/October):13-38.

Manning, T. E. 1986. The why, what, and who of assessment: The accrediting association perspective. Paper presented at the Educational Testing Services Invitational Conference, New York, October.

Marchese, T. 1993. TQM: A time for ideas. *Change* (May/June):10-13.

Old, H. O. 1992. *Themes and variations for a Christian doxology.* Grand Rapids: Eerdmans.

Patton, M. Q. 1986. *Utilization-focused evaluation.* Newbury Park, CA: Sage.

Rossmann, J. E. and E. El-Khawas. 1987. *Thinking about assessment: Perspectives for presidents and chief academic officers*. Washington, DC: American Council on Education and the American Association for Higher Education.

Sandin, R. T. 1982. *The search for Excellence: The Christian college in an age of educational competition*. Macon, GA: Mercer University Press.

Van Harn, G. 1986. Student outcomes. Unpublished Paper. Grand Rapids: Calvin College Library.

Ward, T. 1992. A final exam for Christian higher education. *Faculty Dialogue* 18 (Fall):5-11.

Westling, J. 1988. The assessment movement is based on a misdiagnosis of the malaise afflicting American higher education. *The Chronicle of Higher Education*, October 19, B1.

Contributors

Nicholas P. Barker

Nicholas Barker is Dean of Faculty at Covenant College. He received his B.A. from Princeton University and his M.A. and Ph.D. from the University of Minnesota. He was co-author of three editions of *Themes and Exercises* and author of *Purpose and Function in Prose*.

Bayard D. Baylis

Bayard O. Baylis is Associate Dean for Curriculum at Messiah College in Grantham, PA. He is a graduate of the University of Delaware. Prior to his present position, he served as a professor of mathematics and college registrar.

H. David Brandt

David Brandt is currently the Provost at Bethel College in St. Paul. Before moving to Minnesota in 1988, he served as Dean of the College at Messiah College for over ten years. David's undergraduate degree is from Wheaton College (IL) and his graduate degrees in physics are from the University of Oklahoma.

Delana Gerber Brinkman

Delana Gerber Brinkman is currently an adolescent and family therapist in the Twin Cities. She is a graduate of Bethel College and later served as a Resident Director while completing a M.A. in Counseling and Student Personnel Psychology from the University of Minnesota.

Ronald Burwell

Ronald Burwell is professor of sociology at Messiah. He is a graduate of Wheaton College (IL), Trinity Evangelical Divinity School, and New York University. He has conducted research on refugee resettlement as well as on a variety of student outcomes.

Richard E. Butman

Richard Butman is a professor of psychology at Wheaton College in Illinois. His clinical and research interests include the impact of fathers on their children across the lifespan, psychosocial development in young adulthood, and the assessment of religiosity. He recently co-authored *Modern Psychotherapies: A Comprehensive Christian Appraisal.*

Carlyle C. Dewey

Carlyle C. Dewey was the Assistant to the President for Planning at Messiah and is currently serving with SIM/International in Addis Ababa, Ethiopia, as director of the Good Shepherd School. His degrees are from the University of Minnesota.

Harold Faw

Harold Faw has been a member of the Psychology department at Trinity Western University since 1978, where his primary research interests are in human memory and the relationships between biblical and psychological truth.

Paula Smalligan Foster

Paula Smalligan Foster graduated from Calvin College in 1991. She is currently a graduate student in social psychology at Wayne State University in Detroit, Michigan.

David S. Guthrie

David S. Guthrie works at Calvin College as the Dean of Student Development, as an Adjunct Assistant Professor of Sociology, and as a Research Scholar in the Calvin Center for Christian Scholarship. He recently co-edited a monograph entitled *Agendas for Church-related Colleges and Universities*.

Jim Koch

Jim Koch is the Director of Counseling Services and an associate professor of psychology at Bethel College. He graduated from the New School for Social Research with a Ph.D. in clinical psychology.

D. John Lee

D. John Lee is an associate professor of psychology at Calvin College. He co-edited *Ethnic-minorities and Evangelical Christian colleges* and is editor of *Storing ourselves: A narrative perspective on Christians in psychology*.

Steven P. McNeel

Steve McNeel is professor of psychology at Bethel College, Minnesota and has also taught at the University of Leuven, Belgium and Southern Illinois University. He has conducted research on how colleges facilitate student development, particularly in moral judgment, moral sensitivity, and empathy.

Judith Moseman

Judith Moseman is the Vice-President for Student Affairs at Bethel College and received her M.Ed. from the University of Minnesota. She is presently the President-elect of the Association of Christians in Student Development.

Harry Pinner

Harry Pinner is Covenant College's Director of Planning. After 13 years in the marketing department of New Jersey Bell Telephone, he became Director of Admissions at the college and in 1987, he began his present position and is responsible for the planning and assessment programs.

Rodger R. Rice

After eight years in academic administration at Calvin College, Rodger Rice returned to the Sociology and Social Work department, where he continues to teach and direct the Social Research Center. He earned his Ph.D. in sociology from Michigan State University and has taught and conducted research in sociology and demography at Calvin and the University of Southern California.

Gloria Goris Stronks

Gloria Goris Stronks is a professor of education at Calvin College. She is the author of *The Christian Middle School: An Ethos of Caring* and co-edited *A Vision with a Task: Educating for Responsive Discipleship*.

Harley Schreck

Harley Schreck is presently an associate professor of anthropology and Chairman of the Cultural Studies Department at Bethel College. After graduating from the University of Washington with a Ph.D. in anthropology he was a Senior Researcher with World Vision International. A continuing research interest has been the formation and meaning of community in modern urban life.

Steven R. Timmermans

Steven Timmermans is an associate professor of education and Director of Student Academic Services at Calvin College. He received his doctorate from the Combined Program in Education and Psychology at the University of Michigan in 1985.

Harro Van Brummelen

Harro Van Brummelen is Assistant Dean, Faculty of Social Sciences and Education at Trinity Western. His publications include *Walking with God in the Classroom* as well as other books and articles related to the impact of worldviews on school curriculum.

John Van Wicklin

John Van Wicklin is a professor of psychology at Houghton college in New York. He is a graduate of Wheaton College, Columbia University, and the New School for Social Research.

Carolina Warner

Carolina Warner is a graduate from Bethel Seminary and is presently a Ph.D. candidate in Marriage and Family Therapy at the Fuller Theological Seminary's Graduate School of Psychology.